THE
CONSULTANT'S
SCORECARD

About the Author

Jack Phillips, Ph.D., is the founder of Performance Resources Organization, now the world's leading consulting firm specializing in accountability issues. The author or editor of more than 20 books and 100 articles, including *The Handbook of Training Evaluation and Measurement* and *Accountability in Human Resources Management*, he has served as a bank president, Fortune 500 training and development manager, senior human resources officer, and professor of management at a major state university. His clients in 20 countries include such internationally respected companies as AT&T, Federal Express, Lockheed-Martin, Motorola, and Xerox. In addition, he has provided consulting services to three of the world's largest consulting firms: Andersen Consulting, PriceWaterhouse Coopers, and Deloitte and Touche.

THE CONSULTANT'S SCORECARD

Tracking Results and Bottom-Line Impact of Consulting Projects

JACK J. PHILLIPS

McGraw-Hill

New York   San Francisco   Washington, D.C.   Auckland   Bogotá
Caracas   Lisbon   London   Madrid   Mexico City   Milan
Montreal   New Delhi   San Juan   Singapore
Sydney   Tokyo   Toronto

Library of Congress Cataloging-in-Publication Data

Phillips, Jack J.
  The consultant's scorecard : tracking results and bottom-line impact of consulting
projects / Jack J. Phillips.
    p. cm.
  Includes index.
  ISBN 0-07-134816-6
  1. Consultants. 2. Business consultants. I. Title.
HD69.C6 P468 2000
001'.068—dc21   99-049210

McGraw-Hill

A Division of The McGraw·Hill Companies

    5 6 7 8 9 0   AGM/AGM   0 9 8 7 6 5 4 3 2

ISBN 0-07-134816-6

This book was set in Janson Text by North Market Street Graphics.

Printed and bound by Quebecor, Martinsburg.

McGraw-Hill books are available at special quality discounts to use
as premiums and sales promotions, or for use in corporate training
programs. For more information, please write to the Director of
Special Sales, McGraw-Hill, Professional Publishing, Two Penn
Plaza, New York, NY 10121-2298. Or contact your local bookstore.

This book is printed on recycled, acid-free paper containing
a minimum of 50% recycled, de-inked fiber.

To Patti Pulliam Phillips,
my partner, friend, and wife

Contents

Acknowledgments

In no way has developing this book been a single-handed effort. Many individuals have helped shape the content and issues contained in each chapter. Much appreciation goes to the clients of Performance Resources Organization (PRO), who have provided us an opportunity to continually experiment with the return on investment (ROI) process. Together we have developed many of the issues presented in this book.

Although we have had the opportunity to work with hundreds of individuals in excellent organizations around the world, a few stand out as being very helpful in the development of the issues for this book: Jac Fitz-enz, Saratoga Institute; Toni Hodges, Bell Atlantic; Debi Wallace, First Union National Bank; Brent Peterson, FranklinCovey; Kathy Jones and Debi Harrel, Nortel; Mike Sullivan, AllState; Rob Schriver, Lockheed-Martin; Rick Irwin, ComEd; Mijin Cho, Motorola; Chris King, Walt Disney; Ferdinand Tersoro, Dell Computer; Pauline Stamp, formerly with Guthrie Healthcare Systems; Mark Jones, PricewaterhouseCoopers; Brenda Sayers, Deloitte & Touche; Dan McLinden, formerly with Andersen Consulting; and Peter Howes, HRM Consulting.

Much appreciation goes to PRO's associates, who have provided ideas, suggestions, and helpful information to enable us to fine-tune the ROI process and build a truly successful consulting practice. Among these individuals are Judy Estrin, Patrick Whalen, Dianne Hill, Bob Sutton, Heather Barfoot, and Robert McCarty.

Within our own family at PRO, many individuals have helped make this a reality. My long-time friend and business partner, Ron Stone, who directs our consulting efforts, continues to provide refinements and improvements to our process. Ron is a very methodical and effective consultant with this process. Frank Ashby, a friend and board member, provided encouragement and suggestions for the manuscript. My associate and life partner, Patricia Pulliam, offered many useful ideas and techniques throughout the manuscript's production and provided an overall quality review at the end. A special thanks goes to Jaime Beard for meticulously working through the manuscript and making sense of all the notes, tapes, sketches, and materials. She was very focused and thorough during the entire project. Don Milazzo provided excellent editing. Kelly Chappell rearranged priorities to allow the book to be completed on time, and Michelle Garcia provided assistance on the project in the early stages and again during the final editing. To these individuals I owe much appreciation and a big "Thank you."

Special Credit

Thanks and special credit go to Gulf Publishing Company, Houston, Texas, for allowing us to use limited portions of the material from my previous works. Gulf has published three books on our processes. Small amounts of edited material were used in this book and were taken from *Return on Investment in Training and Performance Improvement Programs* (1997.)

Jack J. Phillips

Introduction

Interest in ROI

In the past, the consulting process was evaluated based on the quality of the relationship between the consultants and the client. The chemistry had to be just right, and interpersonal relationships needed to be appropriate for projects to be successful. Success was often defined in vague and general terms, reflecting qualitative judgments based on alignment, fit, and relationships. There were only a few attempts to actually connect consulting to bottom-line values.

Today, things are different. Executive management requires greater accountability for the consulting investment. With expenditures growing for consulting services and with increasing dissatisfaction with the quality and success of consulting assignments, there is tremendous pressure to show accountability measured in terms that managers clearly understand—ROI.

Several issues are driving the increased interest in and application of the ROI process for consulting assignments. Pressure from clients and executive managers to show the actual return on their consulting investment is probably the most influential driver. Competitive economic pressures are causing intense scrutiny of all expenditures, including consulting costs. A variety of change programs have entered the workplace, including total quality management, reengineering, and continuous process improvement. These initiatives have created renewed interest in measurement and evaluation because of the desire of senior management to show the actual results of these processes.

While these and other change processes have brought great expectations, they have failed to deliver the results promised or expected. In essence, the lack of results has caused many to question the consulting process and to call for a more comprehensive approach for showing the actual contribution—ideally prior to the implementation of the process. The tremendous growth in consulting budgets, combined with the previously mentioned scrutiny and economic pressures, have created an unprecedented need for the ROI process.

The Consulting ROI Process

The challenging aspect of the consulting ROI process is the nature and accuracy of its development. The process often seems very confusing and is usually surrounded by models, formulas, and statistics that can frighten even the most capable consultants and clients. Coupled with this concern are misunderstandings about the process and the gross misuse of ROI techniques in some consulting interventions. These issues leave consultants with a distaste for the process and clients wondering if an appropriate process actually exists.

Unfortunately, ROI cannot be ignored. To admit to clients and executive management that the impact of a consulting project cannot be measured is to admit that consulting does not add value or that consulting should not be subjected to accountability processes. In practice, ROI must be explored, considered, and ultimately implemented as part of the consulting intervention.

What is needed is a rational, logical approach that can be simplified and implemented within most budget constraints and resources. This book presents a proven consulting ROI process based on nearly 20 years of development. It is a process that is rich in tradition and refined to meet the demands facing the consulting field. It meets the requirements of three very important groups. First, the consultants who have used this model and implemented the ROI process in their consulting interventions continue to report satisfaction with the process and the success it has achieved. The ROI process is user-friendly and easy to understand, and has been proven again and again to pay for itself. A second important group—the clients and executive managers who approve consulting projects and consulting budgets—wants measurable results, preferably expressed as a return on investment. The ROI process presented here has fared well with these client groups. Senior executives often view the process as credible, logical, practical, and easy to understand. More importantly, they buy into the process, which is critical in gaining their support for future implementation. The third important group is the evaluation researchers who develop, explore, and analyze new processes and techniques for showing accountability. When exposed to the ROI process in a two-day or one-week workshop, the researchers—without exception—give the process very high marks. They often applaud the strategies for isolating the effects of consulting and converting data to monetary values. Unanimously, they characterize the process as an important contribution to the consulting field.

Why This Book at This Time?

There are no books available that show how the ROI process is developed in a consulting intervention. Also, there are few presentations of comprehensive evaluation processes for consulting interventions. No other approach parallels the comprehensive process presented in this book. Most models and representations of measurement and evaluation processes ignore the essential ingredients for a successful ROI process. They generally provide very little insight into how the processes actually work.

This book is not about how to provide consulting services: rather, it shows how to structure consulting so that it produces results. The book provides a mechanism for showing the actual contribution of consulting in six data categories. There are many good books on consulting processes, but none show how to measure the success of consulting from a balanced viewpoint.

The Scorecard Perspective: Six Balanced Measures

This book presents six types of measures that are collected in a consulting intervention, which present a balanced viewpoint of the success of the consulting project. The measures involve both qualitative and quantitative data collected at different time intervals. The result is a rich profile of successful interventions, as well as explanations for those that have been less than successful. In essence, the process delivers the following six types of data:

1. Reaction to and satisfaction with the consulting intervention from a variety of different stakeholders within different time frames.
2. The extent of learning that has taken place as those involved in the consulting intervention learn new skills, processes, procedures, and tasks.
3. The success of the actual application and implementation of the consulting intervention as the process is utilized in the work environment.
4. The actual business impact changes in the work unit where the consulting project has been initiated. These values include hard data as well as soft data.
5. The actual return on investment reported as a ratio or in a percentage format. This measure shows the monetary return on the cost of the project.
6. Intangible measures, which are usually soft data items that are not converted to monetary values for use in the ROI formula.

These six data items provide a comprehensive, balanced profile of success. In addition, the consulting ROI process provides insight into problems and areas where adjustments can be quickly made to enhance the successful application and implementation of the consulting intervention. It is a comprehensive approach that can guarantee success in a consulting intervention.

A Focus on Results

In addition to actually measuring the contribution with the six measures, the consulting ROI process provides a framework for focusing on results throughout the consulting intervention. Beginning with evaluation planning, the process requires concentration on important measures throughout the consulting intervention so that all stakeholders are aware of expectations, measures, and success levels. In addition, in situations for which a forecast of the ROI process is necessary, the process can be adapted to provide a preproject ROI forecast or a forecast at different time frames during the actual consulting intervention. In short, the consulting ROI process is an effective tool for bringing needed accountability to the consulting field.

Target Audience

The primary audience for this book can be divided into two categories, client and consultant, with both having equal coverage and direction. For clients who engage consulting services, the book provides an indispensable process for measuring the success of the consulting intervention and a framework for measuring success throughout the project. No longer will the client be forced to live with whatever evaluation is provided by the consultant. The client may, as a minimum, impose some parts of the process on future consulting interventions, or require the entire ROI process for all major consulting projects, whether internal or external.

For consultants who need a process for showing the value of consulting intervention, this book presents a process that is user-friendly and easy to understand and apply. It can provide all the information needed or demanded by the client. Many aspects of the process can be built into assignments to keep costs and resources to a minimum. More importantly, pursuing this comprehensive evaluation process will build a database of successful ROI projects that clearly shows the impact of consulting, providing one of the best marketing tools for future consulting interventions. For small consulting firms, the consultant can use part or all of the material to focus additional efforts on accountability, stopping short of a complete, comprehensive assessment. In larger firms, the ROI process will mean a complete change in the way consulting is marketed and implemented from the firm's perspective.

There are three secondary audiences for this book. The first is the individuals involved in support roles for the consulting process. These could be people supporting consulting internally in the consulting firm or in the client organization. The book will be a valuable tool to help them understand the need for accountability and how it is integrated into the processes.

The next secondary audience is management. Managers in a client organization are not necessarily the direct clients of the consulting process but are influenced or affected by the results of consulting intervention. They need to understand the processes for bringing accountability to this important area, and this book should fulfill that need.

The third secondary audience is individuals who are in an external or peripheral role in the consulting process, including researchers, seminar presenters, professors, and other educators who are involved in the professional development of consultants. The book provides a proven, reliable, and valid way to measure the success of consulting projects and should become a valuable addition to any workshop, seminar, or college course on the consulting process.

Structure of the Book

This book has several unique features that make it a very useful tool for the target audiences. The material is presented in a very practical and useful way, outlining how the ROI process is used in organizations. The first chapter explores the need for an ROI process from the perspective of the client. It shows how the client can hold the consultant accountable for a consulting intervention. Chapter 2 explains how the ROI process can be used by consultants to show the value of their consulting assignments and reveals how the process can play a part in every consulting situation, regardless of the budget and resources available.

Chapters 3 through 7 present the data collection for the first four measures: reaction and satisfaction, learning, application and implementation, and business impact. Each chapter presents the rationale for measuring success with a particular measure and describes data collection techniques that would be most appropriate for that type of measure. Shortcut possibilities for each measure are also included.

Chapter 8 examines the actual ROI calculation, which is the fifth measure in the consulting ROI process. It shows how the value is developed and interpreted. Chapter 9 explains how the intangible measures, which represent the sixth type of data, are developed. The analysis needed for intangibles is also presented.

Chapter 10 covers perhaps the most critical issue: isolating the effects of consulting. A variety of useful strategies are presented to separate the influence of the consulting intervention from other factors that may affect output data. Chapter 11 examines the critical issue of converting data to monetary values, explaining the different techniques for developing the overall monetary benefit from a consulting intervention. Shortcut methods are presented in both chapters.

Chapter 12 focuses on the cost of the intervention, showing all the costs that should be monitored and how those costs should be reported. This is an essential part of the process of developing the cost of a consulting intervention because it allows the costs to be compared to benefits.

Chapter 13 focuses on how to forecast the ROI process when a pre-project estimate is needed. Chapter 14 shows how the various types of data are communicated to the various targeted audiences. More specifically, it shows in detail how an impact study is developed and communicated to the client group, how to build an appropriate communications tool for the senior management team, and how routine feedback is provided during the consulting intervention.

Finally, Chapter 15 focuses on ways in which the process can become internalized as a routine part of consulting assignments. The chapter explains how to overcome resistance to using the process and presents a variety of ways in which the consulting ROI process can be implemented effectively in organizations.

Collectively, these chapters provide a comprehensive framework for the consulting ROI process, addressing all of the key issues necessary to make the method an important and essential ingredient in consulting interventions.

Dispelling the ROI Myths

Measuring the consulting ROI is a hot topic. ROI appears routinely on conference agendas and in professional journals and networking meetings. Internally, from a client's perspective, ROI discussions are popping up in executive planning sessions, senior management staff meetings, and board meetings. Externally, ROI strategies are being developed by progressive consulting firms all over the globe.

Although most major consulting firms recognize ROI as an important addition to measurement and evaluation, they often struggle with how to address the issue. Many consultants see the ROI process as a ticket to increased funding and prosperity for consulting. They believe that without it, they may be lost in the shuffle, whereas with it, they may gain the respect they need to continue to achieve funding for consulting. Regardless of the motivation for pursuing ROI, the key question is this: "Is ROI a feasible process that can be implemented with reasonable resources, and will it provide the benefits necessary to make it a useful, routine tool?"

Performance Resources Organization (PRO) is the global leader in the ROI process, having conducted its first ROI impact study in 1976.

Since that time, the process has been refined and is now used by more than 1000 organizations in 20 countries. PRO consultants have been involved in more than 300 ROI impact studies, and more than 500 individuals from 25 countries have completed PRO's ROI certification program. A professional organization with more than 200 members has also been formed to provide a forum for sharing information about the ROI process. From this evidence, it is clear that conducting an ROI impact study is feasible and is a way of life in many organizations and consulting firms.

The controversy surrounding ROI stems from misunderstandings about what the process can and cannot do, and how it can or should be implemented in an organization. These misunderstandings are summarized in the following myths about the ROI process. The myths were developed by PRO and are based on years of experience with the ROI process and the perceptions discovered during consulting projects and workshops. Each myth is presented in the list that follows, along with an explanation of the truth.

1. *ROI is too complex for most users.* This issue has been a problem because of a few highly complex models that have been presented publicly. Unfortunately, these models have done little to help their users and have actually caused confusion about ROI. The ROI process is a basic financial formula for accountability that is simple and understandable: earnings are divided by investments, earnings equate to net benefits from the consulting intervention, and the investment equals the actual cost of the project. Straying from this basic formula can add confusion and create tremendous misunderstanding. The consulting ROI model, as presented in this book, is simplified with a step-by-step, systematic process.

2. *ROI is expensive, consuming too many critical resources.* The ROI process can become expensive if it is not carefully organized and controlled and properly implemented. The cost of a consulting ROI impact study can be significant, but several options are available to keep costs down. For example, the skills for developing ROI studies can be developed internally using existing measurement and evaluation staff, if available. Also, the process can be built into projects at the design and implementation stages, which should significantly reduce the amount of resources

needed for a study. The responsibilities for different parts of the ROI process can be shared with others, reducing the need to use special resources for an ROI study. More importantly, the process should only be applied to a sampling of projects—those critical and important enough to be subjected to this level of analysis. Throughout this book, strategies and techniques for conserving resources are presented.

3. *If senior management does not require ROI, there is no need to pursue it.* This myth captures the most innocent bystanders. It is easy to be lulled into providing evaluation and measurement that simply meets the status quo, believing that no requests means no desire for the information. If senior executives have only been provided reaction and satisfaction data, they may not be asking for higher-level data. In some cases, consultants have convinced top management that consulting interventions cannot be evaluated at the ROI level or that the specific impact of a project cannot be determined. Given these conditions, it comes as no surprise that senior managers may not be asking for ROI data.

   There is another problem with this thinking. Paradigms are shifting—not only within consulting firms but within senior management teams as well. Senior managers are beginning to request ROI data. Changes in corporate leadership sometimes initiate important paradigm shifts, as new leadership often requires proof of accountability. The process of integrating ROI into an organization takes time. It is not a quick fix, and when senior executives suddenly ask the consultants to produce ROI data, they may expect the results to be produced quickly. Because of this, consulting firms should initiate the ROI process and develop ROI impact studies long before senior management begins asking for ROI data.

4. *ROI is a passing fad.* Unfortunately, this comment does apply to many of the processes being introduced to organizations today. Accountability for expenditures will always be present, and ROI provides the ultimate level of accountability. ROI has been used as a tool for years. In 1923, the initial publication year of the *Harvard Business Review*, ROI was the noted measurement tool. For years ROI has been used to measure investments in equipment and new plants. Now it is being utilized in many other

areas, including consulting solutions. With its rich history, ROI will continue to be used as an important tool in measurement and evaluation.

5. *ROI is only one type of data.* This is a common misunderstanding. The actual consulting ROI process depicted in this book reports the following six types of data:

   1. Reaction to and satisfaction with the project
   2. Amount of learning of those directly involved in the project
   3. Application or implementation of the project
   4. Business impact
   5. Return on investment
   6. Intangible data, representing important data not converted to monetary value

   This profile of data includes both qualitative and quantitative data and often involves data from different sources, making the ROI process a rich source for a variety of types of data.

6. *ROI is not future oriented. It only reflects past performance.* Unfortunately, many evaluation processes are oriented toward the past and reflect only what has already happened with a project. This is the only way to gain an accurate assessment of impact. However, the ROI process can easily be adapted to forecast the actual ROI. The challenge is to estimate the actual impact on the measures that will be influenced by a particular project. The rest of the process remains the same. While this is a novel idea and is a routine request, the accuracy of forecasting is limited in any forecasting model. However, several techniques are presented in this book for achieving a reasonably accurate assessment of what a project can provide, removing much of the risk of the forecasting concept and reducing the likelihood of resource misuse.

7. *ROI is rarely used by organizations.* This myth is easily dispelled when the evidence is fully examined. More than 1000 organizations and consulting firms use the ROI process, and there are at least 100 published case studies of the ROI process. Leading organizations throughout the world, including businesses of all sizes and sectors, use the ROI process to increase accountability and improve projects. This process is also being used in the non-

profit, educational, and government sectors. There is no doubt that it is employed and growing in use.

8. *The ROI process cannot by easily replicated.* This is an understandable concern. In theory, any process worthy of implementation must be able to be replicated not only from one study to another but within the same situation as well. For example, if two different individuals conducted an ROI impact study, would they obtain the same results? Fortunately, the ROI process is a systematic process with certain standards and guiding principles. Therefore, the likelihood of two different individuals obtaining the same results is quite high. Because this process involves step-by-step procedures, it can also be replicated from one project to another.

9. *ROI is not a credible process. It is too subjective.* This myth has evolved because some ROI studies involving estimates have been publicized and promoted in the literature and conferences. Many ROI studies can be and have been conducted without the use of estimates. The problem with estimates often surfaces when attempting to isolate the effects of other factors. Using estimates from the participants directly involved in the project is only one of several different techniques for isolating the effects of a project. Other techniques involve extremely precise and analytical approaches such as use of control groups and trend line analysis. Sometimes estimating is used in other steps of the process, such as converting data to monetary values or estimating output in the data collection phase. In each of these situations, other options are often available, but for convenience or economics an estimation is often used. While estimations often represent the worst-case scenario in ROI, they can be extremely reliable when obtained carefully, adjusted for error, and reported appropriately.

10. *ROI is not possible for soft data projects—only for production and sales.* ROI often works best in soft skills projects. Soft consulting solutions often drive hard data items such as output, quality, cost, or time. Case after case shows successful application of the ROI process to projects such as customer satisfaction, team building, communications, and transformation. Additional examples of successful ROI application can be found in compliance projects such as diversity, risk management, and policy implementation.

Any type of project can be evaluated at the ROI level. The issue occurs when ROI is used for projects that should not be evaluated at this level. The ROI process should be reserved for projects that are expensive, that address operational problems and issues related to strategic objectives, or that attract the interest of management in terms of increased accountability.

11. *ROI is for manufacturing and service organizations only.* Although initial ROI studies appeared in the manufacturing sector, the service sector quickly picked up the process as a useful tool. Then it migrated to the nonprofit sector as hospitals and health care firms began endorsing and using the process. Now, the ROI process is moving through government sectors around the world.

12. *It is not possible to isolate the influence of other factors.* Isolating the effects of other factors is always achieved when using the ROI process. There are seven ways to do this, and at least one method will work in any given situation. The challenge is to select an appropriate isolation method for the resources and accuracy needed in a particular situation.

13. *ROI is appropriate only for large organizations.* While it is true that large organizations with enormous consulting budgets have the most interest in ROI, smaller organizations can also use the process, particularly when it is simplified and built into projects. Organizations with as few as 500 people have successfully applied the ROI process, using it as a tool to bring increased accountability to consulting. One-person consulting firms have successfully implemented the ROI process.

14. *There are no standards for the ROI process.* An important problem facing measurement and evaluation is a lack of standardization or consistency. People often ask, "What is an adequate ROI?" "What should be included in the cost so I can compare my data with other data?" "When should specific data be included in the ROI value instead of reported as an intangible?" While these questions are not easily answered, some help is on the way. A professional association called The ROI Network is developing standards for the ROI process, using as its base a group of guiding principles. Also under development is a database that will contain thousands of studies so that best practices, patterns, trends, and standards are readily available.

Conclusion

The ROI process is not for every organization or individual consultant. The use of the ROI process represents a tremendous paradigm shift as an organization attempts to bring more accountability and results to the consulting process. It is client focused, requiring much contact, communication, dialog, and agreement with the client.

Admittedly, there are some natural obstacles to this process that may hinder its use. The good news is that the ROI process is being adopted by thousands of organizations in virtually every type of setting. The myths described here are quickly being debunked as consultants recognize ROI as a useful tool that can add tremendous value to the mission and goals of the consulting process.

THE
CONSULTANT'S
SCORECARD

PART
I

Setting the Stage

The Need for Consulting Accountability from the Client Perspective

Why Measuring Results Is Worth the Trouble

T HE CONSULTING BUSINESS has enjoyed tremendous success during the past two decades, with its growth exceeding that of many professions. According to most estimates, the consulting industry is predicted to grow in the range of 15 to 20 percent each year. Whether in restructuring, implementing systems, developing staff, changing procedures, buying new companies, or bringing out new products and services, consultants are being asked to assist in a variety of ways. Companies are fervently seeking consultants for their external perspectives and expert opinions, hoping they can provide solutions that will improve business. Unfortunately, clients are often disappointed when products and services fail to deliver anticipated results, leaving both the client and the consultant frustrated over the outcome of the project.

Trouble in Paradise

While some have regarded the consulting profession as a highly desirable occupation, others have characterized it by the lack of effectiveness of consultants and the consulting industry. The problems facing consultants, although varying with the industry and the type of consulting activities, generally fall into three major categories: lack of accountability, tarnished image, and excessive costs. Each of these brings a cloud over the industry, causing some to question the contributions of consulting projects. This chapter explores the current status of consulting, examines the causes behind the accountability crisis, and suggests ways to overcome this problem.

Lack of Accountability

Perhaps one of the most damaging reports about the consulting industry was presented in a major book focusing on large consulting companies. *Dangerous Company*, by James O'Shea and Charles Madigan, illustrates how consulting powerhouses are inflicting damages on many organizations. The opening paragraph best summarizes the concerns for accountability:

> **A secretive and elite army of management consultants is at work deep inside corporations everywhere, from the giants of the *Fortune* 500 to middle-sized and smaller companies. It is also expanding its influence all over the developing world, wherever economies are coming to life. And it has become partner to government, adviser to heads of state, and confidant to countless interests eager to exploit the promise of a growing world economy. It collects top dollar for its work, sometimes delivering all the sparkle and success it promises, and sometimes failing so remarkably that its clients seem more victim than customer. A relative newcomer to the world of business, management consulting has escaped all but the most cursory of levels of scrutiny. It has only good things to say about itself. But there is a growing sense of unease about this exploding and occasionally explosive enterprise, a feeling that it is a palace built on a foundation of shifting sand. From a distance, it glistens like alabaster. Up close, a different image emerges. It cen-**

ters on a key question: "Whose interest is being served?" All too often, the answer is that it is not the best interest of the client.[1]

It would be unfair to label all consultants and consulting firms as incapable of producing results or supplying a useful product or service. There are many success stories recounting how consulting firms have enhanced organizations and even turned them around. However, in far too many cases, the results are just not there. And sometimes, the process itself causes a breakdown in accountability.

Consider, for example, the following consulting project for a regional financial institution. A well-known and respected consulting firm was engaged to analyze areas where efficiency could be developed to add immediate bottom-line value to the organization. The consultants pored through financial records, analyzed operating reports, and interviewed dozens of managers and specialists. In the end, the consulting firm seized the ideas and suggestions of the operating managers, taking projects that were already under way or in the planning stages and presenting them as recommendations to improve operating efficiencies. When the senior staff of the firm objected to the consultants' report, the CEO, who had hired the consultants previously, praised the work of the consultants and suggested their recommendations be adopted. The staff resisted in every way and ultimately did nothing with what was originally planned. The recommendations were never implemented by the senior staff. In a reference check by another organization seeking consulting advice, the CEO praised the report and gave the consulting firm very high marks for its efforts. Privately, he said, "Although we did not implement all the recommendations and some were already in planning, it was a good exercise for the organization."

From most perspectives, this scenario represents a failure in the consulting assignment. Although the project was completed, recommendations were made, and the primary client—the CEO—was satisfied, the assignment fell short of what should have been accomplished—and, more importantly, what could have been accomplished. The problem involves a breakdown in the processes that led to the consulting intervention and its ultimate result.

Many consultants agree with this assessment and have developed a new approach. According to Robert Schaffer, in his book *High-Impact Consulting*:

Most management consultants subscribe to a model of consulting that is inherently loaded against success. This consulting paradigm, followed throughout the world by external and staff consultants alike, is unnecessarily labor-intensive, long in cycle time, and low in return on investment. It locks both clients and consultants into a fundamentally ineffective mode of operation. In this, the conventional consulting model, there is a clear divide between the parties: The experts are accountable for creating the best possible solutions and tools, and the clients are accountable for exploiting those solutions and tools to improve organization results. In too many cases, however, clients do not or cannot implement the consultant-developed solutions in ways that yield significant improvement.[2]

Beyond the flawed issues surrounding implementation and support are the problems of a lack of clear definition up front, focus on specific objectives, and emphasis on obtaining results throughout the process. While many consulting projects do yield results, they often fall short of the significant results they could achieve, and in far too many cases they produce no results at all.

This book presents the tools and processes needed to measure the success of consulting projects, ensure that consulting projects are properly initiated (with the end in mind), and place the necessary emphasis on results, including various feedback mechanisms to keep the project clearly on track. When implemented, this process will ensure that a consulting project not only produces results, but also produces the significant results that should be expected from major interventions.

Tarnished Image

Closely related to a lack of accountability in the consulting industry is its problem with a tarnished image. Elaine Biech, in her book *The Business of Consulting*, lists as one of her myths that "consulting is a respected profession." Elaine explains that she thought she had chosen a respected profession, but was shocked the first time she was called a "beltway bandit"—a term assigned to consulting firms in and around the Washington, DC beltway. Since her initial encounter she has been called a "pest" and a "con-person."[3] Indeed, the consulting profession has come under fire, particularly from the employees who have to work with consultants and deal with the outcomes of consulting assignments. Perhaps this is underscored best, or at least in a more visible way, in the role of consultants depicted in the *Dilbert* comic strip. In Scott Adams's best-selling book, *The Dilbert Principle*, which was a number one *New York Times* best-seller, nearly 10 percent of the book's coverage is devoted to consultants and consulting. *Dilbert* depicts the petty and stupid requests and activities of consultants and consulting projects that litter cubicles throughout the corporate world.[4] Some of Adams's observations of consultants are:

- A consultant is a person who takes your money and annoys your employees while tirelessly searching for the best way to extend the consulting contract.
- Consultants will hold a seemingly endless series of meetings to test various hypotheses and assumptions. These exercises are a vital step toward tricking managers into revealing the recommendation that is most likely to generate repeat consulting business.
- After the correct recommendation is discovered, it must be justified by a lengthy analysis. Analysis is designed to be as confusing as possible, thus discouraging any second-guessing by staff members who are afraid of appearing dense.
- Consultants use a standard set of decision tools that involve creating alternative scenarios based on different assumptions. Any pesky assumption that does not fit the predetermined recommendation is quickly discounted as being uneconomical by the consultants.
- Consultants will often recommend that you do whatever you are not doing now.
- Consultants do not need much experience in industry in order to be experts; they learn quickly.

Adams continues with his list of advantages that consultants bring to a company:

- Consultants eventually leave, which makes them excellent scapegoats for major management blunders.
- Consultants can schedule time on your boss's calendar because they do not have your reputation as a troublemaker who constantly brings up unsolvable issues.
- Consultants often are more trusted than your regular employees.

- Consultants will return phone calls because it is all billable time to them.
- Consultants work preposterously long hours, thus making the regular staff feel worthless for only working 60 hours a week.

While this is a humorous attack on the consulting field, it unfortunately rings true for many consultants, bringing confirmation at least on some of the points.

Certainly some of the criticism of consulting is unjustified. Employees who are the subjects of job loss, job redesign, transfer, or relocation as a result of a consulting initiative will undoubtedly view the process as unfair and distasteful. However, the hostility and negative attacks go beyond the outcome of the consulting process. They underscore the fact that many consulting interventions are not a value-added process—they do not provide a payoff to the organization for its time and resources allocated to the process. A well-designed and properly focused project that brings value to the organization will not be subjected to the type of ridicule and negative comments consulting interventions often draw.

Excessive Costs

The cost of consulting is increasing significantly. The story of the employee who was fired and rehired as a consultant at twice the salary is becoming commonplace, except that these days it is three or four times the salary. While most employees understand that an hourly rate for a consultant must be more than a corresponding hourly rate for an employee, the differential is staggering. An MBA fresh out of school may command $200 an hour for a big consulting firm working hand-in-hand with employees who know far more about the process than the consultant. In essence, the consultant is learning on the job with a resulting increase in salary. The middle-level or senior consultants in a large consulting firm may command $250 to $350 an hour, while a senior partner will charge more than $500 an hour. These are not short-term assignments but often long-term projects that continue for as much as a year. The notion of a higher hourly rate was built on the idea that there are only a certain number of billable days—usually 60 percent of all possible workdays. Today that number has increased, and in some firms junior consultants bill between 80 and 90 percent of their time—sometimes on a requirement or expectations. These costs, when spread over a large organization, add up quickly. AT&T, for example, spent roughly $100 million a year on outside consultants until a recent CEO put a clamp on the spending.[6] Other firms are beginning to put a stop on such spending until there is some sense of control and more evidence of additional value.

The underlying theme of the three issues is the lack of a focus on results—the absence of a process that defines results, emphasizes results, and delivers results throughout the project. While this book is not about how to consult, it does show how the value of consulting is determined. It provides a process with which any type of consulting intervention can be measured, quickly and routinely, to keep it on track to reach its ultimate objectives, including the actual return on investment.

What Can Happen When Consultants Are Not Accountable

The previous section provides a glimpse of the problems in the consulting industry from both the consultant and client perspectives. Although the issues sometimes overlap, the following five consequences can come from a flawed consulting assignment that has gone astray.

Wasted Resources

Perhaps the most important consequence is that precious funds are wasted on the consulting intervention. Consulting projects are usually very expensive; in larger organizations the funding for a consulting project can be significant and often grows without accountability. These funds could be used for other worthwhile projects that may address the same issues that precipitated the consulting assignment.

Wasted Time

Consultants eat up precious staff time, as dozens and sometimes hundreds of employees perform tasks for and provide information to consultants. This is often done with the assumption that the current staff can provide this information at less cost. Also, staff members often know where to find the information and how to interpret it. If the consulting intervention has gone astray and not produced results, this experience represents a tremendous waste of internal time—time that could be devoted to important, profit-generating activities.

Demoralized Staff

Connected very closely with the waste of time is the effect the consulting project has on the staff. Too many employees see consultants as individuals who collect information from them and pass their recommendations on to the executives. They see little contribution from consultants. In short, they view consultants the way they are depicted in Scott Adams's comic strip *Dilbert*. This should not come as a surprise. According to Adams, his own experiences with these activities have led to many of the cartoon depictions of consultants.[7]

Harmful Advice

If improper advice is given, the consequences can be devastating. If a system is implemented improperly or a product line is introduced incorrectly, business is unnecessarily harmed. If an acquisition is pursued improperly, the business may suffer irreversible damage. Although these consequences are not the routine, they occur with enough frequency to be alarming. In some cases, bad advice can be so devastating that it brings the company to bankruptcy. In other cases, it causes reduced revenues or diminished profits. Unfortunately, many articles appear routinely in business publications explaining how organizations are now taking consultants to court and holding them legally liable for their bad advice.[8]

Devastated Careers

Consulting assignments have been known to tarnish the careers of those individuals who have advocated or supported faulty assignments. When it is seen that the company has misspent money or has received very little advice for the money spent, the executive or executives involved in the process often lose their luster (and sometimes their jobs). In a very political environment, those who resist consulting interventions often suffer career anxieties and disappointments as well. The use of consultants is often a political activity within organizations.

Many of these consequences of ineffective consulting interventions can be prevented if proper steps are taken to hold consultants accountable from the beginning of the process and throughout to the end of the assignment. The tools presented in this book show how to avoid these disasters that can wreak havoc within an organization.

Shifting Paradigms

Consulting paradigms are shifting for both consultants and clients. Processes are being developed to focus directly on accountability. For years, consulting activity, consulting processes, and consulting progress have been focused on activity or input, with success being derived from the inputs into the process rather than the outcomes. The situation is changing, though, as consulting interventions and processes are now results based. Table 1.1 shows the shift from activity-based consulting to results-based consulting. This represents an important paradigm shift for the consulting profession.

Table 1.1   Paradigm Shift in Consulting Accountability

Activity-Based Consulting	Results-Based Consulting
No business need for the consulting intervention	Intervention linked to specific business needs
No assessment of performance issues	Assessment of performance effectiveness
No specific, measurable objectives for implementation and business impact	Specific objectives for implementation and business impact
No effort to prepare stakeholders/participants to achieve results	Results/expectations communicated to stakeholders/participants
No effort to prepare the work environment to support implementation	Environment prepared to support implementation
No efforts to build partnerships with key managers	Partnerships established with key managers and clients
No measurement of results or cost-benefit analysis	Measurement of results and cost-benefit analysis
Planning and reporting on consulting intervention is focused on input	Planning and reporting on consulting interventions are focused on output

Consulting interventions are being linked to specific business needs that are measurable impact variables having a significant influence on the business. This linkage is part of an up-front analysis that includes:

- A detailed reassessment of performance issues and performance effectiveness to determine the specific causes or inhibitors of the improvement of business impact needs.
- Specific objectives developed not only for learning needs, but for actual application of the consulting solution and the resulting business impact.
- Expectations of results communicated through a variety of individuals, particularly for those stakeholders and participants directly involved in the consulting intervention. This helps keep the end in mind in very specific, measurable terms.
- Full exploration and preparation of the work environment to support the implementation of the consulting solution, which is essential for a successful consulting intervention.
- Partnerships with key managers and clients to build their support for the process, helping to ensure that they will provide the resources and commitment to make the project a success.
- Measurement of results, including a cost-benefit analysis showing the actual payoff of the consulting assignment.
- Output-focused planning and reporting on consulting interventions, indicating the successes obtained through the intervention rather than the resources deployed. This represents a dramatic shift in reporting as organizations report data in terms of the six measures outlined in this book.

This paradigm shift is long overdue. Fortunately, many consulting firms have adopted the results-based philosophy and are delivering results, meeting the expectations of their clients.

Needing a New Approach to Measure Impact

Clients—who must approve consulting budgets, request consulting projects, and live with the results of consulting interventions—have a strong interest in the accountability of interventions. The interest aligns in four major areas. First, clients want to see what actually changes as a result of the consulting assignment. They want to know if the recommendation was implemented properly, on time, on schedule, and as planned, and if the appropriate support was delivered. This is critical to the success of the intervention. Second, clients want to know if the process had an impact on the business units. Third, clients want to know if this assignment was a good investment for the organization. Was the payoff appropriate? Did it exceed the cost of the assignment? Finally, did the project drive key intangible measures, which are often difficult to quantify yet critical to the success of an organization? These four concerns of the client group represent four of the six key measures advocated in this book.

Clients have been skeptical of attempts to quantify the success of consulting interventions. Sometimes, other influences or factors were not considered; the costs were not fully loaded, or the benefits were actually overstated. Attempts to develop a process have been met with much skepticism and sometimes even criticism. While the evaluation process described in this book is explained in more detail in the following chapter, it is important to consider the requirements for this type of process from the viewpoint of the client. The client group is often seeking a process that provides quantifiable results using a method similar to the one utilized to evaluate other investments, namely return on investment (ROI). They want a process that is simple and easy to understand, but credible and conservative in its approach. Any assumptions made in the calculations and methodology used should reflect the frame of reference, background, and level of understanding of the client. Clients do not want or need a string of formulas or complicated models. Instead, they need a process they can explain to others if necessary. More importantly, they need a process with which they can identify—one that is sound and realistic enough to earn their confidence. This book will show how a sound ROI process can be used to provide accountability for consulting projects.

To satisfy the needs of clients, an ROI process must meet several requirements. Ten essential criteria for an effective ROI process are:

1. The ROI process must be *simple*, void of complex formulas, lengthy equations, and complicated methodologies. Most ROI attempts have failed on this requirement. In an attempt to obtain statistical perfection and use as many theories as possible, several ROI models and processes have become too complex to understand and use. Consequently, they have not been implemented.

2. The ROI process must be *economical*, with the ability to be implemented easily. The process should be capable of becoming a routine part of consulting without requiring significant additional resources. Sampling for ROI calculations and early planning for ROI are often necessary to making progress without adding staff.

3. The assumptions, methodology, and techniques must be *credible*. Logical, methodical steps are needed to earn the respect of practitioners, senior managers, and researchers. This requires a very practical approach to the process.

4. From a research perspective, the ROI process must be *theoretically sound* and based on generally accepted practices. Unfortunately, this requirement can lead to an extensive, complicated process. Ideally, the process must strike a balance between maintaining a practical and sensible approach and a sound and theoretical basis for the process. This is perhaps one of the greatest challenges to those who have developed models for an ROI process.

5. The ROI process must *account for other factors* that have influenced output variables. One of the most often overlooked issues—isolating the influence of consulting—is necessary to build credibility and accuracy within the process. The ROI process should pinpoint the contribution of the intervention when compared to the other influences.

6. The ROI process must be appropriate for a *variety of consulting projects*. Some models apply to only a small number of interventions, such as sales or productivity consulting. Ideally, the process should be applicable to all types of consulting interventions, including marketing, systems, product development, and major change initiatives.

7. The ROI process must have the *flexibility* to be applied on a preintervention basis as well as a postintervention basis. In some situations, an estimate of the ROI is required before the actual intervention is developed. Ideally, the process should be adjustable to a range of potential time frames.

8. The ROI process must be *applicable with all types of data*, including hard data (typically represented as output, quality, costs, and time) and soft data (including job satisfaction, customer satisfaction, grievances, and complaints).

9. The ROI process must *include the costs of intervention*. The ultimate level of evaluation is comparing the benefits with costs. Although the term *ROI* has been loosely used to express any benefit of consulting, an acceptable ROI formula must include costs. Omitting or underestimating costs will only destroy the credibility of the ROI values.

10. Finally, the ROI process must have a successful *track record* in a variety of applications. In far too many situations, models are created but never successfully applied. An effective ROI process should withstand the wear and tear of implementation and should produce the expected results.

Because these criteria are considered essential, an ROI process should meet the vast majority if not all of them. The bad news is that most ROI processes fail to do this. The good news is that the ROI process presented in this book meets all of the criteria.

Potential Steps to Take to Ensure a Focus on Results

Now comes the key question: what can the client do to make sure the consultant focuses on results? Actually, the client is in the driver's seat. The client can demand, require, and specify as well as expect results. How is this done? From a practical basis, it can be achieved by focusing on several issues—up to and including the following 15 issues. All of these issues may not be appropriate for a particular consulting intervention, but they represent important areas to consider to make sure that the project is developed properly, is structured adequately, and delivers the results needed and promised. The checklist in Table 1.2 will help the client determine the degree to which the consultant focuses on results.

Ask for Results from Other Projects

As a first step in a new consulting encasement possibility, clients should ask for results from other projects. These could be presented as a final report, impact study, or other measure of success. Ideally, the results should include the actual return on investment from the consulting project. Although results achieved in previous projects do not guarantee success in another project, they do show the extent to

Table 1.2 How to Make Sure Your Consultant Focuses on Results

	Yes	No
Does your consultant have results from other projects?	___	___
Will your consultant agree to guarantee results?	___	___
Has your consultant currently specified the requirements for the project?	___	___
Is there a clear focus on results up front in the proposal and early discussions?	___	___
Has there been a detailed analysis and needs assessment indicating the specific business impact and job performance needs?	___	___
Is it possible to forecast the actual ROI?	___	___
Have multiple levels of objectives been established for the project?	___	___
Is there an evaluation plan developed?	___	___
Have expectations been communicated to all stakeholders?	___	___
Is there a method for routinely providing feedback to enable adjustments to be made?	___	___
Can the consultant develop an impact study?	___	___
Has the consultant isolated the effects of the consulting intervention?	___	___
Has the consultant examined a variety of data on different sources at different times?	___	___
Are the data collection, analysis, and reporting independent?	___	___
Is there a plan to monitor the long-term effects of the project?	___	___

which the consulting firm focuses on results and reviews the methodology, the process, and more importantly the effectiveness of the consulting intervention. If there is no success, then there should be cause for concern. If the consultant or consulting firm cannot produce results or prefers not to disclose confidential information from previous assignments, then the client should beware. Reports can be desensitized and names changed to protect client confidentiality. In today's environment, there is no justification for not having reports of previous successes to provide a glimpse of what might happen in a proposed project.

Seek a Guarantee for Results

Some firms are willing to guarantee results. Unfortunately, not enough are taking this approach. Perhaps it is time to ask for a guarantee. Consultants will quickly comment that there are so many factors out of their control that it is impossible to guarantee results. While this is true, guarantees can be conditional. For example, one consulting firm will guarantee the results of a project on the condition that management supports the project and endorses the recommended solutions. The firm goes on to detail specifically what is meant by "management support," including time frames and specific activities. This provides the consultant leverage but also addresses concerns about other influences.

Other consulting firms will have a contingency for results. They will share the savings or profits from the consulting assignment, placing everything at risk with much to gain if it is successful. Still others will have lower-than-normal consulting fees, barely capturing the direct cost for the consulting intervention and adding a contingency for splitting cost savings after a 25 percent return on investment is achieved. The important issue is the message this sends to the client. Now it is time to ask for a guarantee of results or inject some type of risk from the consultant's standpoint.

Scope the Project and Specify Requirements

There can never be too many details specified on a project in advance. Too often, projects go astray because the expectations of the client are different from the expectations of the consultants. There is not enough detail. The project should be scoped in terms of specific timing, issues, events, activities, deliverables, costs, steps, and, most importantly, expected results. Specific requirements, timetables, time frames, issues, required resources, and other items should be fully detailed and explored. This eliminates confusion and makes expectations crystal clear.

Focus on Results Early, with the End in Mind

As with so many issues or situations, a project should begin with the end in mind in terms of clear expectations of implementation and business impact. Ideally, the business impact measures should form the beginning point, specifying exactly what should change or improve as a result of the consulting intervention. Then the project builds on these results. When results are the starting point, measurement of results at the conclusion of the project becomes much easier. Also, all of the activities in between focus on those end results. Therefore, the client should insist on a results-focused project at the outset.

Insist on Needs Assessment and Analysis

Most consulting projects focus on solving a particular problem or capitalizing on an opportunity. Sometimes the project itself involves an analysis of the problem to arrive at the recommended solutions. In other cases, the consulting project might involve the implementation of solutions identified either by the client or by another consulting firm. Either way, there must be a complete assessment of needs to arrive at a particular solution, and these needs must include issues at several different levels. Not only is there a need to specify the business impact desired, but the desired payoff and job performance requirements, as well as specific learning needs and preferences for implementation, should be included. Table 1.3 shows the levels of needs for a project ranging from payoff to preference. This hierarchy of levels of needs will be explored in Chapter 3 when the linkage between needs assessment and evaluation is clearly established. However, at this point it is important to insist that an appropriate analysis be conducted to reveal needs at all five levels.

Table 1.3 Levels of Needs

Level	Focus
5 Payoff	Potential payoff if problem is addressed or opportunity is pursued
4 Business needs	Business measures that need to change or improve
3 Job performance needs	On-the-job behavior, work design, systems, or environment that need to change to support business
2 Learning needs	Skills/knowledge needed to support job performance needs
1 Preference	Desired structure of solution

Consider an ROI Forecast—with an Update

In some projects it is helpful, and sometimes essential, to forecast the ROI prior to the actual consulting intervention. This is particularly useful if the project is large in scale or if there is tremendous cost associated with the project. The client may need to know the actual impact and anticipated payoff prior to engaging the consulting services. Preconsulting forecasts can be developed for many situations, although they suffer from accuracy and credibility problems because they are estimates. Ideally, if an estimate is needed for a preproject ROI, it should be obtained using the best data available, often from previous studies or experts who can provide input on the expected results. More importantly, when the consulting intervention involves the performance of individuals, input should be obtained directly from them so they can indicate the likelihood of obtaining certain performance levels within the intervention. The important point is that the forecast for ROI can be obtained early—not only prior to the project, but actually during its implementation—using different types of data, including reaction or satisfaction data. Sometimes even learning data can help in forecasting the ROI. While this topic is covered in more detail in a later chapter, it is important to realize that a forecast may be needed, can be required, and should be a consideration with any consulting project.

Specify Multiple-Level Objectives

When solutions are implemented, multiple levels of objectives should be required or specified. These objectives focus on implementation issues and business impact issues. Implementation objectives involve the timing, the actual use of the process, and the progress achieved in making an intervention successful in the organization. Impact objectives define the specific business needs or measures that must change or improve as a result of implementation. They define success in terms of business measures and are often the most critical objectives for consulting projects. These multiple levels of objectives ensure that there is a focus on results. Table 1.4 shows the five levels of objectives involved in implementing solutions for a consulting intervention.

Table 1.4 Multiple Levels of Objectives

Levels of Objectives	Focus of Objectives
Level 1: reaction and satisfaction	Defines a specific level of reaction and satisfaction with the consulting solution as it is explained and communicated to the stakeholders
Level 2: learning	Defines specific skills and knowledge changes expected as the stakeholders learn information about the consulting solution
Level 3: implementation	Defines key issues necessary for the implementation of the solution in the workplace to be successful
Level 4: business impact	Defines the business measures that will change or improve as a result of the implementation
Level 5: ROI	Defines the specific return on investment expected from the implementation of the solution, comparing costs to benefits

Develop an Evaluation Plan

An evaluation plan should be developed for any major project, specifying exactly how data will be collected, analyzed, and reported. Table 1.5 shows a list of the topics contained in an evaluation plan that is typically divided into two parts: a data collection plan and an impact analysis plan.

Addressing these items, which will sometimes require a half a day to a full day, will aid in all the major decisions about how data are collected, analyzed, and reported to various target audiences.

Communicate Expectations to Stakeholders

The stakeholders directly involved in the process should understand what is expected from the consulting assignment, particularly from the implementation and impact objectives. Continuous communication of expectations maintains the focus on the desired results and helps in making adjustments when things are off track or out of line.

Provide Feedback Routinely to Make Adjustments

Different types of data must be collected at different intervals from different sources to make adjustments. If there is some concern about the

Table 1.5   Items for Evaluation

Data Collection Plan	Impact Analysis Plan
• Multiple levels of objectives • Specific measures and data • Data collection method • Sources of data • Timing of data collection • Key responsibilities for data collection	• Business measures analyzed • Methods for isolating the effects of consulting • Methods for converting data to monetary values • Proposed intangible benefits • Project cost categories • Communication target audience • Communication media

project, adjustments may be made. If there appear to be design or analysis flaws, adjustments need to be made. If the implementation is off track or the environment is not conducive to implementation, changes must be made. Many issues can cause a consulting project to go astray. Free-flowing data from different points and different sources can help keep the process on track and the focus on the outcome.

Require an Impact Study with ROI

In many consulting projects, an impact study is desired. This shows a variety of data up to and including the business impact resulting from the consulting intervention. It also shows the actual return on investment where benefits are compared to costs and intangible benefits are identified. All of this may be an extra expense, but it may be worth it for the client to see the actual impact of the consulting intervention, which otherwise may never be known. If the project becomes too costly for the client, perhaps some agreement between the consulting firm and the client to share the costs may be appropriate. The important point is to discuss the impact study up front and include it in the deliverables.

Isolate the Effects of the Consulting Intervention

Perhaps the most important issue that is often omitted from the evaluation of consulting assignments is the isolation of the effects of the consulting intervention. Other factors and influences are almost always present during any consulting intervention. A key challenge is to focus on methods or techniques that isolate the effects of the consulting influence. At least one method should always be used, and the issue must always be addressed. Otherwise the results for a consulting intervention may not be known, or the study may be invalid.

Examine a Variety of Data

Both qualitative and quantitative data need to be collected at different time frames from different sources to provide a complete profile of the success of the project. This book suggests that six types of data representing the six basic measures be collected on every consulting project. These represent both qualitative and quantitative data, as listed in Table 1.6.

Ensure that Data Collection, Analysis, and Reporting Are Independent

In any evaluation data there should be some attempt to make sure the process is independent. A consulting firm reporting the success of its own consulting project is much like a fox guarding a henhouse. There must be some process to ensure that the data are collected, analyzed,

Table 1.6   The Six Measures

Type of Data	Description
Satisfaction/ reaction	Measures the satisfaction/reaction directly involved in the consulting intervention.
Learning	Measures the actual learning taking place for those individuals who must implement or support the process.
Implementation/ application	Measures the success of implementation and the utilization of the consulting intervention solution.
Business impact	Measures the change in business impact measures directly related to the consulting intervention.
ROI	Measures the actual cost versus benefits of the consulting intervention.
Intangible benefits	Measures important intangible benefits not utilized in the benefit-cost formula.

and reported independently of the consulting firm. One option is for the client to review the data and make the analysis. A more viable option may be to employ a firm that specializes in impact analysis, including ROI. If both options are unacceptable, perhaps some initial understanding of how the data are analyzed, collected, or reported is necessary. Perhaps all of the raw data are presented along with the consulting firm's analysis. The most important point is that this issue must be addressed as the evaluation data are collected.

Monitor Long-Term Effects of Projects

The final item is a provision to monitor the long-term effects of these projects. Many consulting projects will not fully pay off for several years. Although no one wants to wait for an extended time period to measure success, there should be some mechanism considered to measure the long-term impact. Perhaps a predetermined follow-up, conducted externally by a third party or jointly by the client and the consulting firm, would be appropriate. Many projects are revisited each year to measure their success, and although the accuracy begins to deteriorate as other influences enter the process, there is a focus on long-term effects.

Shortcut Ways to Secure Results

Following these steps appears to be quite a lengthy process, since they are designed to be comprehensive to cover many consulting situations. A simpler process for small consulting projects would not require these steps as they would represent overanalysis. The following simplified steps should be considered when time is critical, funds are short, or the consulting project is small:

1. Discuss the specific results that are expected in terms of business measures (output, quality, cost, and time) and implementation requirements.
2. Detail the specific requirements and expectations showing what is required of all parties and the ultimate outcomes.
3. Discuss the concept of a guarantee or the consequences of a failed project, addressing the issue in some creative way.

4. Provide a simple mechanism for giving feedback to the appropriate individuals to make necessary adjustments as the project is implemented and the results are developed.

5. Measure the success of the project in terms of implementation, impact, and ROI if possible. This can provide excellent information for future projects.

Final Thoughts

This chapter has explored major changes in the consulting landscape. While there are various reasons for flawed consulting interventions, many are caused by the fact that some consultants are not accountable. The situation is changing in the consulting field and there is more focus on business results than ever before. Processes are available to ensure that there is a focus on results, but the focus must be driven by the client in terms of expectations, demands, and requirements. The next chapter will outline a specific process developed for overall accountability and discuss how this process was developed. The remaining chapters will address the six measures and discuss various issues surrounding implementation of this process.

References

1. O'Shea, James, and Charles Madigan. *Dangerous Company: The Consulting Powerhouses and the Businesses They Save and Ruin.* New York: Times Business/Random House, 1997.

2. Schaffer, Robert H. *High-Impact Consulting: How Clients and Consultants Can Leverage Rapid Results into Long-Term Gains.* San Francisco: Jossey-Bass, 1997.

3. Biech, Elaine. *The Business of Consulting: The Basics and Beyond.* San Francisco: Jossey-Bass/Pfeiffer, 1999.

4. Adams, Scott. *The Dilbert Principle: A Cubicle's-Eye View of Bosses, Meetings, Management Fads & Other Workplace Afflictions.* New York: Harper Business, 1996.

6. *Dangerous Company.*

7. *The Dilbert Principle.*

8. *Dangerous Company.*

Further Reading

Connors, Roger, and Tom Smith. *Journey to the Emerald City: Achieve a Competitive Edge By Creating a Culture of Accountability*. Englewood Cliffs, NJ: Prentice Hall, 1999.

Dauphinais, G. William, and Colin Price (eds.). *Straight from the CEO: The World's Top Business Leaders Reveal Ideas that Every Manager Can Use*. London: Brealey, 1998.

Donovan, John, Richard Tully, and Brent Wortman. *The Value Enterprise: Strategies for Building a Value-Based Organization*. Toronto: McGraw-Hill/Ryerson, 1998.

Gates, Bill, with Collins Hemingway. *Business @ the Speed of Thought: Using a Digital Nervous System*. New York: Warner, 1999.

Hiebeler, Robert, Thomas B. Kelly, and Charles Ketteman. *Best Practices: Building Your Business With Customer-Focused Solutions*. New York: Simon & Schuster, 1998.

Mitchell, Donald, Carol Coles, and Robert Metz. *The 2,000 Percent Solution: Free Your Organization from "Stalled" Thinking to Achieve Exponential Success*. New York: AMACOM/American Management Association, 1999.

O'Shea, James, and Charles Madigan. *Dangerous Company: The Consulting Powerhouses and the Businesses They Save and Ruin*. New York: Times Business/Random House, 1997.

Rasiel, Ethan M. *The McKinsey Way: Using the Techniques of the World's Top Strategic Consultants to Help You and Your Business*. New York: McGraw-Hill, 1999.

Redwood, Stephen, Charles Goldwasser, and Simon Street. *Action Management: Practical Strategies for Making Your Corporate Transformation a Success*. New York: Wiley, 1999.

Trout, Jack, with Steve Rivkin. *The Power of Simplicity: A Management Guide to Cutting Through the Nonsense and Doing Things Right*. New York: McGraw-Hill, 1999.

2

What's in It for Me?

How Consultants Can Prove the Value of Their Work to Clients

CHAPTER 1 FOCUSED on the rationale for comprehensive measurement and evaluation from the client's perspective. This chapter approaches the same issue from the consultant's perspective. Several important accountability questions must be answered by consultants: what is involved in the process? What is my role in the process? How should I approach evaluation? Is a credible process available? Can it be implemented within my resources? What will happen if I do nothing? These and other critical issues will need attention. This chapter explores each of these issues and others as the case is presented for consultants to adopt a more comprehensive measurement and evaluation process, including the consulting ROI process.

In this chapter a rational, credible approach to measurement and evaluation is presented, showing how the process can be applied within the resources of the consulting firm. It shows the various elements and issues necessary to build credibility with a process that meets the needs of today's organizations.

Is This Necessary? Why Measure Consulting ROI?

Developing a balanced set of measures, including measuring the consulting ROI, has earned a place among the critical issues in the consulting field. The topic routinely appears on conference agendas and at professional meetings. Journals and newsletters embrace the concept, devoting increasing print space to it. Several consulting experts are recommending ROI calculations. Even top executives have increased their appetites for ROI information.

Although interest in the topic has heightened and progress has been made, it is still an issue that challenges even the most sophisticated and progressive consulting firms. Some consultants argue that it is not possible to calculate the ROI in consulting interventions, while others quietly and deliberately proceed to develop measures and ROI calculations. Regardless of the position taken on the issue, the reasons for measuring the ROI are still there. Most consultants share a concern that they must eventually show a return on their consulting interventions. Otherwise, consulting funds may be reduced, or the firm may not be able to maintain or enhance its present status with clients.

Although the rationale for focusing on ROI may be obvious, it is helpful to explore the various reasons why now is the time to pursue the actual calculations for the consulting ROI. The consulting industry has been in existence for many years and has earned an important place in the mainstream activities of most medium and large organizations. Why is now the time to begin measuring the success in more detail than ever imagined? Several issues create a logical answer to this question.

Client Demands

Today, more clients are requesting additional evaluation data, up to and including measuring the actual ROI. It is common for clients to ask the key question at the beginning of most consulting projects: "How do I know if this will pay off for me, and will this be a good return on my investment?" Although the accountability issue has always been there, it has never reached the level of concern that exists today. When the client demands a process, it must be explored and implemented, and the process must be credible enough for the client to believe the results. Client questions must be addressed in a simple, rational way. Avoiding the issue will create distrust between the client and consultant and ultimately may cause the business to get off track.

Competitive Advantage

Perhaps one of the most important reasons to pursue a more comprehensive measurement and evaluation, including ROI, is to meet or beat the competition. Many firms are beginning to develop the ROI around consulting assignments to stay competitive or perhaps stay ahead of others who are developing similar processes. It is imperative to address the issue in a proactive manner with a comprehensive approach to consulting ROI. It just may be the best way to position the consulting firm ahead of much of the competition.

Increased Revenues and Profits

When a consulting firm can show the actual contribution of the consulting engagement in monetary terms, an excellent case can be made for additional fees, or at least additional projects. Some firms are taking the process to the level of using it to drive additional compensation—for example, discounting regular fees in a consulting intervention and placing the rest of the compensation at risk with a payoff linked to a target ROI. The payment can be a set amount or savings beyond the target. This approach provides an excellent way to increase revenues and build profits while generating client satisfaction and loyalty.

Enhanced Marketing Database

Developing a history of ROI applications ultimately builds an important database of results. Not only will the database show clients what has happened in previous engagements, but it can eventually show various trends and patterns in consulting interventions throughout different industries. A substantial database of projects using a credible, undisputed process can be a crucial advantage and a persuasive selling point.

Self-Satisfaction

Individuals engaged in professional work want to know that their efforts make a difference. Consultants need to see that they are making a contribution in terms that managers respect and appreciate. Showing the consulting ROI may be one of the most self-satisfying parts of an excellent consulting project. Not only do things go well in terms of schedule, budget, and client feedback, but the actual value added in monetary terms with an impressive ROI adds the final touch to a major project. This provides additional evidence that what we do does make a difference.

The Dilemma of ROI Accountability

The dilemma surrounding consulting ROI is a source of frustration to many clients and consultants and even within the consulting field itself. Most clients realize that consulting is a basic necessity when organizations are experiencing problems, significant growth, or increased competition. In these cases, consultants can prepare employees and organizations to meet competitive challenges. Consulting interventions are also important during business restructuring and rapid change, in which employees find themselves doing much more work in a dramatically downsized workforce.

Many clients see the need for consulting and intuitively feel that there is value in a consulting intervention. They can logically conclude that consulting can pay off in important bottom-line measures such as productivity improvements, quality enhancements, cost reductions, and time savings. Also, they believe that a consulting project can enhance customer satisfaction, improve morale, and build teamwork. The frustration comes from the lack of evidence showing that the process is really working. While the payoffs are assumed to be there, and the consulting intervention appears to be needed, more evidence is needed for consulting funds to be allocated in the future. The consulting ROI process represents the most promising way to show this accountability through a logical, rational approach.

What Is Causing This Concern for Accountability?

Another important issue to face is examining the drivers for the ROI process. Just what is causing so much focus on accountability, including consulting ROI? Several key forces are coming together at this time to create a tremendous pressure to pursue consulting ROI.

Failure of Consulting Interventions

As mentioned in Chapter 1, many consulting projects have not lived up to their promises or expectations. They have not delivered the results that the clients and the consulting firms expected—at least not in the terms that management understands, primarily bottom-line contributions. As more and more consulting projects are undertaken, consuming precious resources in an organization, the results have simply not materialized for many projects. And when the results are reported, there is often skepticism and concern about the credibility and objectivity of the data and the thoroughness of the analysis. This has caused many clients to rethink the role as well as the accountability of consulting and to place more restraints and demands on consultants.

Economic Pressures of Clients

As firms strive to be successful in a global economy, there are tremendous pressures on costs and efficiency. Companies must squeeze all the savings possible out of every process, activity, and resource. They must account for every expenditure and every project. For some, survival is an issue. This competition for resources has caused organizations to examine the payoff of consulting to make sure they are getting the most out of their consulting expenditures.

Budget Growth

With the increased use of consultants comes increased spending for consulting activities. Coupled with this is the increased cost of consultants, as their fees and charges become a bigger target for critics of the process. It is one thing to spend $50,000 on a consulting project, but it is another to spend $1 million and still have nothing to show for it. Consulting has secured a greater percentage of many firms' operating budgets. These firms see the percentage of expenditures dedicated to consulting growing significantly, not only in magnitude but also as a percentage of operating costs. This growth makes consulting a likely target for increased accountability—if nothing else—to satisfy critics of the process.

Accountability Trends

Today, the trend toward increased accountability is sweeping across organizations not only in consulting activities, but in almost every type of process. Quality initiatives, technology implementation, human resources programs, and major change initiatives are all being subjected to increased accountability. In today's environment, any new process implemented must address accountability. This focus on accountability is not a new issue. It has been increasing for years, but only recently has it been growing in intensity across organizations.

Balanced Measures

For years there has been debate over what should or should not be measured and how. Some prefer soft data directly from the client or customers. Others prefer hard data focused on key issues of output, quality, cost, and time. Some others have argued for a balance of measures, and this camp seems to be winning. There is a critical need to examine data from a variety of groups at different time frames and for different purposes. This mixture of data, often referred to as a *balanced approach*, is driving additional need for the process described in this book and is an important part of the consulting ROI process.

Executive Interest

ROI is now enjoying increased interest in the executive suite. Top executives who have watched their consulting budgets grow without the appropriate accountability measures have become frustrated and, in an attempt to respond to the situation, have demanded a return on investment for consulting. The payoff of consulting is becoming a conversation topic in executive publications. *The Wall Street Journal*, the *Financial Times*, *Fortune*, *Business Week*, and *Forbes* regularly feature articles about consulting and the need for increased accountability, describing the frustration of senior executives as they search for results from major consulting projects. Measuring the consulting ROI is becoming a global issue, as executives from all over the world are concerned about accountability of consulting. Whether an economy is mature or developing, the economic pressures of running a global enterprise are making the accountability of consulting an issue.

Passing Fads

Finally, ROI applications have increased because of the growing interest in a variety of organizational improvement and change interventions offered by consulting firms, particularly in North America. Organizations have embraced almost any trend that appears on the horizon. Unfortunately, many of these change efforts have not worked and have turned out to be nothing more than passing fads, however well intentioned. The consulting firm is often caught in the middle of this activity, either by supporting the process with interventions or actually coordinating the new process in these organizations. Unfortunately the consulting ROI process was not used to measure the accountability of these interventions. An implementation of the complete process requires thorough assessment and significant planning before the ROI process is attempted. If these two elements are in place, unnecessary passing fads doomed for failure can be avoided. With the ROI process in place, a new change program that does not produce results will be exposed. Management will be fully aware of it early so that adjustments can quickly be made.

Figure 2.1 shows the five reasons for developing ROI in today's environment and the seven forces previously described, which are driving the need for ROI. Together they develop the rationale for consulting ROI today.

Finally, a Credible Approach

To develop a credible approach for calculating the consulting ROI, several pieces of an important puzzle must be developed. Figure 2.2 shows the major elements of the puzzle. First, there should be an evaluation framework that defines the various levels of evaluation. It should show how data is captured at different times from different sources to develop a comprehensive set of measures. Next, an ROI process model must be developed that shows a step-by-step procedure for developing the actual ROI calculation. Inherent in this process is the isolation of the

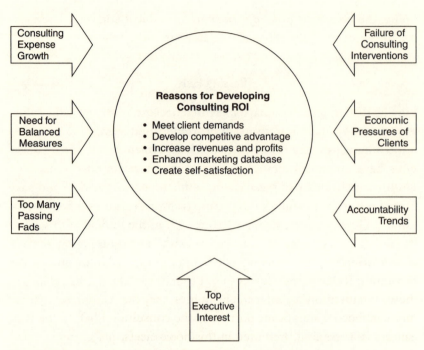

Figure 2.1 Drivers of the need for ROI.

effects of consulting and other factors and actually showing the monetary payoff compared to the cost of the consulting assignment. A process model with many options and sequential steps helps ensure that the process can be replicated. Next, there should be some set of operating guidelines or operating standards. These illustrate the philosophy behind the particular process and are designed to keep processes on track so that the likelihood of replication is enhanced. In other words, if two individuals conducted the same study, the same results would be obtained. Also, the operating standard builds credibility in the process because it is a very conservative approach. Next, appropriate resources should be devoted to implementation issues, addressing responsibilities, policies, procedures, guidelines, goals, and internal skill building. Finally, there should be ample case applications that build experience with a process to show how it actually works in real-world settings. Together, these five pieces of the puzzle are necessary to develop an evaluation system that contains a balanced set of measures, has credibility with the various stakeholders involved, and can be replicated from one group to another.

For a consulting ROI process to be feasible, it must balance many issues, including feasibility, simplicity, credibility, and soundness. More specifically, three major target audiences must be satisfied. First, the consultants who use a process must have a simple approach. Unfortunately, when many consultants have attempted to look for an ROI process, they have found long formulas, complicated equations, and complex models. These make the process appear confusing and complex. This has caused many consultants to give up in a fit of frustration, making the assumption that the ROI cannot be developed or that it would be too expensive for most applications. Because of these concerns, many consultants seek a process that is simple and easy to understand so that they can implement the steps and strategies. Also, they need a process that will not take an excessive amount of time to implement and will not consume too much precious consulting time. Finally, the consultants need a process that is not too expensive. Given the fierce competition for financial resources, they need a process that will not command a significant portion of the consulting budget. The consulting ROI process presented in this book meets this important challenge from the perspective of the consultant.

A consulting ROI process is needed that will meet the unique requirements of clients. Clients, who request consulting interventions and approve consulting projects, need a process that will provide quan-

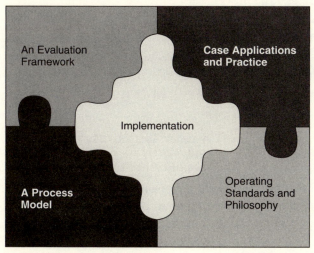

Figure 2.2   Building a credible process.

titative and qualitative results. They need a process that will develop a calculation similar to the ROI formula applied to other types of investments. And as with consultants, they want a process that is simple and easy to understand, and that reflects their point of reference, background, and level of understanding. They neither want nor need a string of formulas, charts, or complicated models. Instead, they need a process that they can explain to others if necessary. More importantly, they need a process with which they can identify—one that is sound and realistic enough to earn their confidence. The process outlined in this book meets the important needs of the client group.

Finally, researchers in measurement and evaluation need a process they can support—one that measures up to their scrutiny and close examination. Researchers want to use models, formulas, assumptions, and theories that are sound and based on commonly accepted practices. Also, they want a process that produces accurate values and consistent outcomes. They want a process that can be replicated from one situation to another and that provides the reliability of having the same measurements if two different consultants are pursuing a project. They want a process that uses estimates very carefully. If estimates are necessary, the researchers want a process that provides the most accuracy within the constraints of the situations, recognizing that adjustments need to be made when there is uncertainty in the process. Fortunately, the process presented in this book has met the needs of researchers who have examined the process very closely.

Not only does the ROI process meet the critical challenges of these three important groups, it also provides consultants with a useful, helpful tool that can be a routine and integral part of consulting interventions. The next five sections describe the five critical parts of the puzzle that come together to create a viable consulting ROI process.

The Framework: Evaluation Levels

The consulting ROI process adds a fifth level to the four levels of evaluation developed for the training profession almost 40 years ago by Donald Kirkpatrick.[1] The concept of different levels of evaluation is both helpful and instructive in understanding how the return on investment is calculated. Table 2.1 shows a modified version of the five-level

Table 2.1   Characteristics of Evaluation Levels

Level	Brief Description
1. Reaction and satisfaction	Measures consulting participants' reaction to the intervention and stakeholder satisfaction with the project and the planned implementation
2. Learning	Measures skills, knowledge, or attitude changes related to the consulting intervention and implementation
3. Application and implementation	Measures changes in behavior on the job and specific application and implementation of the consulting intervention
4. Business impact	Measures business impact changes related to the consulting intervention
5. Return on investment	Compares the monetary value of the business impact with the costs for the intervention, usually expressed as a percentage

framework used in this book. Incidentally, the levels represent the first five of the six measures for consultants presented in this book. At Level 1, reaction and satisfaction, reaction from consulting participants is measured, along with input on a variety of issues. Almost all consulting firms evaluate at Level 1, usually with generic questionnaires and surveys. While this level of evaluation is important as a customer satisfaction measure, a favorable reaction does not ensure that participants will implement the improvements. At Level 2, learning, measurements focus on what consulting participants have learned during the intervention. A learning check is helpful to ensure that consulting participants have absorbed new skills and knowledge and know how to use these to make the consulting intervention successful. However, a positive measure at this level is no guarantee that the intervention will be successfully implemented. At Level 3, application and implementation, a variety of follow-up methods are used to determine if participants have applied on the job what is needed to make the project successful. The frequency and use of skills are important measures at Level 3. In addition, this measure includes all the steps, actions, tasks, and processes involved in the implementation of the intervention. While Level 3 evaluation is important to gauge the success of the intervention's implementation, it still does not guarantee that there will be a positive impact on the organization. At Level 4, business impact, the measurement focuses on the actual results achieved by the consulting intervention. Typical Level 4 measures include output, quality, cost, time, and customer satisfaction. Although the consulting intervention may produce a measurable business impact, there is still a concern that the intervention may have cost too much. At Level 5, return on investment—the ultimate level of evaluation—intervention's monetary benefits are compared with the consulting costs. Although the ROI can be expressed in several ways, it is usually presented as a percentage or benefit-cost ratio. The evaluation cycle is not complete until the Level 5 evaluation is conducted.

While almost all consulting firms conduct evaluations to measure satisfaction, very few actually conduct evaluations at the ROI level. Perhaps the best explanation for this is that ROI evaluation is often characterized as a difficult and expensive process. Although business results and ROI are desired, it is very important to evaluate the other levels. A chain of impact should occur through the levels as the skills and knowledge learned (Level 2) in the consulting project are applied on the job as the project is implemented (Level 3) to produce business impact (Level 4). If measurements are not taken at each level, it is difficult to conclude that the results achieved were actually produced by the consulting project. Because of this, it is recommended that evaluation be conducted at all levels when a Level 5 evaluation is planned.

The Process: Consulting ROI

The consulting ROI process, presented briefly in this chapter and explored throughout this book, had its beginnings several years ago as the process was applied to a variety of interventions. Since then, the process has been refined and modified until it appeared as shown in Figure 2.3. As the figure illustrates, the process is comprehensive, as data are developed at different times and gathered from different sources to develop the six types of measures that are the focal point of this book. To date there have been more than 300 case studies utilizing the ROI process, and the number is growing rapidly. The process meets all of the criteria outlined in the previous chapter and also meets the needs of the three groups mentioned earlier. Each part of the

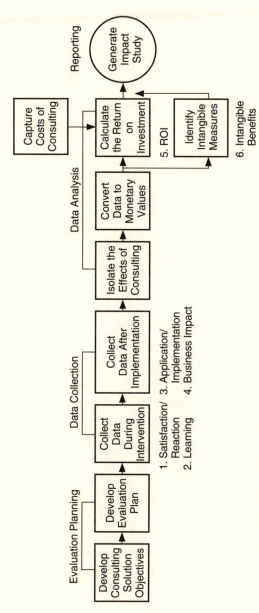

Figure 2.3 The consulting ROI process.

process is briefly mentioned in this chapter. More detail is provided in later chapters.

Evaluation Planning

The first two parts of the consulting ROI process focus on two critical planning issues. The first step is to develop appropriate objectives for the consulting solution. These are often referred to as the ultimate objectives as a particular solution to a problem is implemented. They range from developing objectives for satisfaction to developing an objective for the ROI and are defined in more detail in the next chapter.

With the objectives in hand, the next step is to develop a detailed evaluation plan. This involves two important documents. A data collection plan indicates the type of data collected, the method for data collection, data sources, the timing of collection, and the various responsibilities. The next document, the ROI analysis plan, details how the consulting initiative is isolated from other influences, how data are converted to monetary values, the appropriate cost categories, the expected intangible measures, and the anticipated target audience for communication. These planning documents are necessary for the process to be implemented appropriately.

Collecting Data

Data collected during the intervention measure reaction and satisfaction at Level 1 and learning at Level 2. Collecting data during the intervention ensures that adjustments are made and the process is altered as necessary to make sure the assignment is on track. The reaction, satisfaction, and learning data are critical for immediate feedback and necessary to make the intervention successful.

Data collection is central to the calculation of the ROI. Postintervention data are collected and compared to preintervention situations, control group differences, and expectations. Both hard data (representing output, quality, cost, and time) and soft data (including work habits, work climate, and attitudes) are collected. Data are collected using a variety of methods outlined in Table 2.2.

The important challenge in data collection is selecting the method or methods appropriate for the setting and the specific intervention within the time and budget constraints. Data collection methods are covered in more detail in Chapters 4 through 7.

Table 2.2 Methods of Data Collection

- Follow-up surveys measure satisfaction from stakeholders.
- Follow-up questionnaires measure reaction and uncover specific application issues with consulting interventions.
- On-the-job observation captures actual application and use.
- Tests and assessments are used to measure the extent of learning (knowledge gained or skills enhanced).
- Interviews measure reaction and determine the extent to which the consulting intervention has been implemented.
- Focus groups determine the degree of application of the consulting solution in job situations.
- Action plans show progress with implementation on the job and the impact obtained.
- Performance contracts detail specific outcomes expected or obtained from the consulting intervention.
- Business performance monitoring shows improvement in various performance records and operational data.

Isolating the Effects of Consulting
An often overlooked issue in most evaluations is the process of isolating the effects of a consulting intervention. In this step of the process, specific strategies are explored that determine the amount of performance improvement directly related to the intervention. This step is essential because there are many factors that will influence performance data after a consulting intervention. The specific strategies in this step will pinpoint the amount of improvement directly related to the intervention. The result is increased accuracy and credibility of the ROI calculation. The strategies shown in Table 2.3 have been utilized by organizations to tackle this important issue. Collectively, these strategies provide a comprehensive set of tools for tackling the important and critical issue of isolating the effects of consulting. Chapter 10 is devoted to this important process.

Converting Data to Monetary Values
To calculate the return on investment, business impact data are converted to monetary values and compared to intervention costs. This requires a value to be placed on each unit of data connected with the

Table 2.3 Methods for Isolating the Effects of Consulting

- A pilot group with consulting is compared to a control group without consulting to isolate consulting intervention impact.
- Trend lines are used to project the values of specific output variables, and projections are compared to the actual data after a consulting intervention.
- A forecasting model is used to isolate the effects of a consulting intervention when mathematical relationships between input and output variables are known.
- Participants/stakeholders estimate the amount of improvement related to a consulting intervention.
- Supervisors and managers estimate the impact of a consulting intervention on the output measures.
- External studies provide input on the impact of a consulting intervention.
- Independent experts provide estimates of the impact of a consulting intervention on the performance variable.
- When feasible, other influencing factors are identified and the impact is estimated or calculated, leaving the remaining unexplained improvement attributable to the consulting intervention.
- Customers provide input on the extent to which the consulting intervention has influenced their decision to use a product or service.

---

consulting intervention. Table 2.4 shows most of the key strategies that are available to convert data to monetary values. The specific strategy selected usually depends on the type of data and the situation.

This step in the consulting ROI model is very important and is absolutely necessary for determining the monetary benefits from a consulting intervention. The process is challenging, particularly with soft data, but can be methodically accomplished using one or more of these strategies. Because of its importance, Chapter 11 is devoted to this issue.

Tabulating the Cost of the Intervention

The other part of the equation in a benefit-cost analysis is the consulting intervention cost. Tabulating the cost involves monitoring or developing the cost related to the intervention. A fully loaded approach is recommended in which all direct and indirect costs are tabulated. The cost components that should be included are outlined in Table 2.5.

Table 2.4 Methods for Converting Data to Money

- Output data are converted to profit contribution or cost savings and reported as a standard value.
- The cost of a quality measure, such as a reject, is calculated and reported as a standard value.
- Employee time saved is converted to wages and benefits.
- Historical costs of preventing a measure, such as a customer complaint, are used when they are available.
- Internal and external experts estimate a value of a measure.
- External databases contain an approximate value or cost of a data item.
- Participants estimate the cost or value of the data item.
- Supervisors or managers provide estimates of costs or value when they are both willing and capable of assigning values.
- The consulting staff estimates a value of a data item.
- The measure is linked to other measures for which the costs are easily developed.

The conservative approach is to include all of these costs so that the total is fully loaded. Chapter 12 is devoted to this issue.

Calculating the Return on Investment
The return on investment is calculated using benefits and costs. The benefit-cost ratio (BCR) is the benefits of consulting divided by cost. In formula form this is:

Table 2.5 Recommended Consulting Costs

- The cost of initial analysis and assessment, possibly prorated over the expected life of the intervention
- The cost of developing solutions
- The cost of acquiring solutions
- The cost for application and implementation of the intervention
- The cost of maintenance and monitoring
- The cost of evaluation and reporting
- The costs of administration and overhead for the consulting intervention, allocated in some convenient way

$$BCR = \frac{\text{Consulting Benefits}}{\text{Consulting Costs}}$$

Sometimes this ratio is stated as a cost-benefit ratio, although the formula is the same as BCR. The return on investment uses the net benefits divided by consulting costs. The net benefits are the consulting benefits minus the costs. In formula form, the ROI becomes:

$$ROI\% = \frac{\text{Net Consulting Benefits}}{\text{Consulting Costs}} \times 100$$

This is the same basic formula used in evaluating other investments where the ROI is traditionally reported as earnings divided by investment. Chapter 8 is devoted to ROI calculations.

The BCR and the ROI present the same general information, but from slightly different perspectives. An example will illustrate the use of these formulas: a consulting intervention produces benefits of $581,000 at a cost of $229,000. Therefore, the benefit-cost ratio is:

$$BCR = \frac{\$581,000}{\$229,000} = 2.54 \text{ (or 2.5:1)}$$

As this calculation shows, for every $1 invested, $2.50 in benefits are returned. In this example, net benefits are $581,000 − $229,000 = $352,000. Thus, the ROI is:

$$ROI\% = \frac{\$352,000}{\$229,000} \times 100 = 154\%$$

This means that for each $1 invested in the consulting intervention, there is a return of $1.50 in *net* benefits, after costs are covered. The benefits are usually expressed as annual benefits for short-term consulting interventions, representing the amount saved or gained for a complete year after the consulting solution has been implemented. While the benefits may continue after the first year, the impact usually diminishes and is omitted from calculations in short-term situations. For long-term projects, the benefits are spread over several years. This conservative approach is used throughout the application of the ROI process described in this book.

Identifying Intangible Benefits
In addition to tangible, monetary benefits, most consulting interventions will drive intangible, nonmonetary benefits. During data analysis,

every attempt is made to convert all data to monetary values. All hard data such as output, quality, and time are converted to monetary values. The conversion of soft data is attempted for each data item. However, if the process used for conversion is too subjective or inaccurate, and the resulting values lose credibility in the process, then the data are listed as intangible benefits with the appropriate explanation. For some consulting interventions, intangible, nonmonetary benefits are extremely valuable, often commanding as much influence as the hard data items. Intangible benefits include items such as:

- Improved public impact
- Increased job satisfaction
- Increased organizational commitment
- Enhanced technology leadership
- Reduced stress
- Improved teamwork
- Improved customer service
- Reduced customer response time

Chapter 9 is devoted to intangible benefits.

Reporting with an Impact Study

A final operational step of the consulting ROI process is to generate an impact study that is used to document the results achieved by the consulting intervention and communicate them to various target audiences. The impact study shows the basic process used to generate the six measures of data. The methodology, assumptions, key concepts, and guiding principles are all outlined before the actual results are presented. Next, the six categories of data, beginning with reaction and satisfaction and moving through ROI and intangible measures, are presented in a rational, logical process, showing the building blocks to success for the study. This becomes the official document that presents the complete assessment of the success of the consulting. Its length ranges from 20 to 30 pages for a small project to 200 to 300 pages for a substantial, long-term consulting impact study.

Because there are a variety of target audiences, different reports may need to be generated. All of the stakeholders involved, including key clients who are not interested in knowing the full details, will need some communication regarding the success of the consulting. A stakeholder report may be appropriate for stakeholders who are involved but not directly responsible for the project. Still other reports may be necessary for different target audiences. The key issue in this step of the consulting ROI process is to analyze the target audiences (detailed in the evaluation planning) and develop the appropriate report to meet their specific needs. Chapter 14 is devoted to communicating the results of measurement and evaluation, including the impact study.

The Operating Standards: Guiding Principles

To ensure that each study takes the same conservative philosophy and to increase the likelihood of replication, a set of guiding principles has been developed for the consulting ROI process. Table 2.6 shows the guiding principles used throughout this book. While the principles may be obvious, each will be explored and revisited throughout the book. However, they do need some explanation at this time. The first principle focuses on the need for an initial analysis to ensure that the proper solutions are identified for the problem or opportunity creating the consulting intervention. In other words, it is important that the right problem is addressed and that the proper implementation is planned.

The number two principle focuses on the levels of objectives described in more detail in the next chapter. Although in theory the ROI can be developed for consulting projects even if there were no objectives, the process is much more efficient and effective and the evaluation is more accurate if there are detailed objectives all the way through to business impact and ROI.

The third general principle represents a way to conserve important resources. Shortcuts can perhaps be taken on lower-level evaluations, whereas more emphasis is regularly placed on higher levels. This is important when the client wants to see the business impact. In those cases, shortcuts can be taken perhaps at Levels 2 and 3 (measuring learning and application/implementation).

Principle 5 adds to the credibility of the process. Without some method to isolate the effects of consulting, the studies are considered to be highly inaccurate and overstated in their results.

Principle 6 addresses missing data from individuals involved in consulting projects. If the participants are no longer on the job or no longer

Table 2.6 Ten Guiding Principles

1. If a consulting intervention is not needed, the economic benefits will be negligible.
2. An evaluation can be taken to the highest level of the consulting solution's objectives.
3. When an evaluation is planned for a higher level, the previous level does not have to be comprehensive.
4. When a higher-level evaluation is conducted, data must be collected at lower levels.
5. At least one method must be used to isolate the effects of consulting.
6. If no improvement data are available for a consulting participant, it is assumed that little or no improvement has occurred.
7. Estimates of improvement should be adjusted for the potential error of the estimate.
8. Extreme data items and unsupported claims should not be used in ROI calculations.
9. The first year of benefits (annual) should be used in the ROI analysis of short-term consulting interventions.
10. Consulting costs should be fully loaded for ROI analysis.

performing the work, it is assumed that little or no improvement has occurred. This is an ultraconservative approach.

Principles 7 and 8 build on the conservative approach to data analysis. Principle 9 focuses on the issue of timing of the actual stream of benefits from a consulting assignment. A conservative approach is recommended, usually dictating one year of benefits for short-term assignments but multiple years for a more extensive consulting intervention.

The last principle focuses on the issue of fully loaded costs, ensuring that all direct and indirect costs of the consulting intervention are included. Collectively, these principles will ensure that the proper conservative approach is taken and that the impact study can be replicated and compared to other studies.

Implementation of the Process

The best tool, technique, or model will not be successful unless it is properly utilized and becomes a routine part of the consulting process. As a new process, it will be resisted by both the consultants and clients, just as with any other significant change. Some of the resistance is based on realistic barriers, while some will be based on misunderstandings and perceived problems that may be mythical. In either case, specific steps must be taken to overcome the resistance by carefully and methodically implementing the ROI process. Implementation involves many issues, including assigning responsibilities, building necessary skills, and developing plans and goals around the process. It will also involve preparing the environment, individuals, and support teams for this type of comprehensive analysis. The firms that have the most success with this process are those that have devoted adequate resources to implementation and that have deliberately planned for the transition from the current state to where they desire the organization to be in terms of accountability. Chapter 15 covers the implementation issues.

Case Applications: The Progress

Although a significant number of case applications have been developed, the consulting status of ROI among practitioners in the field is difficult, if not impossible, to pinpoint. Top consulting firms and senior consultants are reluctant to disclose internal practices and, even in the most progressive consulting firms, they confess that too little progress has been made. It is difficult to find cases in the literature that show how a consulting firm has attempted to measure the return on investment in a consulting intervention. Recognizing this void, the American Society for Training and Development (ASTD) undertook an ambitious project to develop a collection of cases that illustrate real-world examples of measuring the return on investment in a variety of consulting and training interventions. To find cases, more than 2000 individuals were contacted for the initial volume, including practitioners, authors, researchers, consultants, and conference presenters. In addition, organizations perceived to be respected and admired were contacted.

The result was the publication of *In Action: Measuring Return on Investment*. Volume 1[2] was published in 1994 and Volume 2[3] in 1997. Volume 3 is planned for publication in 2000. Combinations of books and cases have been published in other fields. *Measuring the Return on Investment in Technology-Based Learning: A Special Report*[4] and *Measuring the Return on Investment in Human Resources: The Process and Case Application*[5] both offer case studies on the ROI process in their respective fields. This book marks the first publication to focus on the ROI in consulting.

One of the most interesting signs of progress in consulting measurement and evaluation comes from industry newsletters designed for and distributed to consultants, consulting managers, and specialists in the consulting field. These newsletters routinely report about consulting successes, often using qualitative data mixed with some quantitative data. They occasionally express the need for more data and more accountability in the profession. The editors believe that many consultants are finding innovative ways to measure their successes.

While examples of the progress of consulting ROI are available, it has become a critical topic that is constantly haunting the consulting field. The need is clear. The interest in ROI will persist as long as consulting budgets continue to increase and consulting holds the promise of helping organizations improve. More progress must be made to meet this important need.

What Gets in the Way? Barriers to Consulting ROI

Although some progress has been made in the implementation of ROI, barriers can inhibit implementation of the concept. Some of these barriers are realistic, while others are actually myths based on false perceptions. Each barrier is briefly described in this section.

Costs and Time

The consulting ROI process will add some additional costs and time to the consulting intervention, although the added amount should not be excessive. As will be described throughout this book, a comprehensive ROI process will probably not add more than 3 to 5 percent to the consulting intervention budget. The additional investment in ROI would perhaps be offset by the additional results achieved from these interventions and the elimination or prevention of unproductive or unprofitable interventions. This barrier alone stops many ROI implementations early in the process.

Lack of Skills and Orientation for Consultants

Many consultants do not understand ROI, nor do they have the basic skills necessary to apply the process within their scope of responsibilities. Also, the typical intervention does not focus on results, but more on qualitative data. Consequently, a tremendous barrier to implementation is the change needed for the overall orientation, attitude, and skills of consultants. As the cartoon character Pogo once said, "We have met the enemy and he is us." This certainly applies to consulting ROI implementation.

Faulty Initial Analysis

Many consulting interventions do not have adequate initial analysis and assessment. Some of these interventions have been implemented for the wrong reasons and are based on management requests or efforts to chase a popular fad or trend in the industry. If the consulting intervention is not needed, the intervention probably won't produce enough benefits to overcome the costs. An ROI calculation for an unnecessary consulting intervention will likely yield a negative value. This is a realistic barrier for many interventions.

Fear

Some consultants do not pursue ROI because of fear of failure or fear of the unknown. Fear of failure appears in many guises. There may be a concern about the consequences of a negative ROI. Also, a comprehensive measurement process will stir up the traditional fear of change. This fear, often based on unrealistic assumptions and a lack of knowledge of the process, is so strong that it becomes a real barrier to many ROI implementations.

Discipline and Planning

A successful consulting ROI implementation requires much planning and a disciplined approach to keep the process on track. Implementation schedules, evaluation targets, ROI analysis plans, measurement and evaluation policies, and follow-up schedules are required. The consultant may not have enough discipline and determination to stay on course. This becomes a barrier, particularly when there are no immediate pressures to measure the return. If the client is not requiring ROI, the consultant may not allocate time for planning and coordination.

Also, other pressures and priorities will often eat into the time necessary for ROI implementation. Only carefully planned implementations will be successful.

False Assumptions

Many consultants have false assumptions about the ROI process that keep them from attempting ROI. Typical of these assumptions are the following:

- ROI can be applied to only a few narrowly focused projects.
- Senior managers do not want to see the results of consulting interventions expressed in monetary values.
- If the client does not ask for ROI, it should not be pursued.
- If the CEO does not ask for ROI, then he or she is not expecting it.
- Our consultants are professional and competent. Therefore, we do not have to justify the effectiveness of our consulting interventions.
- Consulting is a complex but necessary activity. It should not be subjected to a quantitative evaluation process.

These false assumptions form realistic barriers that impede the progress of ROI implementation. They will be addressed in this book, along with concrete ways to overcome them.

How Evaluation Data Can Be Used: Benefits of Consulting ROI

Although the benefits of adopting a comprehensive measurement and evaluation process (including consulting ROI) may be obvious, several important benefits can be derived from the routine use of this process.

Show the Contribution of Selected Consulting Projects

With the consulting ROI process, the consultant and the client will know the specific contribution of the consulting project in terms that were neither previously developed nor in a language understood by the client group. The ROI will show the actual benefits versus the cost, elevating the evaluation data to the ultimate level of analysis. This process presents indisputable evidence to convince the client that the project was successful.

Earn the Respect of Senior Management

Measuring the ROI of a consulting project is one of the best ways to earn the respect and support of the senior management team—not only for a particular consulting project, but for other consulting interventions as well. Managers will respect processes that add bottom-line value presented in terms they understand. The result of this analysis is comprehensive, and when it is applied consistently and comprehensively in several projects, it can convince the management group that consulting is an important investment and not just an expense. Middle-level managers will see that consulting is making a viable contribution to their immediate objectives. This is a critical step toward building an appropriate partnership with the senior management team.

Gain the Confidence of Clients

The client, who requests and authorizes a consulting project, will now have a complete set of data to show the overall success of the process. This provides a complete profile from different sources, at different time frames, and with different types of data, revealing the process that has occurred and validating the client's initial decision to move forward with the consulting intervention.

Improve the Consulting Processes

Because there is a variety of feedback data collected during the consulting intervention, a comprehensive analysis (including consulting ROI) provides data to drive changes in consulting processes and make adjustments during a project. It also provides data that help improve consulting interventions in the future when it is realized that certain processes are nonproductive while others add value. Thus, the consulting ROI is an important process improvement tool.

Develop a Results-Focused Approach

The communication of data at different time frames and with the detailed planning that is involved with the consulting ROI focuses the entire team, including stakeholders, on bottom-line results. This focus often enhances the results that can be achieved because the ultimate goals are clearly in mind. In essence, the process begins with the end in mind. All of the processes, activities, and steps are clearly focused on the ultimate outcomes. As the project shows success, confidence is built in using the process, which enhances the results of future projects.

Alter or Enhance Consulting Interventions

This benefit is twofold. First, if an intervention is not going properly, and the results are not materializing, the consulting ROI process will prompt changes or modifications to move the intervention back on track. On rare occasions, the project may have to be halted if it is not adding the appropriate value. While that will take courage, it will reap important benefits with the client if it is clearly evident that the project will not produce results. The other part of this benefit is that if the consulting assignment is very successful, perhaps the same type of intervention can be applied to other areas. It makes a convincing argument that if one division has a successful intervention and another division has the same needs, the intervention may add the same value and enhance the overall success and replication of all consulting projects.

Shortcut Ways to Develop Consulting ROI

The process described in this chapter is very comprehensive and represents an approach recommended for major consulting projects. The more complex the project, the more comprehensive the evaluation process must be. There are a variety of shortcuts that may help reduce the time and resources necessary to develop consulting ROI. The following techniques or approaches are helpful for conserving resources while at the same time taking advantage of the key issues involved in the consulting ROI process.

Plan Early for the Evaluation

This issue will be emphasized several times throughout this book. Planning early for the evaluation is critical to a successful process in terms of accuracy, credibility, and completeness. In addition, it can conserve resources, as planning can take advantage of the most efficient and resourceful way to capture and analyze data and report results.

Build Evaluation into the Consulting Process

When data collection and other evaluation steps are built into the consulting intervention, the time requirements are reduced significantly. Participants directly involved in the intervention can provide important data, thus eliminating the need for some of the data collection. Other key stakeholders may be able to provide some of the initial analysis, such as isolating the effects of the consulting or converting data to monetary values. All of these key issues can be built into the process, thereby reducing the amount of time and cost for the process.

Share Responsibilities for the Evaluation

While the consultant or consulting project leader may have the ultimate responsibility for driving the evaluation, it may be helpful to share the responsibilities with others, including the client team within the organization. This is not only a way to reduce the amount of resources required for the evaluation; it also helps maintain the objectivity that is often needed. Key individuals within the client organization will take on important responsibilities for the measurement and evaluation, including data collection and analysis. In addition, other stakeholders may have important responsibilities for the evaluation.

Use Shortcut Methods for Major Steps

Throughout this book, several shortcut methods are provided to collect data, isolate the effects of consulting, convert data to monetary values, and capture costs. Shortcuts are available for every step of the process. While the accuracy may be slightly inhibited by shortcut methods, the trade-off is savings in money and time.

Use Sampling to Select Appropriate Projects for Detailed Analysis

The comprehensive, detailed analysis should be reserved only for those consulting projects that are long-term, complex, and expensive. A shortened analysis and reduced process is appropriate for simpler projects and involves less cost and shorter time frames. The important message here is to match the analysis with the complexity of the project, reserving a comprehensive ROI analysis for critical, important, and involved consulting interventions.

Use Estimates in Collection and Analysis of Data

The process of estimating values, factors, or even improvement data represents a very useful tool in this analysis. Estimates are simple and easy to obtain, and keep cost and time to a minimum. The accuracy and reliability of estimates can be improved significantly if the proper steps are taken to ensure that data are provided within the proper framework and environment and that appropriate adjustments are made in the analysis.

Develop Internal Capability to Implement the Process

It may be helpful to transfer skills for building the ROI process internally to the client so the client can use the process to show the value of consulting assignments. This places the client in the position of fully evaluating consulting processes. Also, it significantly reduces the amount of time and resources needed to measure the success of consulting. Sometimes, just offering the process and the willingness to develop the process internally will satisfy clients' accountability needs.

Streamline the Reporting Process

One of the most time-consuming steps in the process is developing detailed reports in the form of an impact study. This important process can be streamlined significantly by having a standard reporting process or even a shortcut method to present the data. In one organization, the results of the consulting intervention are reported on a single sheet showing the six types of measures.

Utilize Web-Based Software to Reduce Time

Fortunately, as with many complex processes, there is software that can be used to save time. An Internet-based software tool is available that will cut in half the amount of time needed to conduct an impact study.

Application of the Consulting ROI Process: A Case Example

To illustrate how the data collected in the consulting ROI are reported, an actual example is presented. The problem addressed by the consulting firm focuses directly on sexual harassment. In this hospital chain, the actual number of internal and external sexual harassment complaints has steadily increased and is considered excessive by the senior management group. In addition, there appears to be a linkage to turnover, as the turnover rate exceeds industry averages. The consultants were asked to analyze the causes of the problem, develop solutions, and implement those solutions to bring harassment complaints and turnover down. The complete analysis is presented in detail elsewhere, but is included here in tabular form as Table 2.7.[6]

As the project profile illustrates, the project involved virtually all employees and was comprehensive in that it required an analysis to develop solutions and implement those solutions. The solution objectives were developed at Levels 1 through 4. It was not considered appropriate to develop a Level 5 objective, although the actual ROI is calculated. The remainder of the table presents the methods selected for data collection during the intervention as well as after the implementation of the solution. In addition, the methods used to isolate the effects of consulting and the methods to convert data to monetary values are shown. The results are then presented, beginning with Level 1 and ranging through Level 5 and on to the intangibles. Collectively, the monetary benefits in a 1-year time frame achieved from reducing complaints and turnover amounted to $3,200,908. The cost of the program is presented in the table and shows a fully loaded cost profile of $277,987. A summary is included to show how the report is developed.

This brief example shows the richness of this approach in terms of presenting a comprehensive profile of success, ranging from reaction to ROI to the intangible benefits. Additional detail on this case study is found in other parts of the book.

Table 2.7 A Case Study: Healthcare, Inc.

Project Profile

Title:	Preventing Sexual Harassment
Target audience:	First and second supervisors and administrators (655) and nonsupervisory employees (6,844)
Duration:	Six months—from initial analysis and assessment, solution development, and implementation
Program objective:	Determine the cause of excessive sexual harassment complaints, the potential linkage to employee turnover, and recommended solutions. The project also includes the implementation of solutions.
Origination:	Management directive with needs analysis and assessment
Facilitation and coordination:	HR coordinators/managers

Solution Objectives

After implementing this project:

- All employees should react favorably to the new emphasis on sexual harassment and this project.
- All supervisors and administrators should be able to understand and administer the company's policy on sexual harassment.
- All employees should be able to identify inappropriate and illegal behavior related to sexual harassment.
- All supervisors should be able to investigate and discuss sexual harassment issues.
- All supervisors should conduct a meeting with all employees to discuss policy and expected behavior.
- The workplace should be free from sexual harassment, actions, activities, and behavior.
- The number of sexual harassment complaints should reduce by 20%.
- Employee turnover should reduce to 20%.

Data Collection During Intervention

- Interview
- Questions
- Tests

Table 2.7 A Case Study: Healthcare, Inc. (*Continued*)

Data Collection After Implementation

- Surveys
- Questionnaires
- Business performance monitoring

Isolating the Effects of Consulting

- Complaints—trend analysis and estimates as a backup
- Turnover—trend analysis, forecasting, and estimates as a backup

Converting Data to Monetary Values—Techniques

- Complaints—historical costs of complaints and expert input
- Turnover—external studies, same industry

Monetary Benefits from Complaint Reduction

- Value of 1 internal complaint = $24,343
- Annual improvement related to program = 14.8 complaints
- $24,343 × 14.8 = $360,276

Monetary Benefits from Turnover Reduction

- Value of one turnover statistic = $20,887
- Annual improvement related to program = 136 turnovers (prevented)
- $20,887 × 136 = $2,840,632

Consulting Intervention Costs

• Initial analysis and assessment (fees)	$ 9,000
• Solution development	15,000
• Coordination/facilitation fees	9,600
• Travel and lodging for facilitators and coordinators	1,520
• Program materials (655 @ $12)	7,860
• Food/refreshments (655 @ $30)	19,650
• Facilities (17 meetings @ $150)	2,550
• Client salaries plus benefits ($130,797 × 1.39)	181,807
• Evaluation and reporting	31,000
Total	**$277,987**

Table 2.7   A Case Study: Healthcare, Inc. (*Continued*)

Level 1 Results—From Supervisors and Administrators

* Overall satisfaction rating: 4.11 out of a possible 5
* 93% of supervisors and managers provided list of action items

Level 2 Results—From Supervisors and Administrators

* Pretest scores average 51
* Posttest scores average 84 (improvement: 65%)
* Successful skill practice demonstration

Level 3 Results—Key Issues

* 96% of supervisors and administrators conducted meetings with employees and completed meeting record
* On a survey of nonsupervisory employees, significant behavior change was noted—4.1 on a scale of 5
* 68% of supervisors and administrators reported that all action items were completed
* 92% of supervisors and administrators reported that some action items were completed

Level 4 Results

Sexual Harassment Business Performance	*One Year Prior to Intervention*	*One Year After Intervention*	*Factor for Isolating the Effects of Consulting*
Internal complaints	55	35	74%
External charges	24	14	62%
Litigated complaints	10	6	51%
Legal fees and expenses	$632,000	$481,000	
Settlement/losses	$450,000	$125,000	
Total cost of sexual harassment	$1,655,000	$852,000	
Prevention, investigation, and defense			
Turnover (nonsupervisory annualized)	24.2%	19.9%	

Table 2.7   A Case Study: Healthcare, Inc. (*Continued*)

ROI Calculation

$$BCR = \frac{\text{Consulting Benefits}}{\text{Consulting Costs}} = \frac{\$2,840,632 + \$360,276}{\$277,987} = \frac{3,200,908}{277,987} = 11.5{:}1$$

$$ROI = \frac{\text{Net Consulting Benefits}}{\text{Consulting Costs}} = \frac{\$3,200,908 - \$277,987}{\$277,987} \times 100 = 1051\%$$

Intangible Benefits

- Job satisfaction improvement
- Absenteeism reduction
- Stress reduction
- Community image enhancement
- Recruiting image

Final Thoughts

This chapter has provided a brief overview of the process presented in the remainder of the book. It clearly underscores the urgency of the challenge: now is the time to develop a comprehensive measurement and evaluation process, including the consulting ROI. It also shows how various forces create this important need for a comprehensive evaluation process. Finally, the process presented in the book is defined by four important elements: evaluation framework, consulting ROI process model, implementation, and guiding principles. When these are combined with experience in case application, a reliable, credible process is developed that can be replicated from one project to another. This process is not without its concerns and barriers, but many of these can be overcome with simplified, economical methods. Realistic strategies to develop ROI are discussed. The remainder of the chapters will detail many of the issues developed in this chapter.

References

1. Kirkpatrick, Donald L. *Evaluating Training Programs: The Four Levels.* San Francisco: Berrett-Koehler, 1994.

2. Phillips, Jack J. (ed.). *In Action: Measuring Return on Investment* (vol. 1). Alexandria, VA: American Society for Training and Development, 1994.
3. Phillips, Jack J. (ed.). *In Action: Measuring Return on Investment* (vol. 2). Alexandria, VA: American Society for Training and Development, 1997.
4. Phillips, Jack J., and Brandon Hall. *Measuring the Return on Investment in Technology-Based Learning*. Birmingham, AL: PRO, 1999.
5. Phillips, Jack J., Patricia F. Pulliam, and Ron D. Stone. *Measuring the Return on Investment in Human Resources: The Process and Case Applications*. Houston, TX: Gulf, in press.
6. Hill, Dianne, and Jack J. Phillips, "Preventing Sexual Harassment: Healthcare, Inc.," in *Measuring Return on Investment* (vol. 2). Alexandria, VA: American Society for Training and Development, 1997, pp. 17–35.

Further Reading

Biech, Elaine. *The Business of Consulting: The Basics and Beyond*. San Francisco: Jossey-Bass/Pfeiffer, 1999.

Epstein, Marc J., and Bill Birchard. *Counting What Counts: Turning Corporate Accountability to Competitive Advantage*. Reading, MA: Perseus, 1999.

Hale, Judith. *The Performance Consultant's Fieldbook: Tools and Techniques for Improving Organizations and People*. San Francisco: Jossey-Bass/Pfeiffer, 1998.

Hiebeler, Robert, Thomas B. Kelly, and Charles Ketteman. *Best Practices: Building Your Business With Customer-Focused Solutions*. New York: Arthur Andersen/Simon & Schuster, 1998.

LaGrossa, Virginia, and Suzanne Saxe, *The Consultative Approach: Partnering for Results!* San Francisco: Jossey-Bass/Pfeiffer, 1998.

Lambert, Tom. *High Income Consulting: How to Build and Market Your Professional Practice* (2d ed.). London: Brealey, 1997.

O'Shea, James, and Charles Madigan. *Dangerous Company: The Consulting Powerhouses and the Businesses They Save and Ruin*. New York: Times Business/Random House, 1997.

Phillips, Jack J. *Return on Investment in Training and Performance Improvement Programs*. Houston, TX: Gulf, 1997.

Rasiel, Ethan M. *The McKinsey Way: Using the Techniques of the World's Top Strategic Consultants to Help You and Your Business.* New York: McGraw-Hill, 1999.

Schaffer, Robert H. *High-Impact Consulting: How Clients and Consultants Can Leverage Rapid Results into Long-Term Gains.* San Francisco: Jossey-Bass, 1997.

Swanson, Richard A., and Elwood F. Holton III. *Results: How to Assess Performance, Learning, and Perceptions in Organizations.* San Francisco: Berrett-Koehler, 1999.

Tuller, Lawrence W. *Cutting Edge Consultants: Succeeding in Today's Explosive Markets.* Englewood Cliffs, NJ: Prentice Hall, 1992.

3

Initial Analysis and Planning

Key to a Successful Evaluation

F EW THINGS ARE more important in a consulting process than the initial analysis and planning, particularly the planning for account-ability processes. When measurement of the success of consulting interventions is attempted after the project is complete—as an add-on, follow-up project—an obvious conclusion is often reached: there should have been more planning. Initial analysis and planning have several advantages and involve several key issues explored in this chapter. The first issue is specifying in detail what the project will involve. Next, and perhaps more importantly, the chapter shows how to determine the success of the project—in advance, in specific detail. Then the chapter examines the process of ensuring that all of the key measures or groups of measures are identified to reflect the success of the project, focusing on different levels of analysis. Finally, a variety of planning tools are introduced that can be helpful in setting up the initial consulting inter-vention.

Pinning Down the Details: Project Requirements

When it comes to specifying the requirements of a consulting intervention, there can never be too much detail. Projects often go astray and fail to reach full success because of misunderstandings and differences in expectations about the consulting intervention. This section shows the key issues that must be addressed before the consulting intervention actually begins. These issues are often outlined in the project proposal or sometimes in the outline and scope of the project's documentation. In other cases, they are dealt with in the planning or implementation document for the actual consulting intervention. Regardless of when the documentation is developed, or for what purpose it is developed, each of the areas listed should be identified in some way. More importantly, the client and the consultant need to reach an agreement on these key issues.

Objectives of the Project

When it comes to consulting interventions, there are objectives and then there are objectives. First, there are the objectives for the consulting project itself, indicating specifically what will be accomplished and delivered in the consulting assignment. The other set of objectives are called *solution objectives* and focus on the goals of the actual solution that will ultimately add value to the organization. The solution objectives are discussed later. Here, our focus is on the objectives of the project.

Every consulting intervention should have a major project objective, and in most cases there should be multiple objectives. The objectives should be as specific as possible and should be focused directly on the assignment. Examples of project objectives are presented in Table 3.1. As this table illustrates, the objectives are very broad in scope, outlining from an overall perspective what is to be accomplished. The details of timing, specifications, and specific deliverables come later. The broad consulting project objectives are critical because they bring focus to the project quickly. They define the basic parameters of the project. As they are often the beginning points of the discussion of the consulting intervention, major project objectives are needed to define a project when it involves several phases and issues.

Table 3.1   Examples of Broad Consulting Project Objectives

- Identify the causes of excessive, unplanned absenteeism, and recommend solutions with costs and timetable.
- Evaluate the feasibility of three alternative approaches to new product development and rollout. For each approach, provide data on projected success, resources required, and timing.
- Implement a new accounts payable system that will maximize cash flow and discounts and minimize late payment penalties.
- Design, develop, and implement automated sales-tracking system that will provide real-time information on deliveries, customer satisfaction, and sales forecasts.
- Enhance the productivity of the call center staff as measured in calls completed, without sacrificing service quality.
- Build a customer feedback and corrective action system that will meet customer needs and build customer relationships.
- Reorganize the sales and marketing division from a product-based unit to a regional-based, fully integrated structure.
- Provide review, advice, and oversight input during the relocation of the headquarters staff. Input is provided by memo each week. The project will address concerns, issues, problems, and delays.

Scope

The scope of the project needs to be clearly defined. The scope can pinpoint key parameters addressed by the project. Table 3.2 shows typical scoping issues that should be defined in the project. Perhaps the project is limited to certain employee groups, a functional area of the business, a specific location, a unique type of system, or a precise time frame. Sometimes there is a constraint on the type of data collected or on access to certain individuals, such as customers. Whatever the scope involves, it needs to be clearly defined in this section.

Timing

Timing is very critical in showing specifically when activities will occur. This is not only the timing of the delivery of the final project report, but the timing of particular steps and events—including when data are

Table 3.2 Scoping Issues

- Target group for intervention
- Location of target group
- Time frame for intervention
- Technology used
- Access to stakeholders
- Functional area for coverage
- Product line for coverage
- Type of process/activity
- Category of customers

---

needed, analyzed, and reported and when presentations are made. Table 3.3 shows typical events needing specific time frames.

Deliverables from the Project

This section describes exactly what the client will receive when the project is completed in terms of reports, documents, systems, processes, manuals, forms, flowcharts, or rights to new technology. Whatever the specific deliverables, they are clearly defined here. Most projects will have a final report, but they often go much further, delivering process tools, software, and sometimes even hardware.

Methodology

If a specific methodology is planned for the consulting intervention, it should be defined. Sometimes a reference should be made to the appropriateness of the methodology as well as its reliability, validity, and previous success and how it will accomplish what is needed in this consulting intervention.

Steps

The specific steps that will occur should be defined showing key milestones. This provides the client with a step-by-step understanding and

Table 3.3 Typical Timing Events

- Start of project
- Data collection design complete
- Evaluation design complete
- Data collection begins
- Data collection complete
- Specific data collection issues (e.g., pilot testing, executive interviews)
- Data analysis complete
- Preliminary results available
- Solutions developed
- Implementation started
- Implementation complete
- Phases complete
- Report developed
- Presentation to management

---

tracking of the intervention so that at any given time the client can see not only where progress is made, but where the project is going next.

Resources Required for the Project

This section defines the specific resources required. This could include access to individuals, vendors, technology, equipment, facilities, competitors, or customers. All resources that may be needed should be listed along with amounts and timing.

Cost

The cost section details the specific cost for different parts of the project, tied to the different steps of the process. Sometimes consulting firms are reluctant to detail costs because it exposes the actual consulting hourly charges and reveals some of the mystery of the process. These firms prefer to present the bottom-line cost and leave it up to the client to figure out how it was reached. A better approach is to be very open with the fees, showing the different steps and issues relative to costs. In general, clients will appreciate this openness to show the breakdown of costs, which sets the stage for a trusting relationship between consultant and client.

Guarantees

A final section is satisfaction guarantees, which are now becoming commonplace in consulting assignments. With some firms, a complete satisfaction guarantee is provided, stating that if the client is not satisfied with the project then there is no charge for the consulting intervention. This may be too much for some firms, particularly for long-term engagements. However, the mere presence of this feature makes a statement that helps keep the entire consulting team focused and ensures that the client is satisfied throughout the project and never asks for a refund.

Levels of Objectives for Solutions

Eventually a consulting project leads to solutions. In some situations, the consulting project is aimed at implementing a solution to a particular dilemma, problem, or opportunity. In other situations, the initial consulting project is designed to develop a range of feasible solutions, or one desired solution, prior to implementation. Whatever the case, solutions should have multiple levels of objectives. These levels of objectives, ranging from qualitative to quantitative, define precisely what will occur as a particular solution is implemented in the organization. Table 3.4 shows the different levels of objectives. These objectives are so critical that they need special attention in their development and use.

Satisfaction and Reaction

For any project solution to be successful, various stakeholders must react favorably, or at least not negatively. Ideally, the stakeholders should be satisfied with the solution, since the best solutions offer win-win relationships. The stakeholders are those who are directly involved in implementing or utilizing the solution developed. These can be the employees who are involved in implementing the work, or the supervisors or team leaders who are responsible for the redesigned or changed process. Stakeholders could also be managers who must support or

Table 3.4   Multiple Levels of Objectives

Levels of Objectives	Focus of Objectives
Level 1: Reaction and satisfaction	Defines a specific level of satisfaction and reaction to the consulting solution as it is revealed and communicated to the stakeholders
Level 2: Learning	Defines specific skills and knowledge requirements as the stakeholders learn information about the consulting solution
Level 3: Implementation	Defines key issues around the implementation of the solution in the workplace
Level 4: Business impact	Defines the specific business measures that will change or improve as a result of the solution's implementation
Level 5: ROI	Defines the specific return on investment from the implementation of the solution, comparing costs against benefits

assist the process in some way. Finally, the stakeholders could include the teams and task forces involved in project solutions. Table 3.5 shows some of the typical areas for specific satisfaction objectives. It is important to obtain this type of information routinely through a consulting project so that feedback can be used to make adjustments, keep the project on track, and perhaps even redesign certain parts of the solution. One problem with many consulting interventions is that specific objectives at this level are not developed, and data collection mechanisms are not put in place to ensure appropriate feedback for making needed adjustments.

Learning Objectives

Almost every consulting intervention solution will involve a learning objective. In some cases involving major change projects, the learning component is quite significant. To ensure that the various stakeholders have learned what they need to in order to make the solution effective, learning objectives are developed. Learning objectives are critical to measuring learning because they communicate expected outcomes of the learning solution and define the desired competence or perfor-

Table 3.5 Typical Areas for Satisfaction Objectives

- Usefulness of solution
- Relevance of solution
- Economics of solution
- Difficulty in understanding the solution
- Difficulty in learning the solution
- Difficulty in implementing the solution
- Difficulty in maintaining the solution
- Perceived support for the solution
- Appropriate resources for the solution
- Overall satisfaction with the solution

mance necessary to make the consulting solution successful. These objectives provide a basis for evaluating the learning since they often reflect the type of measurement process. Perhaps more importantly, learning objectives provide a focus for participants to clearly indicate what they must learn—sometimes with precision.

The best learning objectives describe the behaviors that are observable and measurable, which are necessary for success with the consulting solutions. The objectives are often outcome based, clearly worded, and specific. They specify what the particular stakeholder must do as a result of implementing the learning solutions. Learning objectives often have three components:

- *Performance:* what the participant or stakeholder will be able to do at the end of the consulting project
- *Conditions:* the circumstances under which the participant or stakeholder will perform the various tasks and processes
- *Criteria:* the degree or level of proficiency necessary to perform a new task, process, or procedure that is part of the solution

The three types of learning objectives are often defined. These include:

- *Awareness:* Familiarity with terms, concepts, and processes

- *Knowledge:* general understanding of concepts, processes, or procedures
- *Performance:* ability to demonstrate skills at least on a basic level

Implementation and Application Objectives

As a solution is actually implemented in the workplace, the implementation and application objectives define clearly what is expected and often to what level of performance. Application levels are very similar to learning level objectives but reflect the actual use on the job. They also involve particular milestones, indicating specifically when intervals of the process are reached or the entire process is implemented. Application objectives are critical because they describe the expected outcomes in the intermediate area, that is, the interval between the learning of new tasks and procedures and the impact that will be improved. Application or implementation objectives describe how things should perform or the state of the workplace after the solution is implemented. They provide a basis for the evaluation of on-the-job changes and performance. The emphasis is on what has occurred on the job as a result of the learning objectives.

The best application objectives identify behaviors that are observable and measurable or action steps in a process that can easily be observed or measured. They specify what the various stakeholders will change or have changed as a result of the consulting intervention solution. As with learning objectives, application or implementation objectives may have three components:

- *Performance:* what the stakeholders have changed or have accomplished in a specific time frame after the implementation of the learning solution
- *Condition:* the circumstances under which the stakeholders have performed or are performing the tasks or implementing the solution
- *Criteria:* the degree or level of proficiency under which the solution is implemented, the task is being performed, or the steps are completed

There are two types of basic application objectives: *knowledge based*, in which the general use of concepts, processes, and procedures is important, and *behavior-based*, in which the participant is able to demonstrate the actual use of skills, accomplishments of particular tasks, or completion of particular milestones. Table 3.6 shows typical key questions asked regarding application and implementation objectives.

Application objectives have almost always been included to some degree in consulting interventions, but have not been as specific as they could be or need to be. To be effective, they must clearly define the environment at the work site when the solution is successfully implemented.

Impact Objectives

Every consulting solution should result in improving business impact—the key business measures that should be improved as the application or implementation objectives are achieved. The impact objectives are critical to measuring business performance because they define the ultimate expected outcome from the consulting intervention. They describe business unit performance that should be connected to the consulting solution. Above all, they place emphasis on achieving bottom-line results that key client groups expect and demand.

The best impact objectives contain measures that are linked to the solution from the consulting intervention. They describe measures that

Table 3.6 Typical Questions for Application and Implementation Objectives

---

1. What new or improved knowledge will be applied on the job?
2. What is the frequency of skill application?
3. What specific new task will be performed?
4. What new steps will be implemented?
5. What action items will be implemented?
6. What new procedures will be implemented or changed?
7. What new guidelines will be implemented?
8. What new processes will be implemented?
9. Which meetings need to be held?
10. Which tasks, steps, or procedures will be discontinued?

---

are easily collected and are well known to the client group. They are results based and clearly worded, and specify what the stakeholders have ultimately accomplished in the business unit as a result of the consulting intervention.

The four major categories of hard data impact objectives are output, quality, cost, and time. The major categories of soft data impact objectives are customer service, work climate, and work habits. Examples of the measures that frame the objectives are presented in Chapter 7.

Return on Investment Objectives

A fifth level of objectives for consulting solutions is the expected return on investment. These objectives define the expected payoff from the learning solution and compare the input resources (the cost of the consulting project) with the value of the ultimate outcome (the monetary benefits). This is typically expressed as a desired return on investment percentage that compares the annual monetary benefits minus the cost divided by the actual cost and multiplied by 100. A 0 percent ROI indicates a break-even consulting solution. A 50 percent ROI indicates that the cost of the consulting project is recaptured and an additional 50 percent "earnings" are achieved.

For many consulting interventions, the ROI objective is larger than what might be expected from the ROI of other expenditures, such as the purchase of a new company, a new building, or major equipment; but the two are related. In many organizations the consulting ROI objective is set slightly higher than the ROI expected from other interventions because of the relative newness of applying the ROI concept to consulting interventions. For example, if the expected ROI from the purchase of a new company is 20 percent, the ROI from a consulting intervention might be in the 25 percent range. The important point is that the ROI objective should be established up front and in discussions with the client.

Importance of Specific Objectives

Developing specific objectives at different levels for consulting intervention solutions provides important benefits. First, these objectives provide direction to the consultants involved in the process to help keep them on track. Objectives define exactly what is expected at different time frames from different individuals and what different types of data are involved. They provide guidance to the support staff and the client so that these people fully understand the ultimate goal and impact of the consulting intervention. Also, they provide important information and motivation for the stakeholders. In most consulting interventions, the stakeholders are actively involved and will influence the results of the solution. Specific objectives provide goals and motivation for the stakeholders so that they will clearly see the gains that should be achieved. More importantly, objectives provide important information for the key client groups to enable them to clearly understand what the landscape will look like when the consulting solution is complete. Finally, from an evaluation perspective, the objectives provide a basis for measuring success.

How Is It All Connected? Linking Evaluation with Needs

There is a distinct linkage between evaluation objectives and original needs driving a consulting project. The previous chapter focused on the five levels of evaluation and showed how they are critical to providing an overall assessment of the impact of a consulting intervention—particularly when a solution is implemented as part of the consulting project. The earlier material in this chapter showed the importance of setting objectives around the consulting solution. The objectives define the specific improvements sought. In this section, we will make a further connection to the original needs assessment. Figure 3.1 shows the connection between evaluation and needs assessment. This figure shows the important linkage from the initial problem or opportunity that created the needs to the evaluation and measurement. Level 5 defines the potential payoff and examines the possibility for a return on investment before the project is even pursued. Level 4 analysis focuses directly on the business needs that precipitated the need for a consulting intervention. At Level 3, the specific issues in the workplace focus on job performance in detail. At Level 2, specific knowledge, skill, or attitude deficiencies are uncovered as learning needs are identified. Finally, the preferences for the structure of the solution define the Level 1 needs. This connection is critical and very important to under-

Needs Assessment	Consulting Solution Objectives	Evaluation	
5 Potential Payoffs	→ ROI	→ ROI	5
4 Business Needs	→ Impact Objectives	→ Business Impact	4
3 Job Performance Needs	→ Application and Implementation Objectives	→ Application and Implementation	3
2 Skill/Knowledge/ Attitude Deficiencies	→ Learning Objectives	→ Learning	2
1 Preference for Solutions	→ Reaction and Satisfaction Objectives	→ Reaction and Satisfaction	1

Figure 3.1   Linking needs assessment with evaluation.

standing all of the elements that must go into an effective consulting intervention and overall consulting project.

An example will help illustrate this linkage. Figure 3.2 shows an example of linking needs assessment with the evaluation for a consulting project involving a reduction in absenteeism. As the figure shows, the first step is to see if the problem is great enough at Level 5. However, this sometimes causes a validation of the problem using Level 4 data. Four benchmarks are used to compare the current absenteeism problem. These are as follows:

- Absenteeism is higher than it used to be.
- Absenteeism is higher than at other locations within the company.
- Absenteeism is higher than at other facilities in the local area.
- Absenteeism is higher than the general manager desires.

With the confirmation in Level 4 that there is a problem, a potential payoff is estimated. This involves estimating the cost of absenteeism and estimating the actual potential reduction that can come from the consulting intervention. This develops a profile of potential payoff to aid in determining if the problem is worth solving.

At Level 3, the causes of excessive absenteeism are explored using a variety of techniques. One issue that is uncovered is that a positive disci-

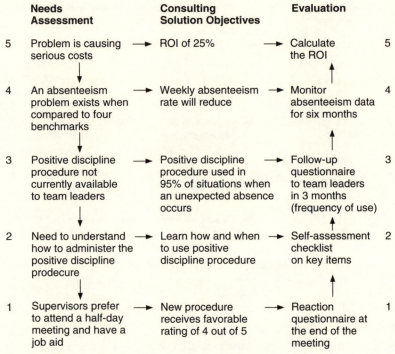

Figure 3.2 Sample needs assessment–evaluation linkage.

pline procedure is not currently available to team leaders when there is an unexpected absence. A learning component is also uncovered, as the team leaders need to understand how and when to administer the positive discipline procedure. Finally, the specific way in which the solution should be implemented is explored in terms of preferences. In this case, supervisors preferred to attend a half-day meeting to learn the procedure and leave with a job aid that helps them with the process as they apply it.

These five levels provide an overall profile for determining if the problem is worth solving to begin with; they also align problems with key measures and data necessary to develop the program objectives. The consulting solution objectives for each level are shown in the figure as well, as is the evaluation method needed to verify that the appropriate change did occur. This process is important to the development and implementation of a consulting solution. Many consulting projects are involved in developing the actual solution and implementing the solution, as is the case in this particular example. When this occurs, the linkage connects the needs to actual objectives and then to evaluation.

The solution to the problem or opportunity is an important part of this linkage. Some consulting projects may be involved in uncovering needs with the initial analysis to determine the actual causes of the problem and then recommend solutions. It is up to the client to then implement the solution, or implementation becomes part of another consulting project. In either case, the solutions are ultimately developed for a complete consulting project. If this has not been accomplished, multiple levels of analysis may be necessary for the project. While there are other references that focus more specifically on the performance analysis to uncover different levels of needs, a brief summary is presented here.

Payoff Needs

The very first part of the process is to determine if the problem is worth solving or the opportunity is large enough to warrant serious consideration. In some cases, this is obvious when there are serious problems that are affecting the organization's operations and strategy. Other cases may not be so obvious. At Level 5, it is important not only to identify business measures at Level 4 that are needed to improve, but to also convert them into monetary values so the actual improvement can be converted to financial measures. The second part of the process is to develop an approximate cost for the entire consulting project. This could come from a detailed proposal or may be a rough estimate. At this stage it is only an estimate, as the projected cost of the project is compared to the potential benefits to roughly determine if there is a payoff in pursuing the issue. This step may be omitted in some situations when the problem must be solved regardless of the cost, or if it becomes obvious that it is a high-payoff activity. Still other projects may be initiated and the potential payoff is not expected to be developed. For example, as an organization strives to be a technology leader, it may be difficult to place a value on that goal.

Business Needs

In conjunction with Level 5, actual business data are examined to determine which measures need to improve. This includes an examination of organizational records and involves looking at all types of hard and soft data. It is usually one of the data items and its performance that triggers the consulting assignment: for example, market share is not as much as it should be, costs are excessive, quality is deteriorating, or productivity is not as high as should be. These are the key issues that come directly from the data in the organization and are often found in the operating reports or records.

The supporting data may come not only from the operating reports, but also from annual reports, marketing data, industry data, major planning documents, or other important information sources that clearly indicate operating performance in terms of operation or strategy.

Workplace Needs

The Level 3 analysis involves workplace needs. The task is to determine the cause of the problem as determined at Level 4 (i.e., what is causing the business measure not to be at the desired level or to be inhibited in some way). The different types of needs can vary considerably and may include the following, among others:

1. Ineffective or inappropriate behavior
2. Dysfunctional work climate
3. Ineffective systems
4. Improper process flow
5. Ineffective procedures
6. Unsupported culture
7. Inappropriate technology
8. Unsupportive environment

These and other types of needs will have to be uncovered using a variety of problem-solving or analysis techniques. This may involve the use of data collection techniques discussed in this book, such as surveys, questionnaires, focus groups, or interviews. It may involve a variety of problem-solving or analysis techniques such as root cause analysis, fishbone diagrams, and other analysis techniques. Whatever is used, the key is to determine all of the causes of the problem so that solutions can be developed. Often, multiple solutions are appropriate.

Learning Needs

Most problem analysis from Level 3 uncovers specific learning needs. It may be that learning inefficiencies, in terms of knowledge and skills, may contribute to the problem if they are not the major cause of it. In other situations, the actual solution applied may need a particular learning component as participants learn how to implement a new process, procedure, or system. The extent of learning required will determine whether formalized training is needed or whether more informal, on-the-job methods can be utilized to build the necessary skills and knowledge. The learning would typically involve acquisition of knowledge or the development of skills necessary to improve the situation. In some cases, perceptions or attitudes may need to be altered to make the process successful in the future.

Preferences

The final level is to consider the preference for the solution. This involves determining the way in which those involved in the process prefer to have it changed or implemented. It may involve implementation preferences and/or learning preferences. Learning preferences may involve decisions such as when learning is expected and in what amounts, how it is presented, and the overall time frame. Implementation preferences may involve issues such as timing, support, expectation, and other key factors. The important point is to try to determine the specific preferences to the extent possible so that the complete profile of the solution can be adjusted accordingly.

Planning for Measurement and Evaluation

An important ingredient in the success of the consulting ROI process is to properly plan early in the consulting cycle. Appropriate up-front attention will save much time later when data are actually collected and analyzed, thus improving accuracy and reducing the cost of the process. It also avoids any confusion surrounding what will be accomplished, by whom, and at what time. Two planning documents are key and should be completed before the intervention is designed or developed.

Data Collection Plan

Table 3.7 shows a completed data collection plan for the sexual harassment prevention consulting project described in the previous chapter. The project was initiated to reduce sexual harassment complaints and the resulting employee turnover. An ROI calculation was planned to show the value of preventive projects.

This document provides a place for the major elements and issues regarding collecting data for the five evaluation levels. In the first column, broad areas for objectives are stated that are appropriate for planning. Specific, detailed objectives are developed later, before the consulting intervention is designed. In the second column, the specific measures or data descriptors are indicated when they are necessary to explain the measures linked to the objectives. In the next column, the specific data collection method is briefly described using standard terminology. Next, the source of the data is entered. Data sources will vary considerably, but usually include participants, team leaders, company records, and the client. In the next column, the time frame for data collection is usually referenced from the beginning of the project. Finally, the responsibility for data collection is described.

The objectives for reaction and satisfaction usually include positive reactions to the intervention and suggested improvements. Planned actions may be included in the input. Reaction and satisfaction data may be collected at different intervals. In this example, feedback is taken only at one time, at the end of implementation of the solution.

Because Level 2 evaluation focuses on the measures of learning, specific objectives include those areas where participants are expected to learn new tasks, knowledge, skills, or attitudes. The evaluation method is the specific way in which learning is assessed—in this case, a test and observation of skill practice by the facilitator of the meeting. The timing for Level 2 evaluation is at the end of the implementation.

For application and implementation evaluation, the objectives represent broad areas of application, including significant on-the-job activities and implementation steps. In this example, the methods include questionnaires, surveys, and monitoring company records. This information is usually collected a matter of months after the implementation. Because responsibilities are often shared among several groups, including the consulting staff, it is important to clarify this issue early in the process. In this example, four groups share the responsibilities.

For impact evaluation, objectives focus on business impact measures influenced by the intervention. The measures/data column includes the way in which each item is measured. For example, if one of the objectives is to improve quality, a specific measure would indicate how that quality is actually measured, such as defects per thousand units produced. In the example, two very different types of complaints are defined. The third measure, turnover, is also defined. While the preferred evaluation method is performance monitoring, other methods such as questionnaires may be appropriate as in this example. Two sources of data are utilized at this level: company records and questionnaires. The timing depends on how quickly the intervention can generate a sustained impact on the three measures. It is usually a matter of months after the consulting intervention is completed. In this example, data were collected at six-month intervals. A project evaluator is responsible for data collection at this level. If appropriate, an ROI objective (Level 5) is included. It was not considered appropriate in this example.

The data collection plan is an important part of the evaluation strategy and should be completed prior to moving forward with the intervention; the plan is completed before pursuing an ROI evaluation. The plan provides a clear direction as to what types of data will be collected, how they will be collected, where they will be collected, when they will be collected, and who will collect them.

ROI Analysis Plan

Table 3.8 shows a completed ROI analysis plan for the same sexual harassment prevention project. This planning document is the continuation of the data collection plan presented in Table 3.7 and captures information on several key items that are necessary to develop the actual ROI calculation. In the first column, significant data items are listed; usually these are business impact measures (Level 4 data items), but in some cases they could include Level 3 data. These items will be used in the ROI analysis. The method for isolating the effects of consulting is listed next to each data item in the second column. For most projects, the method will be the same for each data item, but there

Table 3.7 Example of Completed Data Collection Plan

Project: Preventing Sexual Harassment **Responsibility:** **Date:**

Level	Broad Objectives	Measures/Data	Data Collection Method	Data Sources	Timing	Responsi-bilities
			Data Collection Plan			
1. Reaction and satisfaction	• Obtain a positive reaction to project and materials • Obtain input for suggestions for improvement • Identify planned actions		• Questionnaire	• Supervisors	• End of Implemen-tation	• Project coordinator
2. Learning	• Knowledge of policy on sexual harassment • Knowledge of inappropriate and illegal behavior • Skills to investigate and discuss sexual harassment	• True/false statements • Skill practices	• Pre- and posttest • Observation	• Supervisors	• Beginning of project and end of implemen-tation • During session	• Meeting facilitator

3. Implementation	• Administer policy • Conduct meeting with employees to explain policy and issues • Ensure that the workplace is free of sexual harassment	• Completed meeting records	• Questionnaire • Company records • Employee survey (25% sample)	• Supervisors • New supervisors and employees	• 6 months after program • 1 month after program • 6 months after program	• Project evaluator • HRIS staff • Employee communi-cations
4. Business Impact	• Reduce internal complaints • Reduce external complaints • Reduce employee turnover	• Formal com-plaints filled with HR VP • Charges filed with EEOC • Monthly voluntary termination	• Performance monitoring • Questionnaire	• Company records • Supervisors	• Monthly for 1 year before and after program • 6 months after program	• Project evaluator

Table 3.8   Example of Completed ROI Analysis Plan

Project: Preventing Sexual Harassment   **Responsibility:**   **Date:**

ROI Analysis Plan

Data Items	Methods of Isolating the Effects of the Intervention	Methods of Converting Data	Cost Categories	Intangible Benefits	Communication Targets	Other Influences/ Issues
Formal internal complaints of sexual harassment	• Trend line analysis • Participant estimation (as a backup)	• Historical costs with estimation form EEO/AA staff (internal expert)	• Initial analysis and assessment solution • Solution development • Coordination/ facilitation • Client time for project • Materials • Food/refreshments • Salaries and benefits for participants • Evaluation and reporting	• Job satisfaction • Absenteeism • Stress reduction • Public image • Recruiting	• All employees (condensed information) • Senior Executives (summary report with detailed backup) • All supervisors and managers (brief report) • HR/consulting staff (full report)	• Several initiatives to reduce turnover were implemented during this time period • Must not duplicate benefits from both internal and external complaints
External complaints of sexual harassment	• Trend line analysis • Participant estimation (as a backup)	• Historical costs with estimation form EEO/AA staff (internal expert) • External studies within industry				
Employee voluntary turnover	• Forecasting using percentage of turnover related to sexual harassment					

could be variations. For example, if no historical data are available for one data item, then trend line analysis is not possible for that item, although it may be appropriate for other items. In this example, a control group arrangement was not feasible, but a trend line analysis was. Participant estimates were used as a backup.

The method for converting data to monetary values is included in the third column. In this example, complaints are converted to monetary values via two approaches: using costs in the company records and collecting expert input from the staff directly involved in the process. The cost categories planned for capture are outlined in the fourth column. Instructions about how certain costs should be prorated are noted here. Normally the cost categories will be consistent from one intervention to another. However, a specific cost that is unique to this intervention is also noted. The anticipated intangible benefits expected from this intervention are outlined in the fifth column. This list is generated from discussions about the intervention with sponsors and subject matter experts.

Communication targets are outlined in the sixth column. Although there could be many groups that should receive the information, four target groups are always recommended: senior management, managers of participants, consulting participants, and the consulting staff. Each of these four groups needs to know about the results of the consulting ROI analysis. Finally, other issues or events that might influence intervention implementation are highlighted in the seventh column. Typical items include the capability of participants, the degree of access to data sources, and unique data analysis issues.

The ROI analysis plan, when combined with the data collection plan, provides detailed information on calculating the ROI, illustrating how the process will develop from beginning to end. When completed, these two plans should provide the direction necessary for a consulting ROI evaluation and should integrate with the overall project plan.

Shortcut Ways to Plan for the Evaluation

This chapter presents a very comprehensive approach to planning the evaluation of consulting projects. The process is wide ranging and thorough, which is the approach often needed in most major consulting projects. When a major project involves hundreds of thousands or even millions of dollars of investment, it is important to allocate the appropriate time and budgets for developing the actual consulting ROI. For smaller-scale projects, a more simplified process is appropriate. Four key issues should be addressed when taking a shortcut approach to planning for the evaluation.

Define Expectations and Requirements

Even in small-scale, simple projects, it is important to detail the specific requirements needed for the consulting project to be successful and to clearly define the expectations. Here, the client should be as specific as possible in terms of desired conduct and expectations regarding the consulting intervention. As much detail as can be developed is recommended. This can be included in the proposal or a very brief working document, but it should highlight the very key issues that can cause the process to go astray.

Define Workforce Changes

It is important to define the anticipated changes at the work site—changes that will be driven by the consulting intervention and, more specifically, the solutions from the consulting intervention. Thinking through the changes will often help identify potential barriers and enablers to the process. It will define what the employees and other stakeholders will experience or be expected to do to make the consulting project successful. Perhaps a checklist of things to be concerned about would be appropriate to ensure that both client and consultant agree on anticipated changes and the work flow, work process, working conditions, and workplace environment.

Define Expected Outcomes

The various levels of objectives are helpful for the simplest projects. It is recommended that some consideration be given to developing these multiple levels of objectives. More importantly, the ultimate impact expected should be clearly defined in terms of the measures that should change or improve if the project is successful. Along with this definition would be the parameters regarding data collection and methods to isolate the effects of the process. The more specifics that are provided around these outcomes, the better the project will be in terms of its results being focused and of having a clear understanding of what is necessary for success.

Develop a Plan

While the two documents presented in Tables 3.7 and 3.8 may be too much detail for a simple project, there is no substitute for detailing these issues. Even a project with a $50,000 price tag is worth the few hours of planning to make sure that the key issues are covered in some way. Shortcut ways to develop some of those processes are possible and are described later in the book. The important point here is to develop some type of simplified plan, although the document may be less detailed than the two formal planning documents presented. Overall, this step is critical and cannot be ignored because the key issues must be addressed.

Final Thoughts

This chapter has presented the initial analysis and planning for the evaluation of a consulting intervention. The rationale for initial analysis and objectives was explored. The linkage of levels of evaluation, objectives, and initial needs was explored. This connection greatly simplifies the consulting accountability process. Next, evaluation planning tools were introduced. When the consulting ROI process is thoroughly planned, taking into consideration all potential strategies and techniques, it becomes manageable and achievable. The remaining chapters will focus on the major elements of this process.

Further Reading

Dean., Peter J., and David E. Ripley (eds). *Performance Improvement Interventions: Performance Technologies in the Workplace* (vol. 3 of the *Performance Improvement* Series. Methods for Organizational Learning). Washington, DC: International Society for Performance Improvement, 1998.

Esque, Timm J., and Patricia A. Patterson (eds.). *Getting Results: Case Studies in Performance Improvement* (vol. 1). Washington, DC: HRD/International Society for Performance Improvement, 1998.

Hiebeler, Robert, Thomas B. Kelly, and Charles Ketteman. *Best Practices: Building Your Business with Customer-Focused Solutions.* New York: Arthur Andersen/Simon & Schuster, 1998.

Kaufman, Roger. *Strategic Thinking: A Guide to Identifying and Solving Problems.* Washington, DC: American Society for Training and Development, 1996.

Kaufman, Roger, Sivasailam Thiagarajan, and Paula MacGillis (eds.). *The Guidebook for Performance Improvement: Working with Individuals and Organizations.* San Francisco: Pfeiffer, 1997.

Langley, Gerald J., Kevin M. Nolan, Thomas W. Nolan, Clifford L. Norman, and Lloyd P. Provost. *The Improvement Guide: A Practical Approach to Enhancing Organizational Performance.* San Francisco: Jossey-Bass, 1996.

Swanson, Richard A., and Elwood F. Holton III. *Results: How to Assess Performance, Learning, and Perceptions in Organizations.* San Francisco: Berrett-Koehler, Inc. 1999.

PART
II

The Six Measures

4

Was It Useful?

How to Measure Reaction and Satisfaction

BECAUSE OF THE complexity and variety of approaches to collecting data at the first four levels (1—reaction and satisfaction; 2—learning; 3—application and implementation; 4—impact), four chapters are devoted to presenting the techniques and issues surrounding the major phases of evaluation. This chapter focuses on measuring reaction and satisfaction. Chapter 5 covers measuring learning, Chapter 6 measuring application and implementation, and Chapter 7 measuring business impact.

Collecting data at all four levels is necessary because of the chain of impact that must exist for a project to be successful. Participants in the consulting project should experience a positive reaction to the project and its potential application, and they should acquire new skills or knowledge to implement the project. There should be changes in on-the-job behavior, actions, and tasks that should prompt a positive implementation. A successful implementation should drive changes in business impact. The only way to know if the chain of impact has occurred is to collect data at all four levels.

Collecting reaction and satisfaction data during the intervention is the first operational phase of the consulting ROI process. Client feedback data are powerful for making adjustments and measuring success. A variety of methods are available to capture reaction and satisfaction data at the appropriate time during consulting. This chapter outlines the most common approaches for collecting these critical intervention data and explores several key issues about the use of the information.

Why Measure Reaction and Satisfaction?

It would be difficult to imagine a consulting project being conducted without collecting feedback from those involved in the project, or at least from the client. Client feedback is critical to understanding how well the process is working or to gauging its success after it has been completed. This feedback is always included in every consulting project because of its crucial importance. However, the advantage of collecting this type of data goes beyond just the satisfaction of the client and includes many other key issues, making it one of the most important data collection efforts.

Customer Service Is Key

In these days of the customer service revolution, it is important to measure customer satisfaction. Without continuous improvement from customer satisfaction data and without sustained, favorable reactions to projects, it would be difficult for a consulting firm to continue in business. It is important to consider the different types of customers involved in projects. Three particular types of customers exist for almost every consulting intervention. First, there are those directly involved in the project. These individuals have a direct role in the project and are often referred to as the *consulting participants.* They are key stakeholders who are directly affected by the consulting intervention and often have to change process procedures and make other job adjustments related to the project. In addition, they often have to learn new skills, tasks, and behaviors to make the project successful. These *participants*, as they are sometimes called, are very critical to the success of the project, and their feedback is critical for making adjustments and changes in the project as it unfolds and is implemented. The second set of customers are those who are on the sidelines and not directly involved, but who have some interest in the project. These *supporters*, as they are sometimes called, are concerned about the project and are supporting it in some way. Their perception of the success or potential success of the project is important feedback, as this group will be in a position to influence the project in the future. The third set of stakeholders is perhaps the most important. This is the client group that actually pays for the project. These individuals, or groups of individuals, request consulting projects, support projects, approve budgets, allocate resources, and ultimately live with the success or failure of the project. This important group must be completely satisfied—or, with today's consulting guarantees, it will not have to pay for the project. The client's level of satisfaction must be determined early (and again at the end of the project), and adjustments must be made. In short, customer satisfaction is key to success and must be obtained in a variety of different ways to focus on the success.

Early Feedback Is Essential

Projects can go astray quickly, and sometimes a specific project is the wrong solution for the specified problem. There are times when a project can be mismatched from the beginning, so it is essential to get feedback early in the process so that adjustments can be made. This helps head off misunderstandings, miscommunications, and, more importantly, misappropriations, enabling an improperly designed project to be altered or changed quickly before more serious problems are created.

Making Adjustments and Changes to the Project

The concept of continuous process improvement suggests that a project must be adjusted and refined throughout its duration. There must be an important linkage between obtaining feedback and making changes and reporting changes back to the groups who provide the information. This survey-feedback-action loop is critical for any type of consulting intervention.

Attention Is Appreciated

Many of the individuals involved in a consulting intervention, particularly the consulting participants, appreciate the opportunity to provide feedback. In too many situations, their input is ignored and their complaints are disregarded. They appreciate the project leader or consultant asking for input—and, more importantly, taking action as a result of that input. Other stakeholders and even clients appreciate the opportunity to provide feedback, not only early on but throughout the process.

For Some, This Is the Most Important Data

Because feedback data are important to the project's success, they are gathered in almost every project. They have become some of the most important data collected. Unfortunately, in some situations, project success is often measured by the feedback. As this book clearly shows, the feedback data are only one part of the evaluation puzzle and represent only one of the six types of data, yet their importance cannot be understated.

Comparing with Data from Other Projects

Some organizations collect reaction and satisfaction data from several sources using standard questions, and the data are then compared with data from other projects so that norms and standards can be developed. This is particularly helpful at the end of a project as client satisfaction is gauged. These satisfaction data can be used not only to compare the success of the project but to relate to overall project success and even correlate with other successful measures. Some firms even base a portion of consulting compensation on the level of client satisfaction, making reaction and satisfaction data very critical to the success of every project. Data collection must be deliberately pursued in a systematic, logical, rational way. This chapter explores the key issues involved in collecting and using these important measures.

Sources of Data

When considering the possible data sources that will provide feedback on the success of a consulting intervention, the categories are easily defined. The major categories of stakeholders are briefly described in this section.

Clients/Senior Managers

One of the most useful data sources for consulting ROI analysis is the client group, usually a senior management team. Whether an individual or a group, the client's perception is critical to project success. Clients can provide input on all types of issues and are usually available and willing to offer feedback. Collecting data from this source is preferred for reaction and satisfaction, since the data usually reflect what is necessary to make adjustments and measure success.

Consulting Participants

The most widely used data source for an ROI analysis is the consulting participants, who are directly involved in the consulting project. They must use the skills and knowledge acquired in an intervention and apply them on the job. Sometimes they are asked to explain the potential impact of those actions. Participants are a rich source of data for almost every issue or part of the project. They are credible, since they are the individuals who must achieve the performance results and are often the most knowledgeable about processes and other influencing factors. The challenge is to find an effective and efficient way to capture data in a consistent manner.

Team Leaders

Another important source of data is those individuals who directly supervise or lead consulting intervention participants. Members of this group often have a vested interest in evaluation, since they have a stake in the process because their employees are directly involved in the consulting intervention. Also, in many situations, they observe the participants attempting to use the knowledge and skills acquired in the intervention. Consequently, they can report on the successes linked to the intervention as well as the difficulties and problems associated with it. Although team leader input is usually best for reaction and satisfaction data, it can also be useful for other levels of evaluation data.

Team Members

In situations where entire teams are involved in or affected by the consulting intervention, all team members can provide information about the perceived changes prompted by the consulting intervention. Input from team members is appropriate for issues directly involved in their work. While collecting data from this source can be very helpful and instructive, it is sometimes avoided because of the potential inaccuracies that can enter the feedback process. Team members must be capable of providing meaningful input.

Internal Customers

The individuals who serve as internal customers of the consulting participants are another source of data for a few types of interventions. In these situations, internal customers provide input on perceived changes linked to the consulting intervention. This source of data is more appropriate when consulting projects directly affect the internal customers. These people report on how the project has influenced (or will influence) their work or the service they receive. Because of the subjective nature of this process and the lack of opportunity to fully evaluate the application of skills of the consulting participants, this source of data may be somewhat limited.

Project Leader

In some situations, the consulting project leader may provide input on the success of the project. The input from these sources may be based on on-the-job observations during the intervention and after it has been completed. Data from this source have limited use because project leaders may have a vested interest in the outcome of evaluation, so their input may lack objectivity.

Areas of Feedback

There are many topics that are critical targets for feedback because there are so many issues and processes involved in a typical consulting project. Feedback is needed in almost every major issue, step, or process to make sure things are moving forward properly. Table 4.1 shows the typical major areas of feedback for most projects. The list shows the key success factors in a consulting intervention, beginning with the documents that reflect the planning of the project. Different stakeholders

Table 4.1   Areas of Feedback

Appropriateness of objectives

Appropriateness of plans

Appropriateness of schedule

Progress made with plans

Relevance of project

Support for project

Resources for project

Integration of project with one system

Project leadership

Project staffing

Project coordination

Project communication

Motivation of project participants

Cooperation of project participants

Capability of project participants

Likelihood of project success

Barriers to project success

Enablers to project success

react to the appropriateness of the project planning schedule and objectives and the progress made with those planning tools. The relevance of the project is critical for the participants because if the project is perceived as irrelevant, more than likely it will not succeed in the workplace. The support for the project—including resources and how the project is integrated with other systems—represents important areas for feedback. Participants must see that the project has the necessary commitment. Several issues are important to management and the organization sponsoring the project, including project leadership, staffing levels, coordination, and communication. Also, it is important to gather feedback on how well the project team is working to address such issues as motivation, cooperation, and capability. A dysfunctional team can spell disaster quickly. Finally, the issues that inhibit or enhance success are important, along with input on the likelihood of success. For a particular project, there can be other issues, and each can have specific parts. Each step, element, task, or part of the project represents an opportunity for feedback. The challenge is to sort out those things that are most important so the participants can provide valuable input.

Timing of Data Collection

The timing of data collection revolves around particular events connected with the consulting intervention. Any particular activity, implementation issue, or milestone is an appropriate time to collect data, beginning with preproject data collection and progressing to implementation. Figure 4.1 shows the timing of feedback on a six-month project. This particular project has preproject data collection. This is important in helping to make sure that the environment is proper and supportive of the project. A preproject assessment can be an eye-opening exercise, as particular inhibitors and barriers can be identified that will need adjustment or alteration in the project to achieve success. In this particular example, assessment is taken at the beginning of the project as the announcement is made and the project is fully described. Next, a one-month follow-up is taken, followed three months later by a four-month follow-up. Finally, at the end of the project—the sixth month—an assessment is taken. Using five time frames for data collection may be too comprehensive for some projects, but is appropriate for major projects. In addition to these data collection opportunities, a six-month follow-up is planned after implementation. Project timing will depend on the resources available, the need to obtain feedback directly from participants, and the magnitude of events or activities scheduled throughout the project. In addition, quick adjustments and changes will need to be made that will also affect the timing. Finally, the need to gain commitment and support and measure the pulse all the way through the process is an important factor in determining the actual timing.

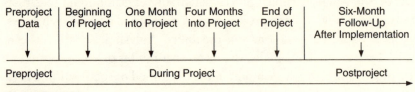

Figure 4.1 Timing of feedback for a six-month project.

Using Questionnaires to Measure Reaction and Satisfaction

The questionnaire is probably the most common method of data collection. Questionnaires come in all sizes, ranging from short reaction forms to detailed instruments. They can be used to obtain subjective data about participants' attitudes as well as to document data for future use in a projected ROI analysis. With this versatility and popularity, it is important that questionnaires be designed properly to satisfy both purposes.

Types of Questions

Five basic types of questions are available. Depending on the purpose of the evaluation, a questionnaire may contain any or all of the following types of questions:

- *Open-ended question:* has an unlimited answer. The question is followed by ample blank space for the response.
- *Checklist:* a list of items. A participant is asked to check those that apply to the situation.
- *Two-way question:* has alternate responses, a yes/no, or other possibilities. This type of question can also include a range of responses from disagree to agree.
- *Multiple choice question:* has several choices. The participant is asked to select the most appropriate.
- *Ranking scales:* requires the participant to rank a list of items.

Figure 4.2 shows examples of each of these types of questions.

Questionnaire Design

Questionnaire design is a simple and logical process. An improperly designed or worded questionnaire will not collect the desired data and will be confusing, frustrating, and potentially embarrassing. The following steps will help ensure that a valid, reliable, and effective instrument is developed.

Determine the Information Needed

The first step in designing any instrument is to itemize the topics, issues, and success factors for the project. Questions are developed later. It

1. Open-ended question:

   What problems will you encounter when attempting to use the system implemented in this project?

2. Checklist:

   For the following list, check all of the business measures that may be influenced by the application of the system in this project in this program.

   ☐ Responsibility   ☐ Cost control

   ☐ Productivity   ☐ Response time

   ☐ Quality   ☐ Customer satisfaction

   ☐ Efficiency   ☐ Job satisfaction

3. Two-way question:
   As a result of this project, I have a better understanding of my job as a customer service representative.

   ☐ Yes   ☐ No

4. Multiple choice question:
   Since the project has been initiated, the customer response time has:

   a. Increased
   b. Decreased
   c. Remained the same
   d. Don't know

5. Ranking scale:
   The following list contains five important factors that will influence the success of this project. Place a one (1) by the item that is most influential, a two (2) by the item that is second most influential, and so on. The item ranked five (5) will be the least influential item on the list.

   __ Rewards systems   __ Training

   __ Job responsibility   __ Management support

   __ Communications   __ Resources

Figure 4.2 Types of questions.

might be helpful to develop this information in outline form so that related questions can be grouped together.

Select the Type(s) of Questions
Determine whether open-ended questions, checklists, two-way questions, multiple choice questions, or ranking scales are most appropriate for the purpose of the questions. Take into consideration the planned data analysis and the variety of data to be collected.

Develop the Questions
The next step is to develop the questions based on the types of questions planned and the information needed. The questions should be simple and straightforward enough to avoid confusion or leading the participant to a desired response. Terms or expressions unfamiliar to participants should be avoided.

Test the Questions
After the questions are developed, they should be tested for understanding. Ideally, questions should be tested on a small sample of participants in the project. If this is not feasible, the questions should be tested on employees at approximately the same job level as the participants. Collect as much input and criticism as possible, and revise the questions as necessary.

Prepare a Data Summary
A data summary sheet should be developed so data can be tabulated quickly for summary and interpretation. This step will help ensure that the data can be analyzed quickly and presented in a meaningful way.

Develop the Completed Questionnaire
The questions should be finalized in a professional questionnaire with proper instructions. After these steps are completed, the questionnaire is ready to be administered. Because questionnaire administration is a critical element in evaluation, several ideas will be presented later in this chapter.

Determining Questionnaire Content

The content for a questionnaire will vary with the particular issue explored. The questions will focus on any of the areas identified in Table 4.1. For example, the issue of progress made with the project is an important topic that should always be included on a questionnaire. It could be presented as a range of responses, an open-ended question, or even a multiple choice response category. The content of the questions is just as important as the design and must receive careful attention to make sure the proper topics are explored and the appropriate information is examined.

Using Surveys to Measure Reaction and Satisfaction

Attitude surveys represent a specific type of questionnaire with several applications for measuring reaction and satisfaction in consulting projects designed to improve work, policies, procedures, the organization, or even the team. Before-and-after intervention measurements are important to show changes. Sometimes an organization will conduct a survey to assess the correct solution with one of the areas previously listed. Then, based on these results, consulting projects will be undertaken to change areas in which improvements are needed.

Measuring satisfaction and reaction is a complex task in which attitudes are crucial. It is impossible to measure an attitude precisely, since information gathered may not represent a consulting participant's true feelings. Also, the behavior, beliefs, and feelings of an individual will not always correlate. Attitudes tend to change with time, and several factors can form an individual's attitude. Recognizing these shortcomings, it is possible to get a reasonable assessment of an individual's attitude.

Surveys are not the only way to measure attitudes. Interviews and observations are two other ways that are discussed later.

Guidelines for Developing Surveys

The principles of survey construction are similar to those of questionnaire design. However, there are a few guidelines unique to the design or purchase of feedback surveys.

Involve Appropriate Management

The key stakeholders involved in this process must be committed to taking action based on survey results. Involve them early in the process, before the survey is constructed. Address management concerns, issues, and suggestions, and try to win commitment.

Determine Precisely the Reactions that Must Be Measured
While this is obvious, it is easy to stray into areas unrelated to the subject. "Let's check on their reaction to this" is a familiar trap. While the information may be interesting, it should be omitted if it is unrelated.

Keep Survey Statements as Simple as Possible
Participants need to understand the meaning of a statement or question. There should be little room for differing interpretations.

Ensure that Participant Responses Are Anonymous
If it is feasible, participants must feel free to respond openly to statements or questions. The confidentiality of their responses is of the utmost importance. If data are collected that can identify a respondent, then a neutral third party should collect and process the data.

Communicate the Purpose of the Survey
Participants tend to cooperate in an activity when they understand its purpose. When a survey is administered, participants should be given an explanation of its purpose and told what will be done with the information. Also, they should be encouraged to give correct and proper statements or answers.

Identify Survey Comparisons
Reactions by themselves are virtually meaningless. They need to be compared to expectations, to data before or after the project, or to another group or project. Data may be compared for all employees, a division, a department, or previous projects. For purchased surveys, information may be available on a national scale in similar industries. In any case, specific comparisons should be planned before the survey is administered.

Design for Easy Tabulation
In an attitude survey, yes/no remarks or varying degrees of agreement and disagreement are the usual responses. Figure 4.3 illustrates these two kinds of responses.

Yes/No Responses		Yes	No	
1. My team leader gives us credit for our work on the project.		☐	☐	
2. My team leader secures our ideas about the project.		☐	☐	

Agreement/Disagreement Responses	Strongly Disagree	Disagree	Neutral	Agree	Strongly Agree
1. My work environment is supportive of this project.	☐	☐	☐	☐	☐
2. Management provides adequate resources for this project.	☐	☐	☐	☐	☐

Figure 4.3 Typical attitude survey questions.

Uniform responses make it easier for tabulation and comparisons. On a scale of *strongly agree* to *strongly disagree*, numbers are usually assigned to reflect the response. For instance, a 1 may represent *strongly disagree* and a 5 *strongly agree*. An average response of 2.2 on a preprogram survey followed by a postprogram average response of 4.3 shows a significant change in attitude. Some argue that a five-point scale merely permits the respondent to select the midpoint and not be forced to make a choice. If this is a concern, an even-numbered scale should be used.

Purchasing an Existing Survey

Some organizations purchase existing surveys to use for evaluating very complex consulting projects. These can offer several advantages. They can save time in development and pilot testing. Most of the reputable companies producing and marketing surveys have designed them to be reliable and valid for their intended purposes. Also, outside surveys make it easier to compare your results with those of other organizations within the same industry or in similar industries. For example, a team effectiveness survey is administered prior to a team-building consulting project. The survey is administered again at the end of the project. Pre-

and postproject results can be compared to the same results in another organization.

Improving the Response Rate for Questionnaires and Surveys

Given the wide range of potential issues to explore in a follow-up questionnaire or survey, asking all of the questions can cause the response rate to be reduced considerably. The challenge, therefore, is to approach questionnaire and survey design and administration for maximum response rate. This is a critical issue when the questionnaire is a key data collection activity and much of the evaluation hinges on the questionnaire results. The following actions can be taken to increase response rate. Although the term *questionnaire* is used, the same rules apply to surveys.

Provide Advance Communication

If it is appropriate and feasible, consulting participants and other stakeholders should receive advance communications about the plans for the questionnaire or survey. This minimizes some of the resistance to the process, provides an opportunity to explain in more detail the circumstances surrounding the evaluation, and positions the evaluation as an integral part of the consulting intervention rather than an add-on activity that someone initiated three months after the intervention.

Communicate the Purpose

Stakeholders should understand the reason for the questionnaire, including who or what initiated this specific evaluation. They should know if the evaluation is part of a systematic process or a special request for this consulting intervention only.

Explain Who Will See the Data

It is important for respondents to know who will see the data and the results of the questionnaire. If the questionnaire is anonymous, it should clearly be communicated to participants what steps will be taken to ensure anonymity. If senior executives will see the combined results of the study, the respondents should know it.

Describe the Data Integration Process

The respondents should understand how the questionnaire results will be combined with other data, if available. Often the questionnaire is only one of the data collection methods utilized. Participants should know how the data are weighted and integrated into the entire impact study, as well as interim results.

Keep the Questionnaire as Simple as Possible

A simple questionnaire does not always provide the full scope of data necessary for a comprehensive analysis. However, the simplified approach should always be kept in mind when questions are developed and the total scope of the questionnaire is finalized. Every effort should be made to keep the questionnaire as simple and brief as possible.

Simplify the Response Process

To the extent possible, it should be easy to respond to the questionnaire. If appropriate, a self-addressed stamped envelope should be included. Perhaps e-mail could be used for responses, if it is easier. In still other situations, a response box is provided near the workstation.

Utilize Local Management Support

Management involvement at the local level is critical to response rate success. Managers can distribute the questionnaires themselves, make reference to the questionnaire in staff meetings, follow up to see if questionnaires have been completed, and generally show support for completing the questionnaire. This direct supervisor support will prompt many participants to respond with usable data.

Let the Participants Know They Are Part of the Sample

For large consulting projects, a sampling process may be utilized. When this is the case, participants should know that they are part of a carefully selected sample and that their input will be used to make decisions regarding a much larger target audience. This action often appeals to a sense of responsibility for participants to provide usable, accurate data for the questionnaire.

Consider Incentives

A variety of incentives can be offered, usually falling into three categories. First, an incentive is provided in exchange for the completed questionnaire. For example, if participants return the questionnaire personally or through the mail, they will receive a small gift, such as a T-shirt or mug. If identity is an issue, a neutral third party can provide the incentive. In the second category, the incentive is provided to make participants feel guilty about not responding. Examples are a dollar bill clipped to the questionnaire or a pen enclosed in the envelope. Participants are asked to "take the dollar, buy a cup of coffee, and fill out the questionnaire." A third group of incentives is designed to obtain a quick response. This approach is based on the assumption that a quick response will ensure a greater response rate. If an individual puts off completing the questionnaire, the odds of his or her completing it diminish considerably. The initial group of participants may receive a more expensive gift or they may be part of a drawing for an incentive. For example, in one project, the first 25 returned questionnaires were placed in a drawing for a $400 gift certificate. The next 25 were added to the first 25 in the next drawing. The longer a participant waits, the lower the odds of winning will be.

Have an Executive Sign the Introductory Letter

Participants are always interested in who sent the letter with the questionnaire. For maximum effectiveness, a senior executive who is responsible for a major area where the participants work should sign the letter. Employees may be more willing to respond to a letter signed by a senior executive than to one signed by a member of the consulting staff.

Use Follow-Up Reminders

A follow-up reminder should be sent a week after the questionnaire is received, and another should be sent two weeks later. Depending on the questionnaire and the situation, these times can be adjusted. In some situations a third follow-up is recommended. Sometimes the follow-up is sent in a different medium. For example, a questionnaire may be sent through regular mail, whereas the first follow-up reminder is from the immediate supervisor and a second follow-up is sent via e-mail.

Send a Copy of the Results to the Participants

Even if it is an abbreviated report, participants should see the results of the questionnaire. More importantly, participants should understand when they are asked to provide the data that they will receive a copy of the impact study. This promise will often increase the response rate, as some individuals want to see the results of the entire group along with their particular input.

Estimate the Length of Time to Complete the Questionnaire

Respondents often have a concern about the time it may take to complete the questionnaire. A very lengthy questionnaire may quickly turn off the participant and cause him or her to discard it. Sometimes lengthy questionnaires can be completed quickly because they contain forced-choice questions or statements that make it easy to respond. However, the number of pages may frighten the respondent. Therefore, it is helpful to indicate the estimated length of time needed to complete the questionnaire, perhaps in the letter itself or at in the communications. This provides extra information so that respondents can decide if they are willing to invest the required amount of time into the process. A word of caution is necessary, though: the amount of time must be realistic. Purposely underestimating it can do more harm than good.

Explain the Timing of the Planned Steps

Sometimes the respondents want to know more detail regarding when they can see the results or when the results will be presented to particular groups. It is recommended that a timeline be presented showing when different phases of the process will be completed. Typical steps for timing are responding to the questionnaire, analyzing the data, presenting the data to different groups, and returning the results to the participants in a summary report. This timetable provides some assurance that the process is well organized and professional, and that the length of time to receive a data summary will not be too long. Another word of caution: the timetable must be followed to maintain the confidence and trust of the individuals.

Give Materials a Professional Appearance

While it should not be an issue in most organizations, unfortunately there are too many cases where a questionnaire is not developed properly, does not appear professional, or is not easy to follow and understand. The participants must gain respect for the process and for the organization. To do this, a sense of professionalism must be integrated throughout data collection, particularly in the appearance and accuracy of the materials. Sloppy questionnaires will usually command sloppy responses, or no response at all.

Explain the Questionnaire During the Intervention

Sometimes it is helpful to explain to the consulting participants and other key stakeholders that they will be required or asked to provide certain types of data. When this is feasible, questionnaires should be reviewed question by question so that the participants understand the purpose, the issues, and how to respond. This will only take 10 to 15 minutes but can increase the response rate, enhance the quality and quantity of data, and clarify any confusion that may exist on key issues.

Collect Data Anonymously

Participants are more likely to provide frank and candid feedback if their names are not on the questionnaire, particularly when the project is going astray or is off target. Anonymous input is desired whenever possible and whenever the groups are large enough to protect anonymity. When this is the case, every effort should be made to protect the anonymous input, and explanations should be provided as to how the data are analyzed to minimize the demographic makeup of respondents so that the individuals cannot be identified in the analysis.

Collectively, these items help boost response rates for follow-up questionnaires. Using all of these strategies can result in a 50 to 70 percent response rate, even with lengthy questionnaires that might take 30 minutes to complete.

Using Interviews to Measure Reaction and Satisfaction

The interview is another collection method that can be helpful, although it is not used as frequently as questionnaires. Interviews can be conducted by the consulting staff, the client staff, or a third party. Interviews can secure data not available in performance records, or data difficult to obtain through written responses or observations. Also, interviews can uncover success stories that can be useful in communicating evaluation results. Consulting participants may be reluctant to describe their results in a questionnaire but will volunteer the information to a skillful interviewer using probing techniques. The interview is versatile and appropriate for reaction, satisfaction, and application data (Level 3). A major disadvantage of the interview is that it is time consuming. It also requires consulting intervention or preparation of interviewers to ensure that the process is consistent.

Types of Interviews

Interviews usually fall into two basic types: structured and unstructured. A structured interview is much like a questionnaire. Specific questions are asked with little room for deviation from the desired responses. The primary advantages of the structured interview over the questionnaire are that the interview process can ensure that the questions are answered and that the interviewer understands the responses supplied by the participant.

The unstructured interview permits probing for additional information. This type of interview uses a few general questions, which can lead to more detailed information as important data are uncovered. The interviewer must be skilled in the probing process. Typical probing questions are:

- Can you explain that in more detail?
- Can you give me an example of what you are saying?
- Can you explain the difficulty you say you encountered?

Interview Guidelines

The design steps for interviews are similar to those for questionnaires. A brief summary of key issues with interviews is outlined here.

Develop Questions to Be Asked

Once a decision has been made about the type of interview, specific questions need to be developed. Questions should be brief, precise, and designed for easy response.

Test Out the Interview

The interview should be tested on a small number of participants. If possible, interviews should be conducted as part of the early stages of the project. The responses should be analyzed and the interview revised if necessary.

Train the Interviewers

The interviewer should have appropriate skills, including active listening, the ability to form probing questions, and the ability to collect and summarize information into a meaningful form.

Provide Clear Instructions

The consulting participant should understand the purpose of the interview and know what will be done with the information. Expectations, conditions, and rules of the interview should be thoroughly discussed. For example, the participant should know if statements will be kept confidential. If the participant is nervous during an interview and develops signs of anxiety, he or she should be made to feel at ease.

Administer Interviews with a Plan in Mind

As with other evaluation instruments, interviews need to be conducted according to a predetermined plan. The timing of the interview, the person who conducts the interview, and the location of the interview are all issues that become relevant when developing an interview plan. For a large number of stakeholders, a sampling plan may be necessary to save time and reduce the evaluation cost.

Using Focus Groups to Measure Reaction and Satisfaction

An extension of the interview, focus groups are particularly helpful when in-depth feedback is needed. The focus group involves a small group discussion conducted by an experienced facilitator. It is designed to solicit qualitative judgments on a planned topic or issue. Group members are all required to provide their input, as individual input builds on group input.

When compared to questionnaires, surveys, or interviews, the focus group strategy has several advantages. The basic premise of using focus groups is that when quality judgments are subjective, several individual judgments are better than one. The group process, in which participants often motivate one another, is an effective method for generating new ideas and hypotheses. It is inexpensive and can be quickly planned and conducted. Its flexibility makes it possible to explore an intervention's unexpected outcomes or applications.

Applications for Evaluation

The focus group is particularly helpful when qualitative information is needed about the success of an intervention program. For example, the focus group can be used in the following situations:

- Evaluating reactions to specific procedures, tasks, schedules, or other components of an intervention
- Assessing the overall effectiveness of an intervention as perceived by the participants immediately following the intervention
- Assessing the potential impact of an intervention

Essentially, focus groups are helpful when evaluation information is needed but cannot be collected adequately with simple, quantitative methods.

Guidelines

While there are no set rules on how to use focus groups for evaluation, the following guidelines should be helpful:

Ensure that Management and the Client Embrace Focus Groups
Because this is a relatively new process for evaluation, it might be unknown to some management groups. Managers need to understand focus groups and their advantages. This should raise their level of confidence in the information obtained from group sessions.

Plan Topics, Questions, and Strategy Carefully
As with any evaluation instrument, planning is the key. The specific topics, questions, and issues to be discussed must be carefully planned and sequenced. This enhances the comparison of results from one group to another and ensures that the group process is effective and stays on track.

Keep the Group Size Small
While there is no magical group size, a range of 6 to 12 seems appropriate for most focus group applications. A group has to be large enough to ensure different points of view but small enough to give every participant a chance to talk freely and exchange comments.

Ensure a Representative Sample of the Target Population
It is important for groups to be stratified appropriately so that participants represent the target population. The group should be homogeneous in experience, rank, and influence in the organization.

Insist on Facilitators with Appropriate Expertise
The success of a focus group rests with the facilitator, who must be skilled in the focus group process. Facilitators must know how to control aggressive members of the group and diffuse the input from those who want to dominate the group. Also, facilitators must be able to create an environment in which participants feel comfortable offering comments freely and openly. Consequently, some organizations use external facilitators.

In summary, the focus group is an inexpensive and quick way to determine the strengths and weaknesses of interventions. However, for a complete evaluation, focus group information should be combined with data from other instruments.

Using Reaction and Satisfaction Data

Sometimes consulting participant feedback is solicited, tabulated, summarized, and then disregarded. The information must be collected and used for one or more of the purposes of evaluation. Otherwise, the exercise is a waste of the participants' time. Too often, project evaluators use the material to feed their egos and let it quietly disappear into their files, forgetting the original purposes behind its collection. A few of the more common reasons to gather reaction and satisfaction data are summarized in the following paragraphs.

Monitor Customer Satisfaction

Because this input is the principal measure taken from the participants, it provides a good indication of their overall reaction to, and satisfaction with, the program. Thus, program developers and owners will know how well satisfied the customers actually are with the product. Data should be reported to clients and others.

Identify Strengths and Weaknesses of the Project

Feedback is extremely helpful in identifying weaknesses as well as strengths in the project. Participant feedback on weaknesses can often lead to adjustments and changes. Identifying strengths can be helpful in future designs so processes can be replicated.

Develop Norms and Standards

Because reaction and satisfaction evaluation data can be automated and are collected in nearly 100 percent of projects, it becomes relatively easy to develop norms and standards throughout the organization. Target ratings can be set for expectations; particular course results are then compared to those norms and standards.

Evaluate Individual Consultants

Perhaps one of the most common uses of reaction and satisfaction data is consultant evaluation. If properly constructed and collected, helpful feedback data can be provided to consultants so that adjustments can be made to increase their effectiveness. Some caution needs to be exercised, though, since consultant evaluations can sometimes be biased; therefore other evidence may be necessary to provide an overall assessment of consultant performance.

Evaluate Planned Improvements

Feedback data from a questionnaire can provide a profile of planned actions and improvements. This can be compared with on-the-job actions as a result of the project, providing a rich source of data in terms of what participants may be changing or implementing because of what they have learned.

Link with Follow-Up Data

If a follow-up evaluation is planned, it may be helpful to link Level 1 data with follow-up data to see if planned improvements have become reality. In most cases, planned actions are often inhibited in some way through on-the-job barriers.

Marketing Future Projects

For some organizations, participant feedback data provide helpful marketing information. Participants' quotes and reactions furnish information that may be convincing to potential participants. Consulting marketing brochures often contain quotes from and summaries of feedback data.

Shortcut Ways to Measure Reaction and Satisfaction

The key question for some at this point is: what are some shortcut ways to measure reaction and satisfaction? While reaction and satisfaction data must always be collected, there are some shortcuts that can be taken. There are some essential items that must be taken care of for very short, low-profile, inexpensive projects. Unfortunately, omitting Level 1 is not an option because of the critical importance of these data. Three particular issues can be helpful.

Use a Simple Questionnaire

A detailed, comprehensive, 100-item questionnaire isn't necessary for every project. A simple 10- to 15-item questionnaire using multiple choice or true/false questions or even a scale rating will be sufficient for many small-scale projects. Although interviews, focus groups, surveys, and questionnaires are all presented as options, the questionnaire can suffice for most situations.

Collect Data Early and React Quickly

Taking an early pulse is critical. Find out if the project is being accepted and if those involved have concerns. This is very critical, and the action must be taken quickly. This will ensure that the process is kept on track and that the consulting intervention enjoys success as planned.

Pay Attention to Participants

The key stakeholders—the consulting participants—are critical to the process. They can make or break any consulting project, and their feedback is very important. A general rule is to always listen to this group and react to its concerns, issues, and recommendations. Sometimes this feedback will need filtering because of biases. The important thing is to listen and react when appropriate.

Final Thoughts

This chapter is the first of four on data collection and represents one of the six measures of data reported in the consulting ROI process. Measuring reaction and satisfaction is included in every study and is a critical part of the success. Although there are many uses for the data, two important ones stand out. The first is making adjustments and changes throughout the consulting intervention as problems or barriers are uncovered. The second is reporting the level of satisfaction with the project and having this finding included as one of the six key types of data. There are several ways to collect satisfaction and reaction data, including questionnaires, surveys, interviews, and focus groups. By far the questionnaire is the most common; sometimes just a simple, one-page reaction questionnaire will be appropriate. Whatever the method used, the important point is to collect data, react quickly, make adjustments, and summarize the data for reporting and for use in preparing the consulting ROI impact study.

Further Reading

Barlow, Janelle, and Claus Moller. *A Complaint is a Gift: Using Customer Feedback as a Strategic Tool.* San Francisco: Berrett-Koehler, 1996.

Gummesson, Evert. *Qualitative Methods in Management Research* (revised ed.). Newbury Park, CA: Sage, 1991.

Hronec, Steven M./Arthur Andersen & Co. *Vital Signs: Using Quality, Time, and Cost Performance Measurements to Chart Your Company's Future.* New York: AMACOM/American Management Association, 1993.

Krueger, Richard A. *Focus Groups: A Practical Guide for Applied Research* (2d ed.). Thousand Oaks, CA: Sage, 1994.

Kvale, Steinar. *InterViews: An Introduction to Qualitative Research Interviewing.* Thousand Oaks, CA: Sage, 1996.

Naumann, Earl, and Kathleen Giel. *Customer Satisfaction Measurement and Management: Using the Voice of the Customer.* Boise, ID: Thomson, 1995.

Rea, Louis M., and Richard A. Parker. *Designing and Conducting Survey Research: A Comprehensive Guide* (2d ed.). San Francisco: Jossey-Bass, 1997.

Renzetti, Claire M., and Raymond M. Lee (eds.). *Researching Sensitive Topics.* Newbury Park, CA: Sage, 1993.

Schwartz, Norbert, and Seymour Sudman (eds.). *Answering Questions: Methodology for Determining Cognitive and Communicative Processes in Survey Research.* San Francisco: Jossey-Bass, 1996.

What Did the Client Organization Learn?

How to Measure Skill and Knowledge Changes During the Consulting Intervention

IT MAY SEEM unnecessary to measure learning in a consulting intervention. After all, when application and implementation are measured, so is the actual progress made in the workplace. And ultimately, when business impact variables are monitored, the success of the project becomes quite clear. However, it is sometimes critical to understand the extent to which learning has occurred, particularly in projects where there are significant job changes, procedure changes, new tools, new processes, and new technology. The extent to which the participants involved in a project actually learn their new jobs and new processes may be one of the biggest determinants of the success of the project. This chapter focuses on very simple techniques for measuring learning. Many of these have been used for years in training programs in terms of formal testing and skill practices; others are less formal in structure and can suffice when time is a concern or when costs need to be minimized.

Is Measuring Learning Really Necessary?

There are four key areas that demonstrate why learning is an important measure in a consulting intervention. Each of these individually will probably justify the need to measure learning. Collectively, they provide a major thrust for measuring the amount of skills, knowledge, or change during an intervention.

The Transfer Problem

A significant problem that has plagued the training and development field for many years is a lack of transfer of what is learned by participants. In many situations, the learning is not transferred to the actual job environment. During a consulting intervention, participants may be involved in several learning activities, and it is critical to make sure this knowledge is transferred to the job. The result of the transfer is measured on the job during Level 3 evaluation, where application and implementation is measured. However, the learning that takes place needs to be measured early to see how much progress is being made, so that the transfer can be expected or, in some cases, even enhanced.

Importance of Knowledge, Expertise, and Competencies

Many organizations are increasing their focus on knowledge, expertise, and competencies. Many large consulting projects involve developing expertise, with employees using tools and techniques not previously used. Some projects focus directly on core competencies and building important skills, knowledge, and behaviors into the organization. With a continuous focus on knowledge management, it is important for knowledge-based employees to understand and acquire a vast array of information, assimilate it, and use it in a productive way. This emphasis on employee knowledge and skills makes measuring learning in a consulting intervention crucial.

The Importance of Learning in a Consulting Intervention

Although some consulting interventions may involve plenty of new equipment, processes, procedures, and technology, the human factor is still critical. Whether there is significant restructuring or the addition of new systems, employees must learn how to work in the new environment and develop new knowledge and skills. Learning is becoming a larger part of consulting interventions than previously because of the variety of tools, techniques, processes, and technologies that are being applied in the learning intervention. Gone are the days when simple tasks and procedures were built into work or automated within the process. Instead, there are complex environments, complex processes, and complicated tools that must be used in an intelligent way to reap the benefits of consulting interventions. Employees must learn in a variety of ways, not just in a formal classroom environment but through technology-based learning and on-the-job facilitation with job aids and other tools. Also, the team leaders and managers serve as reinforcers, coaches, or mentors in some interventions. In a few cases, learning coaches or on-the-job trainers are used in conjunction with consulting interventions to ensure that learning is transferred to the job and is implemented as planned.

Finding Out What Went Wrong When There Is a Problem

When application and implementation does not go smoothly, the most important issue is to find out what went wrong. What areas need to be adjusted? What needs to be altered? When learning is measured, it is easy to see the degree to which the lack of learning is a problem, or, in some cases, to eliminate the learning deficiency as a problem. In other words, without the learning measurement, the consultant may not know why employees are not performing the way they should or why particular parts of the consulting intervention are not being managed the way they should.

These key issues make learning an important issue in consulting interventions, requiring appropriate attention to this measure as with the other five measures in the consulting ROI process.

Measuring Learning with Formal Tests

Testing is important for measuring learning in project evaluations. Pre- and post-intervention comparisons using tests are very common. An improvement in test scores shows the change in skill, knowledge, or attitude of the participant attributed to the consulting project. By any measure, there was a dramatic increase in the use of tests in the United

States throughout the 1990s. The principles of test development are similar to those for the design and development of questionnaires and attitude surveys.

The types of tests used in consulting projects can be classified in three ways. The first is based on the medium used for administering the test. The most common are written or keyboard tests; performance tests, using simulated tools or the actual equipment; and computer-based tests, using computers and video displays. Knowledge and skills tests are usually written, because performance tests are more costly to develop and administer. Computer-based tests and those using interactive video are gaining popularity. In these tests, a computer monitor or video screen presents the questions or situations, and participants respond by typing on a keyboard or touching the screen. Interactive videos have a strong element of realism because the person being tested can react to images, often moving pictures and video vignettes that reproduce the real job situation.

The second way to classify tests is by purpose and content. In this context, tests can be divided into aptitude tests or achievement tests. Aptitude tests measure basic skills or acquired capacity to learn a job, while achievement tests assess a person's knowledge or competence in a particular subject.

A third way to classify tests is by their design. The most common types are objective tests, norm-referenced tests, criterion-referenced tests (CRTs), essay tests, oral examinations, and performance tests. Objective tests have answers that are specific and precise, based on the objectives of a program. Attitudes, feelings, creativity, problem-solving processes, and other intangible skills and abilities cannot be measured accurately with these tests. A more useful form of objective tests is criterion-referenced tests. Oral examinations and essay tests have limited use in consulting intervention evaluations; they are probably more useful in academic settings. Criterion-referenced tests and performance testing evaluations are more common in consulting. Both are described in more detail in the following text.

Criterion-Referenced Test

The criterion-referenced test is an objective test with a predetermined cutoff score. The CRT is a measure against carefully written objectives for the learning components of the consulting project. In a CRT, the interest lies in whether or not a consulting participant meets the desired minimum standards, not how that participant ranks with others. The primary concern is to measure, report, and analyze participant performance as it relates to the learning objectives.

Table 5.1 examines a reporting format based on criterion-referenced testing. This format helps explain how a CRT is applied to an evaluation effort. Four participants have completed a learning component with three measurable objectives that correspond to each of the modules. Actual test scores are reported, and the minimum standard is shown. For example, on the first objective, participant 4 received a pass rating for a test that has no numerical value and is simply rated pass or fail. The same participant met objective 2 with a score of 14 (10 was listed as the minimum passing score). The participant scored 88 on objective 3 but failed it because the standard was 90. Overall, participant 4 satisfactorily completed the learning component. The column on the far right shows that the minimum passing standard for the project is at least two of the three objectives. Participant 4 achieved two objectives, the required minimum.

Criterion-referenced testing is a popular measurement tool in consulting. The approach is helpful when it is necessary for a group of employees to learn new systems, procedures, or technologies as part of a consulting project. Its use is becoming widespread. The process is frequently computer based, making testing more convenient. It has the advantage of being objective based, precise, and relatively easy to administer. It requires clearly defined objectives that can be measured by tests.

Performance Testing

Performance testing allows the participant to exhibit a skill (and occasionally knowledge or attitudes) learned in a consulting intervention. The skill can be manual, verbal, or analytical, or a combination of the three. Performance testing is used frequently in job-related training where the participants are allowed to demonstrate what they have learned. In supervisory and management training, performance testing comes in the form of skill practices or role-playing. Participants are asked to demonstrate discussion or problem-solving skills they have

Table 5.1 Reporting Format for CRT Test Data

	Objective 1 P/F	Raw Score	Objective 2 Std	P/F	Raw Score	Objective 3 Std	P/F	Total Objectives Passed	Minimum Standard	Overall Score
Participant 1	P	4	10	F	87	90	F	1	2 of 3	Fail
Participant 2	F	12	10	P	110	90	P	2	2 of 3	Pass
Participant 3	P	10	19	P	100	90	P	3	2 of 3	Pass
Participant 4	P	14	10	P	88	90	F	2	2 of 3	Pass
Totals 4	3 Pass 1 Fail			3 Pass 1 Fail			2 Pass 2 Fail	8 Pass 4 Fail		3 Pass 1 Fail

acquired. To illustrate the possibilities of performance testing, two examples are presented.

Example 1

Computer systems engineers are participating in a system reengineering project. As part of the project, participants are given the assignment of designing and testing a basic system. The consultant observes participants as they check out the system, then carefully builds the same design and compares his results with those of the participants. These comparisons and the performance of the design provide an evaluation of the project and represent an adequate reflection of the skills learned in the project.

Example 2

As part of a reorganization project, team members learn new products and sales strategies. Part of the evaluation requires team members to practice skills in an actual situation involving a sales presentation. Then, participants are asked to conduct the skill practice on another member of the group using a real situation and applying the principles and steps learned in the project. The skill practice is observed by the consultant, and a written critique is provided at the end of the practice. These critiques provide part of the evaluation of the consulting project.

For a performance test to be effective, the following steps are recommended in the design and administration of the test:

- The test should be a representative sample of the work/task related to the consulting intervention. The test should allow the participants to demonstrate as many skills taught in the program as possible. This increases the validity of the test and makes it more meaningful to the participants.
- The test should be thoroughly planned. Every phase of the test should be planned—the timing, the preparation of the participants, the collection of necessary materials and tools, and the evaluation of results.
- Thorough and consistent instructions are necessary. As with other tests, the quality of the instructions can influence the outcome of a performance test. All participants should be given the same

instructions, which should be clear, concise, and to the point. Charts, diagrams, blueprints, and other supporting information should be provided if they are normally provided in the work setting. If appropriate and feasible, the test should be demonstrated by the consultant so that participants can observe how the skill is practiced.

- Procedures should be developed for objective evaluation, and acceptable standards must be developed for performance tests. Standards are sometimes difficult to develop because varying degrees of speed, skill, and quality are associated with individual outcomes. Predetermined standards must be developed so that employees know in advance what has to be accomplished to be considered satisfactory and acceptable for test completion.
- Information that may bias participants should not be included. The learning module is included to develop a particular skill. Participants should not be led in a particular direction unless they face the same obstacles in the job environment.

Using these general guidelines, performance tests can be utilized as effective tools for consulting evaluation. Although more costly than written tests, performance tests are essential in situations where a high degree of fidelity is required between work and test conditions.

Measuring Learning with Simulation

Another technique for measuring learning is job simulation. This method involves the construction and application of a procedure or task that simulates or models the work involved in the consulting intervention. The simulation is designed to represent the actual job situation as closely as possible. Participants try out their performance in the simulated activity and are evaluated based on how well the task is accomplished. Simulations may be used during the intervention, at the end of the implementation, or as part of a follow-up evaluation.

Advantages of Simulations

Simulations offer several advantages for the consulting professional.

Reproducibility
Simulations permit a job or part of a job to be reproduced in a manner almost identical to the real setting. Through careful planning and design, the simulation can be given all of the central characteristics of the real situation. Even complex jobs, such as that of the manager, can be simulated adequately.

Cost-Effectiveness
Although the initial development of simulations can be expensive, they can be cost-effective in the long run. For example, it is cost-prohibitive to train airline pilots to fly an airplane utilizing a $50 million aircraft. Therefore, an aircraft simulator is used to simulate all of the flying conditions and enable the pilot to learn to fly before boarding the actual aircraft. The cost involved in on-the-job learning can become prohibitive, making simulation much more attractive in other situations as well.

Safety Considerations
Another advantage of using simulations is safety. The safety component of many jobs requires participants to be trained in simulated conditions. For example, emergency medical technicians risk injury and even life if they do not learn emergency medical techniques prior to encountering a real-life situation. Firefighters are trained in simulated conditions prior to being exposed to actual fires. CIA agents are trained in simulated conditions before being exposed to their real-world environment. Safety is an important consideration when deciding on learning methodologies.

Simulation Techniques

There are several simulation techniques used to evaluate learning that has taken place during a consulting initiative. The most common techniques are briefly described in the following text.

Electrical/Mechanical Simulation
This technique uses a combination of electronics and mechanical devices to simulate real-life situations. These devices are used in con-

junction with programs to develop operational and diagnostic skills. Expensive examples of these types include simulated patients, or a simulator for a nuclear power plant operator. Other less expensive types of simulators have been developed to simulate equipment operation.

Task Simulation

Another approach involves a participant's performance in a simulated task as part of an evaluation. For example, in an aircraft company, technicians are trained on the safe removal, handling, and installation of a radioactive source used in a nucleonic oil quantity indicator gauge. These technicians attend a thorough training program on all of the procedures necessary for this important assignment. To become certified to perform this task, technicians are observed in a simulation, where they perform all the necessary steps on a checklist. After they have demonstrated that they possess the skills necessary for the safe performance of this assignment, they are certified by the instructor. This task simulation serves as the evaluation.

Business Games

Business games have grown in popularity in recent years. They represent simulations of part or all of a business enterprise. Participants change the variables of the business and observe the effects of those changes. The game not only reflects the real-world situation, but may also represent a consulting intervention. The participants are provided certain objectives, play the game, and have their output monitored. Their performance can usually be documented and measured. Typical objectives are to maximize profit, sales, market share, or return on investment. Those participants who maximize the objectives are those who usually have the highest performance in the program.

In-Basket

Another simulation technique called the in-basket is particularly useful in team leader, supervisory, and management training. Portions of a supervisor's job are simulated through a series of items that normally appear in an in-basket. These items are usually memos, notes, letters, and reports that create realistic conditions facing the supervisor. The participant must decide what to do with each item while taking into consideration the principles learned. The participant's performance with the in-basket represents an evaluation of the program. In some situations, every course of action for each item in the in-basket is rated, and a combination of the chosen alternatives provides an overall rating on the in-basket. This provides a performance score representing the participant's ability to address the major issues.

Case Studies

A perhaps less effective but still popular simulation technique is a case study. A case study represents a detailed description of a problem and usually contains a list of several questions posed to the participant. The participant is asked to analyze the case and determine the best course of action. The problem should reflect the conditions in the real-world setting and the content in a consulting intervention.

The most common categories of case studies include:

- Exercise case studies, which provide an opportunity for participants to practice the application of specific procedures.
- Situational case studies, which provide participants the opportunity to analyze information and make decisions regarding their particular situation.
- Complex case studies, which are an extension of the situational case study, where participants are required to process a large amount of data and information, some of which may be irrelevant.
- Decision case studies, which require participants to go a step further than the previous categories and present plans for solving a particular problem.
- Critical incident case studies, which provide participants with a certain amount of information and withhold other information until it is requested by the participants.
- Action maze case studies, which present a large case in a series of smaller units. Participants are required to predict at each stage what will happen next.

The difficulty in a case study lies in the objectivity of the evaluation of the participant's performance. Frequently, there can be many possible courses of action, some equally effective as others, making it extremely difficult to obtain an objective, measurable performance rating for the analysis and interpretation of the case.

Role-Playing

In role-playing, sometimes referred to as *skill practice*, participants practice a newly learned skill and are observed by other individuals. Participants are given their assigned role with specific instructions, which sometimes include an ultimate course of action. Then participants practice the skill with other individuals to accomplish the desired objectives. This is intended to simulate the real-world setting to the greatest extent possible. Difficulty sometimes arises when other participants involved in the skill practice make the practice unrealistic by not reacting the way individuals would in an actual situation. To help overcome this obstacle, trained role-players (nonparticipants trained for the role) may be used in all roles except that of the participant. This can possibly provide a more objective evaluation. The success of this technique also lies in the judgment of those observing the role-playing. The skill of effective observation is as critical as the skill of the role-player. Also, the success of this method depends on the participants' willingness to participate in and adjust to the planned role. If participant resistance is extremely high, the performance in the skill practice may not reflect the actual performance on the job. Nevertheless, these skill practices can be very useful, particularly in supervisory and sales training, to enable participants to practice discussion skills.

Assessment Center Method

The final method for measuring learning with simulation is a formal procedure called the assessment center method. Here the feedback is provided by a group of specially trained observers called *assessors*. For years, the assessment center approach has been a very effective tool for employee selection. It now shows great promise as a tool for evaluating the effectiveness of a major learning module in a consulting project.

Assessment centers are not actually centers in the sense of locations or buildings. Instead, the term refers to a procedure for evaluating the performance of individuals. In a typical assessment center, the individuals being assessed participate in a variety of exercises that enable them to demonstrate particular skills, knowledge, or abilities, usually called *job dimensions*. These dimensions are important to on-the-job success for individuals involved in the consulting project. It may take anywhere from four hours to three days for the participants to complete all the exercises.

The assessors then combine ratings of each exercise for each dimension, removing subjectivity to reach a final rating for each participant.

In the assessment center process, a rating or "assessment" of the participants is given prior to the consulting intervention. After the consulting intervention is implemented, the participants are assessed again to see if there are improvements in their performance within the job dimensions. The use of a control group in an evaluation design helps produce evidence of the impact of training.

Although the popularity of this method seems to be growing, it still may not be feasible for many projects. The use of an assessment center is quite involved and time consuming for the participants and the assessors. The assessors have to be carefully trained to be objective and reliable. However, for programs that represent large expenditures aimed at making improvements in the soft data area, the assessment center approach may be the most promising way to measure the impact of the program. This is particularly true for an organization in which the assessment center process is already in use for selection purposes.

In summary, simulations come in a wide variety of types and styles. They offer an opportunity for participants to practice what they have learned in a consulting project and to have their performance observed under simulated job conditions. They can provide extremely accurate evaluations if the performance in the simulation is objective and can be clearly measured.

Measuring Learning with Less Structured Activities

In many situations, it is sufficient to have an informal check of learning to provide some assurance that participants have acquired skills and knowledge, or perhaps that there have been some changes in attitudes. This approach is appropriate when other levels of evaluation are pursued. For example, if a Level 3 application and implementation evaluation is planned, it might not be so critical to conduct a comprehensive Level 2 evaluation. An informal assessment of learning is usually sufficient. After all, the resources are scarce, and a comprehensive evaluation at all levels becomes quite expensive. The following are some alternative approaches to measuring learning when inexpensive, low-key, informal assessments are needed.

Exercises/Activities

Many consulting projects involve activities, exercises, or problems that must be explored, developed, or solved during the program. Some of these are constructed in terms of involvement exercises, while others require individual problem-solving skills. When these tools are integrated into the learning activity, there are several specific ways in which to measure learning:

- The results of the exercise can be submitted for review and for possible scoring by the consultant. This becomes part of the overall score for the course and becomes a measure of learning.
- The results can be discussed in a group situation, with a comparison of the various approaches and solutions, and the group can reach an assessment of how much each individual has learned. This may not be practical in many settings, but can work in a few narrowly focused applications.
- The solutions to the problem or exercises can be shared with the group, and the participant can provide a self-assessment indicating the degree to which the skills and/or knowledge have been obtained from the exercise. This also serves as a reinforcement in that participants quickly see the correct solution.
- The consultant or facilitator can review the individual progress of each participant to determine the relative success. This is appropriate for small groups but can be very cumbersome and time consuming in larger groups.

Self-Assessment

In many consulting situations, self-assessment may be appropriate. Participants are provided an opportunity to assess their acquisition of skills and knowledge. This is particularly applicable in cases where higher-level evaluations are planned and it is important to know if actual learning is taking place. A few techniques can ensure that the process is effective:

- The self-assessment should be made anonymously so that participants feel free to express realistic and accurate assessments of what they have learned.

- The purpose of the self-assessment should be explained, along with the plans for the data. Specifically, if there are implications for project design or individual retesting, this should be discussed.
- If there has been no improvement or the self-assessment is unsatisfactory, there should be some explanation as to what that means and what the implications will be. This will help ensure that accurate and credible information is provided.

Consultant/Facilitator Assessment

A final technique involves the consultants and/or facilitators providing an assessment of the learning that has taken place. Although this approach is very subjective, it may be appropriate when a higher-level evaluation is planned. One of the most effective ways to accomplish this is to provide a checklist of the specific skills that need to be acquired in the course. Facilitators can then check off the assessment of each skill individually. Also, if there is a particular body of knowledge that needs to be acquired, a checklist of the categories should be developed for assuring that the individual has a good understanding of those items. This could create a problem if the participants have not had the appropriate time and opportunity to demonstrate skills or knowledge acquisition, and the instructor may have a difficult time in providing appropriate responses. There is also the question of what to do if there is no evidence of learning. The specific consequences need to be considered and addressed before the method is used.

Administrative Issues

There are several administrative issues that need to be addressed for measuring learning. Each is briefly discussed in the following text and should be part of the overall plan for administering a Level 2 measurement.

Consistency

It is extremely important that different tests, exercises, or processes for measuring learning are administered consistently from one group to another. This includes issues such as the time required to respond, the learning conditions under which the participants complete the process, the resources available to the participants, and the assistance provided by other members of the group. These issues can easily be addressed in the instructions.

Monitoring

In some situations, it is important for participants to be monitored as they are completing the test or other measurement processes. This ensures that each individual is working independently and also that someone is there to provide assistance or answer questions as needed. This may not be an issue in all situations, but it needs to be addressed in the overall plan.

Scoring

The scoring instructions need to be developed for the measurement process so that the person evaluating the responses will be objective in the process and provide consistent scores. Ideally, potential bias in the individual scoring the instrument should be completely removed through proper scoring instructions and other information necessary to provide an objective evaluation.

Reporting

A final issue is reporting the results. In some situations, the participants are provided with the results immediately, particularly with self-scoring tests or with group-based scoring mechanisms. In other situations, the results may not be known until later. In these cases, a mechanism for providing scoring data should be built into the evaluation plan unless it has been predetermined that participants will not know the scores. The worst thing to do is to promise test scores and deliver them late or not at all.

Using Learning Data

Although there can be several uses of learning data, the following are most common:

Providing individual feedback to build confidence. Learning data, when provided directly to participants, give reinforcement for correct answers and enhance learning for the solutions. This reinforces the learning process and provides much-needed feedback to participants in consulting projects.

Ensuring that learning has been acquired. Sometimes it is essential to show the extent and scope of learning. Measuring learning, even if done informally, will provide input on this issue.

Improving consulting interventions. Perhaps the most important use of learning data is to improve the consulting intervention. Consistently low responses in certain learning measures may indicate that inadequate facilitation has been provided on a topic. Consistently low scores for all participants may indicate that the objectives and scope of coverage are too ambitious or are misdirected.

Evaluating consultants/facilitators. Just as reaction and satisfaction data can be used to evaluate consultants and facilitators, learning measures provide additional evidence of the success of the staff. The consultant/facilitator has a significant responsibility to ensure that participants have acquired the new skills and knowledge and that testing is a reflection of the degree to which the skills/knowledge have been acquired and internalized from actual application.

Final Thoughts

This chapter briefly discusses some of the key issues involved in measuring learning—an important ingredient in most consulting assignments. Even if it is accomplished informally, learning must be assessed to determine the extent to which the participants in a consulting intervention are acquiring new skills, techniques, processes, tools, and procedures. Without measuring learning, it is impossible to know what may be wrong should there be an implementation problem later. Also, measuring learning provides an opportunity to make adjustments quickly so that changes can be made to enhance learning. The approach does not have to be formal, except for major projects. A less formal, less structured approach—even a self-assessment activity—is usually appropriate for most learning situations.

Further Reading

Boyce, Bert R., Charles T. Meadow, and Donald H. Kraft. *Measurement in Information Science*. San Diego: Academic, 1994.

Dixon, Nancy M. *Evaluation: A Tool for Improving HRD Quality*. San Diego: University Associates/American Society for Training and Development, 1990.

Fetterman, David M., Shakeh J. Kaftarian, and Abraham Wandersman (eds.). *Empowerment Evaluation: Knowledge and Tools for Self-Assessment & Accountability*. Thousand Oaks, CA: Sage, 1996.

Fitz-enz, Jac. *How to Measure Human Resources Management*. New York: McGraw-Hill, 1995.

Gummesson, Evert. *Qualitative Methods in Management Research* (revised ed.). Newbury Park, CA: Sage, 1991.

Kirkpatrick, Donald L. *Evaluating Training Programs: The Four Levels* (2d ed.) San Francisco: Berrett-Koehler, 1998.

Phillips, Jack J. *Accountability in Human Resource Management*. Houston, TX: Gulf, 1996.

Phillips, Jack J. *Handbook of Training Evaluation and Measurement Methods* (3d ed.). Houston, TX: Gulf, 1997.

Rea, Louis M., and Richard A. Parker. *Designing and Conducting Survey Research: A Comprehensive Guide* (2d ed.). San Francisco: Jossey-Bass, 1997.

Schwartz, Norbert, and Seymour Sudman (eds.). *Answering Questions: Methodology for Determining Cognitive and Communicative Process in Survey Research*. San Francisco: Jossey-Bass, 1996.

Swanson, Richard A., and Elwood F. Holton III. *Results: How to Assess Performance, Learning, and Perceptions in Organizations*. San Francisco: Berrett-Koehler, 1999.

Was the Intervention Implemented Properly?

How to Measure Implementation, Application, and Utilization

Measuring the application and implementation of skills and knowledge is critical because these steps play a pivotal role in the overall success or failure of the consulting implementation. If learned skills and knowledge are not applied effectively, there will be no change in the business function—and no benefit from the consulting intervention.

There are many ways to measure application and implementation that command the rich resources of data collection. This chapter explores the most common ways in which the application of consulting projects is evaluated. The range of possibilities varies from the use of questionnaires to observation and includes several specific methodologies, such as action planning and performance contracting. This chapter will explore the issues faced in applying these processes on the job and provide several examples.

Why Measure Implementation and Application?

In addition to the obvious reasons for measuring application and implementation, there are several specific reasons why this is one of the most important measures to track in the consulting evaluation process.

The Value of the Information

As briefly discussed in Chapter 2, the value of the information increases as progress is made through the chain of impact from Level 1 to Level 5. Thus, information concerning application and implementation at Level 3 is more valuable to the client than information on reaction and satisfaction (Level 1) and learning (Level 2). This is not meant to discount the importance of the lower levels, but to emphasize that measuring the extent to which the consulting process is implemented often provides critical data about not only the success of the project, but the factors that can contribute to greater success as the consulting process is fully integrated within the organization.

A Key Transition Issue

The two previous measures, reaction and satisfaction and learning, occur during the consulting intervention, when there is more attention and focus directly on the consulting project. Level 3, measuring application and implementation, occurs after the project has been implemented and measures the success of the actual implementation. Essentially, this measure tells the degree to which the project is handed off to those who are charged with its success. This is a key transition process and is the first measure that follows the process after the project has been fully implemented. This in itself makes it a critical issue, for this is when various measures of success are identified and enhancements to additional success are pinpointed.

The Key Focus of Many Projects

Because many consulting projects focus directly on implementation and application, the project sponsor often speaks in these terms and is concerned about these measures of success. Many major consulting projects designed to transform an organization and build a stronger customer base will have key issues around Level 3, implementation and application. The sponsor will be interested in knowing the extent to which all of the key stakeholders are adjusting to and implementing the desired new behaviors, processes, and procedures. This interest is at the core of application and implementation.

Problems, Obstacles, and Barriers

When a consulting project goes astray, the first question is, "What happened?" More importantly, when a project appears not to be adding value, the first question should be, "What can we do to change the direction of the project?" In either scenario, it is critical to have information that identifies barriers to success, problems encountered in implementation, and obstacles to the application of the process. It is at Level 3, measuring implementation and application, that these problems are addressed, identified, and examined for solutions. In many cases, the key stakeholders directly involved in the process provide important input into the recommendations for making changes or for using a different approach in the future.

Enablers and Enhancers

When there is success, the obvious question is, "How can we repeat this or even improve on it in the future?" The answer to this question is also found at Level 3. Identifying the factors that contribute directly to the success of the project is critical since those same items can be used to replicate the process to produce specific results in the future and to enhance results. When key stakeholders identify these issues, it helps make the project successful and provides an important case history of what is necessary for success.

Rewards Those Who Are Most Effective

Measuring application and implementation allows the client and consulting team to reward those who are doing the best job of applying the processes and implementing the consulting project. Measures taken at this level provide clear evidence of various efforts and roles, furnishing an excellent basis for performance review or special recognition. This often has a reinforcing value for keeping the project on track and communicating a strong message for future improvements.

Key Issues

When implementing a process to measure the application and implementation of consulting project solutions, several key issues should be addressed. These are very similar to the Level 1 (reaction and satisfaction) issues. A few may differ slightly due to the postconsulting project time frame for this type of data.

Areas of Coverage

To a large degree the areas of coverage for this process parallel the same areas identified in Chapter 4. However, because of the follow-up time frame, the other additional issues become opportunities to measure success. In addition, the follow-up is approached from a postprogram perspective rather than predictively as in Level 1. The areas of coverage are fully detailed in the section on using questionnaires to measure application and implementation. Here, the detailed issues can serve as a guide for finding the areas of coverage for all types of data collection methods at this level.

Sources

The sources of data mirror those identified in Chapter 4. Essentially, all key stakeholders are candidates to be sources of data. Perhaps the most important source is those who are actually involved in the application and implementation. It may involve the entire team, or team leaders charged with the responsibility of implementation.

Timing

The timing of data collection can vary significantly. Since this is a follow-up, the key issue is determining the best time for a postintervention evaluation. The challenge is to analyze the nature and scope of the application and implementation and determine the earliest time that a trend and pattern will evolve. This occurs when the application of skills becomes routine and the implementation is making significant progress. This is a judgment call. The important point is to go in as early as possible so that potential adjustments can still be made, but at the same time to wait until there is significant change in behavior for the implementation to be observed and measured. In consulting projects spanning a considerable length of time in terms of complete implementation, several measures may be taken at three- to six-month intervals. This gives successive input in terms of implementation progress and clearly shows the extent of improvement, using effective measures at well-timed intervals, and identifies the issues that are standing in the way of a successful implementation.

Responsibilities

Measuring application and implementation may involve the responsibility and work of others. Because this time period follows the consulting intervention's completion, an important issue may surface in terms of who is responsible for this follow-up. There is a range of possibilities, from consulting staff to client staff, as well as the possibility of an external, independent third party. This matter should be addressed in the planning stage so that there is no misunderstanding as to the distribution of responsibilities. More importantly, those who are responsible should fully understand the nature and scope of their responsibility and what is necessary to collect the data. Additional information on responsibilities is covered in a later chapter.

Using Questionnaires to Measure Application and Implementation

Because of their flexibility, low cost, and ease of administration, questionnaires have become a mainstream data collection tool for measuring application and implementation. The issues involved in questionnaire design discussed in Chapter 4 apply equally to questionnaire development for measuring application and implementation. This section will be limited to the specific content issues of follow-up questionnaires.

One of the most difficult tasks is to determine specific issues that need to be addressed on a follow-up questionnaire. Although the content items on a follow-up questionnaire can be the same as those on questionnaires used in measuring reaction and satisfaction, the following content items are more desirable for capturing application, implementation, and impact information (Level 3 and 4 data). Figure 6.1 presents a questionnaire used in a follow-up evaluation of a consulting intervention on building a sales culture. The evaluation was designed to capture the consulting ROI, with the primary method of data collection being the follow-up questionnaire. This example will be used to illustrate many of the issues involving potential content items for a follow-up questionnaire.

National Bank, following a carefully planned growth strategy of acquiring smaller banks, initiated a consulting project to develop a strong sales culture. The project involved four solutions. Through a competency-based learning consulting intervention, all branch personnel were taught how to aggressively pursue new customers and cross-sell to existing customers in a variety of product lines. The software and customer database were upgraded to provide faster access and enhanced routines to assist selling. The incentive compensation system was also redesigned to enhance payments for new customers and increase sales of all branch products. Finally, a management coaching and reinforcement system was implemented to ensure that ambitious sales goals were met. All branch employees were involved in the project.

Six months after the project was implemented, an evaluation was planned. Each branch in the network had a scorecard that tracked performance through several measures such as new accounts, total deposits, and growth by specific products. All product lines were monitored. All branch employees provided input via the questionnaire shown in Figure 6.1. Most of the data from the questionnaire covered application and implementation, while some involved impact measures. This type of feedback helps consultants know which parts of the intervention are most effective and useful.

Progress with Objectives

Sometimes it is helpful to assess progress made with the objectives of the project in the follow-up evaluation, as illustrated by question 1 in Figure 6.1. While this issue is usually assessed during the intervention, it is sometimes helpful to revisit the objectives after the participants have had an opportunity to implement the project.

Action Plan Implementation

If an action plan is required in the intervention, the questionnaire should reference the plan and determine the extent to which it has been implemented. If the action plan requirement is very low key, perhaps only one question on the follow-up questionnaire will be devoted to the action

---

Sales Culture at National Bank
Follow-Up Questionnaire

Are you currently in a sales capacity at a branch?   ☐ Yes   ☐ No

1. Listed below are the objectives of the sales culture project. After reflecting on this intervention, please indicate the degree of success in meeting the objectives. Use the following scale:
   1. No success at all
   2. Limited success
   3. Moderate success
   4. Generally successful
   5. Very successful

   As a result of this project,
   branch employees will: 1   2   3   4   5

   a. Use the tools and techniques to
      determine customer needs
      and concerns.   ☐   ☐   ☐   ☐   ☐

   b. Match needs with specific
      projects and services.   ☐   ☐   ☐   ☐   ☐

   c. Use the tools and techniques
      to convince customers to buy/use
      National Bank products and services.   ☐   ☐   ☐   ☐   ☐

   d. Build a productive, long-term
      relationship with customers.   ☐   ☐   ☐   ☐   ☐

   e. Increase sales of each product line
      offered in the branch.   ☐   ☐   ☐   ☐   ☐

2. Did you develop and implement an on-the-job action plan for this project?
   ☐ Yes   ☐ No

   If yes, please describe the nature and outcome of the plan. If not, explain why. _____
   _____
   _____
   _____

Figure 6.1   Sample follow-up evaluation questionnaire.

3. Please rate the relevance to your job of each of the following components of the project using the following scale:
   1. No relevance
   2. Limited relevance
   3. Moderate relevance
   4. Generally relevant
   5. Very relevant in every way

	1	2	3	4	5
Job aids	☐	☐	☐	☐	☐
Group learning activities	☐	☐	☐	☐	☐
Incentive opportunities	☐	☐	☐	☐	☐
Networking opportunities with other Branches	☐	☐	☐	☐	☐
Reading material/videos	☐	☐	☐	☐	☐
Coaching sessions	☐	☐	☐	☐	☐
Software/system changes	☐	☐	☐	☐	☐
Database enhancements	☐	☐	☐	☐	☐

4. Have you used the job aids provided during the intervention?
   ☐ Yes   ☐ No
   Please explain. _____
   _____
   _____
   _____

5. Please indicate the change in the application of knowledge and skills as a result of your participation in the sales culture project. Use the following scale:
   1. No change
   2. Limited change
   3. Moderate change
   4. Much change
   5. Very much change

Figure 6.1   Sample follow-up evaluation questionnaire. (*Continued*)

	1	2	3	4	5	No Opportunity to Use Skill
a. Probing for customer needs	☐	☐	☐	☐	☐	☐
b. Helping the customer solve problems	☐	☐	☐	☐	☐	☐
c. Understanding the features and benefits of all products and services	☐	☐	☐	☐	☐	☐
d. Comparing products and services to those of competitors	☐	☐	☐	☐	☐	☐
e. Selecting appropriate products and services	☐	☐	☐	☐	☐	☐
f. Using persuasive selling techniques	☐	☐	☐	☐	☐	☐
g. Using follow-up techniques to stay in touch with the customer	☐	☐	☐	☐	☐	☐
h. Using new software routines for data access and transactions	☐	☐	☐	☐	☐	☐

6. What has changed about your relationship with your customers as a result of this project? _____

_____

_____

_____

7. Please identify any specific accomplishments/improvements that can be linked to this consulting project. _____

_____

_____

_____

Figure 6.1 Sample follow-up evaluation questionnaire. (*Continued*)

8. What specific value, in U.S. dollars, can be attributed to the above accomplishments/improvements? Use first-year values only. While this is a difficult question, try to think of specific ways in which the above improvements can be converted to monetary units. Along with the monetary values, please indicate the basis of your calculation. $ _____

Basis _____

_____

_____

_____

9. Other factors often influence improvements in performance. Please indicate the percentage of the above improvement that is related directly to this program. _____%

10. What level of confidence do you place in the above estimations? (0% = no Confidence, 100% = certainty) _____%

Please explain. _____

_____

_____

_____

11. Do you think the sales culture project represented a good investment for National Bank?

☐ Yes   ☐ No

Please explain. _____

_____

_____

_____

12. Indicate the extent to which you think this project has influenced each of these measures in your branch. Use the following scale:
   1. No influence
   2. Limited influence
   3. Moderate influence
   4. Much influence
   5. Very much influence

Figure 6.1 Sample follow-up evaluation questionnaire. (*Continued*)

	1	2	3	4	5
a. Productivity	☐	☐	☐	☐	☐
b. Sales	☐	☐	☐	☐	☐
c. Customer response time	☐	☐	☐	☐	☐
d. Cross-sales ratio	☐	☐	☐	☐	☐
e. Cost control	☐	☐	☐	☐	☐
f. Employee satisfaction	☐	☐	☐	☐	☐
g. Customer satisfaction	☐	☐	☐	☐	☐
h. Quality	☐	☐	☐	☐	☐
i. Other	☐	☐	☐	☐	☐

13. Please rate the success of the immediate consulting team and the quality of the team's leadership. Use the following scale:
    1. No success
    2. Limited success
    3. Moderately successful
    4. Generally successful
    5. Very successful

Team Characteristic	1	2	3	4	5
Capability	☐	☐	☐	☐	☐
Motivation	☐	☐	☐	☐	☐
Cooperation	☐	☐	☐	☐	☐
Communication	☐	☐	☐	☐	☐

Leadership Issue	1	2	3	4	5
Leadership style	☐	☐	☐	☐	☐
Organization	☐	☐	☐	☐	☐
Communication	☐	☐	☐	☐	☐
Support for team	☐	☐	☐	☐	☐
Training for team	☐	☐	☐	☐	☐

14. What barriers, if any, have you encountered that prevented this project from being successful? Please explain, if possible.

_____

_____

_____

Figure 6.1   Sample follow-up evaluation questionnaire. (*Continued*)

15. What has helped this project be successful?
    Please explain. _____
    _____
    _____

16. Which of the following statements best describes the level of management support?
    ☐ There was no management support for this project.
    ☐ There was limited management support for this project.
    ☐ There was a moderate amount management support for this project.
    ☐ There was much management support for this project.
    ☐ There was very much management support for this project.

17. Could other solutions have been effective in meeting the business need(s)?
    ☐ Yes   ☐ No
    Please explain. _____
    _____
    _____
    _____

18. What specific suggestions do you have for improving this project? _____
    _____
    _____
    _____

19. Other comments about this project: _____
    _____
    _____
    _____

Figure 6.1   Sample follow-up evaluation questionnaire. (*Continued*)

plan, as illustrated in question 2 in Figure 6.1. If the action plan is quite comprehensive and contains an abundance of Level 3 and 4 data, then the questionnaire takes a secondary role, and most of the data collection process will focus directly on the status of the completed action plan. The action planning process is described later in the chapter.

Relevance of Intervention

Although the relevance of the consulting intervention is often assessed during the project as Level 1 data, it is sometimes helpful to assess the relevance to various aspects of the intervention after application and implementation. This proves that the perceived relevance is applicable and reinforces the Level 1 data.

Use of Job-Related Materials

If participants are provided with job aids and references to use on the job, then it may be helpful to determine the extent to which these materials have been used. This is particularly helpful when operation manuals, reference books, and job aids have been distributed and explained in the consulting intervention and are expected to be used on the job. Question 4 in Figure 6.1 focuses on this issue.

Knowledge/Skill Use

Perhaps one of the most important questions on the follow-up questionnaire focuses on the application of skills and knowledge. As shown in question 5 in Figure 6.1, the specific skills and knowledge areas are listed, with the question framed around the amount of change since the intervention was implemented. This is the recommended approach when there are no preintervention data. If preintervention data have been collected, it is more appropriate to compare postintervention assessments with preintervention assessments using the same type of question. Sometimes it is helpful to determine the most frequently used skills that are directly linked to the intervention. A more detailed variation of this question is to list each skill and indicate the frequency of use. For many skills, it is important to experience frequent use quickly after the skills are acquired so that the skill becomes internalized.

Changes with Work

Sometimes it is helpful to determine what specific features have changed about participants' work that can be connected to the consulting intervention. As question 6 in Figure 6.1 illustrates, the participant explores how the skill application has actually changed the relationship with customers.

Improvements/Accomplishments

Question 7 in Figure 6.1 begins a series of four impact questions that are appropriate for most follow-up questionnaires. The first question in the series seeks specific accomplishments and improvements that are directly linked to the consulting intervention. This question focuses on specific, measurable successes that can be easily identified by the participants. Since this is an open-ended question, it can be helpful to provide examples that indicate the nature and range of responses requested. However, examples can also limit the responses.

Monetary Impact

Perhaps the most difficult question, question 8 in Figure 6.1, asks participants to provide monetary values for the improvements identified in question seven. Although these are business impact data, it may be helpful to collect them here. Only the first-year improvement is sought. Participants are asked to specify net improvements so that the actual monetary values will represent gains from the intervention. An important part of the question is the basis for calculation, where participants specify the steps taken to develop the annual net value and the assumptions made in the analysis. It is very important for the basis to be completed with enough detail to understand the process.

Improvements Linked with Intervention

The next question in the series of impact questions, question 9 in Figure 6.1, isolates the effects of the consulting intervention. Participants indicate the percentage of the improvement that is directly related to the intervention. As an alternative, the various factors that have influenced the results may be listed. Participants are asked to allocate a percentage to each factor.

Confidence Level

To adjust for the uncertainty of the data provided in the impact questions, participants are asked to provide a level of confidence for each estimation. This confidence factor is expressed as a percentage with a range of 0 to 100%, as shown in question 10 in Figure 6.1. This input adjusts the participant estimates to account for their uncertainty. This conservative approach adds credibility to the estimation process.

Investment Perception

The participants' perception of the value of the intervention is useful information. As illustrated in question 11 in Figure 6.1, participants are asked if they believe the project to be a good investment. An option for this question is to present the actual cost of the intervention so that participants can respond more accurately. Also, the question can be divided into two parts, one reflecting the investment of money by the organization and the other the investment of the participants' time in the project. The perceived value is an indicator that the consulting processes are being implemented.

Linkage with Output Measures

Sometimes it is helpful to determine the degree to which the intervention has influenced certain output measures. As shown in question 12 in Figure 6.1, participants are often asked to indicate the degree to which they think certain measures have been influenced by the intervention. However, when this issue is uncertain, listing potential business performance measures known to have been influenced and asking participants to indicate which measures they believe have been influenced will identify the measures most influenced by the intervention.

Success of Consulting Team

Sometimes it is helpful to solicit input about the working relationship between the consulting team and the consulting participants. Large-scale projects rely on the quality of the consulting leadership team. Question 13 in Figure 6.1 asks participants to indicate the degree to which the consulting team is successful and the quality of the team's leadership. This information is helpful in making adjustments in future projects.

Barriers

Several barriers can influence the successful application of a consulting project. Question 14 in Figure 6.1 identifies these barriers. As an alternative, the perceived barriers are listed and participants check all that apply. Still another variation is to list the barriers with a range of responses, indicating the extent to which the barrier inhibited results.

Enablers

Just as important as barriers are the enablers—those issues, events, or situations that have enabled the project to be successful. The same options are available with this question as in the question on barriers. Question 15 in Figure 6.1 addresses this issue.

Management Support

Management support is critical to the successful application of newly acquired skills. At least one question about the degree of management support should be included in the questionnaire. Sometimes this question is structured so that various descriptions of management support are detailed, and participants check the one that applies to their situation. Question 16 in Figure 6.1 is an example of such a question.

Appropriateness of Solution

A recommended process or program in a consulting project is usually only one of many potential solutions to a performance problem. If the initial analysis and needs assessment is faulty or if there are alternative approaches to meeting the desired business need, another solution may achieve equal or greater success. The consulting participant is asked to identify alternative solutions that could have been effective in obtaining the same or similar results. Question 17 in Figure 6.1 represents this type of question. The consulting staff can use this information to help improve processes and understand the use of alternative approaches.

Suggestions for Improvement

Participants are asked to provide suggestions for improving any part of the consulting intervention or process. As illustrated in question 18 in Figure 6.1, the open-ended structure is intended to solicit qualitative responses to be used to make improvements.

Other Comments

A final step is to seek other comments about a project. This provides an opportunity to offer additional intangible benefits, to present concerns, or to suggest issues that will need to be addressed in the future. Question 19 in Figure 6.1 is such a question.

Using Interviews and Focus Groups
to Measure Implementation and Application

Interviews and focus groups can be used on a follow-up basis to collect data on implementation and application. The steps needed to design and administer these instruments are the same as the ones presented in Chapter 4 and will not be repeated here.

Observing Participants on the Job
to Measure Implementation and Application

Another potentially useful data collection method is observing participants on the job and recording any changes in behavior and specific actions taken. This technique is particularly useful when it is important to know precisely how the consulting participants are using new skills, knowledge, tasks, procedures, or systems. Participant observation is often used in sales and sales support projects. The observer may be a member of the consulting staff, the participant's supervisor, a member of a peer group, or an external resource. The most common observer, and probably the most practical, is a member of the consulting staff.

Guidelines for Effective Observation

Observation is often misused or misapplied in evaluation situations, forcing some clients to abandon the process. The effectiveness of observation can be improved with the following guidelines.

Observers Must Be Fully Prepared

Observers must fully understand what information is needed and what skills are covered in the intervention. They must be prepared for the assignment and provided a chance to practice observation skills.

The Observations Should Be Systematic

The observation process must be planned so that it is executed effectively without any surprises. The individuals observed should know in advance about the observation and why they are being observed, unless the observation is planned to be invisible. In this case, the individuals are monitored unknowingly. The timing of observations should be a part of the plan. There are right times to observe a participant, and there are wrong times. If a participant is observed when work situations are not normal (i.e., in a crisis), the data collected may be useless.

Planning a systematic observation is important. Several steps are necessary to accomplish a successful observation:

1. Determine what behavior will be observed.
2. Prepare the forms for the observers' use.
3. Select the observers.
4. Prepare a schedule of observations.
5. Prepare observers to observe properly.
6. Inform participants of the planned observation, providing explanations.
7. Conduct the observations.
8. Summarize the observation data.

The Observers Should Know How to Interpret and Report What They See

Observations involve judgment decisions. The observer must analyze which behaviors are being displayed and what actions are being taken by the participants. Observers should know how to summarize behavior and report results in a meaningful manner.

The Observer's Influence Should Be Minimized

Except for "mystery" or "planted" observers and electronic observations, it is impossible to completely isolate the overall effect of an observer. Participants will display the behavior they think is appropriate, performing at their best. The presence of the observer must be minimized. To the extent possible, the observer should blend into the work environment.

Select Observers Carefully

Observers are usually independent of the participants. They are typically members of the consulting staff. The independent observer is usually more skilled at recording behavior and making interpretations of behavior and is usually unbiased in these interpretations. Using an independent observer reduces the need for consultants to prepare observers and relieves the operating department or division of the responsibility. On the other hand, the independent observer has the appearance of an outsider, and participants may resent this kind of observer. Sometimes it is more feasible to recruit observers from outside the organization. Another advantage is the ability of this approach to neutralize prejudicial feelings entering the decisions.

Observation Methods

Five methods of observation are suggested and are appropriate depending on the circumstances surrounding the type of information needed. Each method is briefly described in the following text.

Behavior Checklist and Codes

A behavior checklist is useful for recording the presence, absence, frequency, or duration of a participant's behavior as it occurs. A checklist does not provide information on the quality, intensity, or possible circumstances surrounding the behavior observed. The checklist is useful, though, since an observer can identify exactly which behaviors should or should not occur. Measuring the duration of a behavior may be more difficult and requires a stopwatch and a place on the form to record time intervals. This factor is usually not as important as whether or not a particular behavior was observed and how often. The behaviors listed in the checklist should be few and should be listed in a logical sequence if they normally occur in a sequence. A variation of this approach involves coding behaviors on a form. While this method is useful when there are many behaviors, it is more time consuming because the observer must enter a code that identifies a specific behavior instead of simply checking an item.

Delayed Report Method

With a delayed report method, the observer does not use any forms or written materials during the observation. The information is either recorded after the observation is completed or at particular time intervals during an observation. The observer tries to reconstruct what has been witnessed during the observation period. The advantage of this approach is that the observer is not as noticeable, and there are no forms being completed or notes being taken during the observation. The observer becomes more a part of the situation and less of a distraction. An obvious disadvantage is that information written later may not be as accurate and reliable as information collected at the time events occurred. A variation of this approach is the 360° feedback process, in which surveys are completed on other individuals based on observations within a specific time frame.

Video Recording

A video camera records behavior in every detail. However, this intrusion may be awkward and cumbersome, and the participants may be unnecessarily nervous or self-conscious while they are being videotaped. If the camera is concealed, the privacy of the participant may be invaded. Because of this, video recording of on-the-job behavior is not frequently used.

Audio Monitoring

Monitoring conversations of participants who are using the skills taught in the consulting intervention is an effective observation technique. For example, in a large communication company's telemarketing department, sales representatives were prepared to sell equipment by telephone. To determine if employees were using the skills and procedures properly, telephone conversations were monitored on a randomly selected basis. While this approach may stir some controversy, it is an effective way to determine if skills are being applied consistently and effectively. For it to work smoothly, it must be fully explained and the rules must be clearly communicated.

Computer Monitoring

For employees who work regularly with a keyboard, computer monitoring is becoming an effective way to "observe" participants as they perform job tasks. The computer monitors times, sequence of steps, use of routines, and other activities to determine if the participant is performing the work according to the guidelines of the consulting intervention. As technology continues to be a significant part of the workplace, computer monitoring holds much promise. This is particularly helpful for application and implementation data.

Using Action Plans and Follow-Up Assignments to Measure Implementation and Application

In some cases, follow-up assignments can develop implementation and application data. In a typical follow-up assignment, the consulting participant is asked to meet a goal or complete a particular task or project by a set date. A summary of the results of the completed assignments provides further evidence of the success of the consulting intervention and actual implementation of new skills and knowledge gained.

The action plan is the most common type of follow-up assignment process and is fully described in this section. With this approach, participants are required to develop action plans as part of the intervention. Action plans contain detailed steps to accomplish specific objectives related to the intervention. The process is one of the most effective ways to enhance support for a consulting project and build the ownership needed for the successful application and implementation of the project.

The plan is typically prepared on a printed form such as the one shown in Figure 6.2. The action plan shows what is to be done and by whom, and the date by which the objectives should be accomplished. The action plan approach is a straightforward, easy-to-use method for determining how participants will change their behavior on the job and achieve success with the consulting intervention. The approach produces data answering such questions as:

- What on-the-job improvements have been realized since the intervention was implemented?
- Are the improvements linked to the intervention?
- What may have prevented participants from accomplishing specific action items?

With this information, consultants can decide if the project should be modified and in what ways, if it is not too late. Collectively, the consultants and the client can assess the findings to evaluate the success of the intervention.

Developing the Action Plan

The development of the action plan requires two major tasks: determining the areas for action and writing the action items. Both tasks should be completed during the consulting intervention and, at the same time, should be related to on-the-job activities. A list of areas for action can be developed with the help of consultants. The list may include an area needing improvement or representing an opportunity for increased performance. Examples of typical questions that should be answered before determination of the areas for action are:

- How much time will this action take?
- Are the skills for accomplishing this action item available?
- Who has the authority to implement the action plan?
- Will this action have an effect on other individuals?
- Are there any organizational constraints for accomplishing this action item?

Usually, it is more difficult to write specific action items than it is to identify action areas. The most important characteristic of an action item is that it should be written so that everyone involved will know when it occurs. One way to help achieve this goal is to use specific action verbs and set deadlines for completion of each action item. Some examples of action items are:

- Implement the new customer contract software by [date].
- Identify and secure a new customer account by [date].

Name: _____ Consultant Signature _____ Follow-Up Date _____

Objective: _____ Evaluation Period _____ to _____

Action Steps	Expected Consequences	Target Date	Responsibility
1. _____	_____	_____	_____
2. _____	_____	_____	_____
3. _____	_____	_____	_____
4. _____	_____	_____	_____
5. _____	_____	_____	_____
6. _____	_____	_____	_____
7. _____	_____	_____	_____
8. _____	_____	_____	_____

Comments: _____
_____
_____

Figure 6.2 Action plan.

- Handle every piece of paper only once to improve my personal time management by [date].
- Probe my customers directly about a particular problem by [date].

If appropriate, each action item should indicate other individuals or resources necessary for completion of the action item. Planned behavior changes should be observable. It should be obvious to the participant and others when the change takes place. Action plans, as used in this context, do not require prior approval or input from the participant's supervisor, although, as in any case, supervisor support may be helpful.

Using Action Plans Successfully

The action plan process can be an integral part of the consulting intervention and is not necessarily considered an add-on or optional activity. To gain maximum effectiveness from action plans to collect data for evaluation, the following steps should be implemented.

Communicate the Action Plan Requirement Early

One of the most negative reactions to action plans is the surprise factor often inherent in the way the process is introduced. When consulting participants realize they must develop a detailed action plan, there is often immediate, built-in resistance. Communicating to participants in advance, when the process is shown to be an integral part of the consulting intervention, will often minimize resistance. When participants fully realize the benefits before they attend the first session, they take the process more seriously and usually perform extra steps to ensure its success.

Describe the Action Planning Process at the Outset of the Project

At the first meeting, action plan requirements are discussed, including an outline of the purpose of the process, an explanation of why it is necessary, and the basic requirements during and after the consulting intervention. Some consultants furnish a separate notepad for participants to collect ideas and useful techniques for their action plans. This is a productive way to focus more attention on the process.

Teach the Action Planning Process
An important prerequisite for action planning success is an understanding of how it works and how specific action plans are developed. A portion of the consulting project time is allocated to teaching participants how to develop plans. In this session, the requirements are outlined, special forms and procedures are discussed, and a positive example is distributed and reviewed. Sometimes an entire half-day module is allocated to this process so that participants will fully understand and use it. Any available support tools, such as key measures, charts, graphs, suggested topics, and sample calculations, should be used in this session to help facilitate the plan's development.

Allow Time to Develop the Plan
When action plans are used to collect data for project evaluation, it is important to allow participants to develop plans during the consulting intervention. Sometimes it is helpful to have participants work in teams so they can share ideas as they develop specific plans. In these sessions, consultants often monitor the progress of individuals or teams to keep the process on track and to answer questions.

Have the Consultant Approve Action Plans
It is essential for the action plan to be related to consulting project objectives and, at the same time, to represent an important accomplishment for the organization when it is completed. It is easy for participants to stray from the intent and purpose of action planning and not give it the attention it deserves. Consequently, it is helpful to have the consultant actually sign off on the action plan, ensuring that the plan reflects all of the requirements and is appropriate for the consulting intervention. In some cases, a space is provided for the consultant's signature on the action plan document.

Ask Participants to Isolate the Effects of the Consulting Intervention
Although the action plan is initiated because of the consulting intervention, the actual improvements reported on the action plan may be influenced by other factors. Thus, the action planning process should not be given full credit for the improvement. For example, an action plan to reduce product defects could receive only partial credit for an improve-

ment because of the other variables that will usually affect the defect rate. While there are several ways to isolate the effects of a consulting intervention, participant estimation is usually the most appropriate in the action planning process. Consequently, the participants are asked to estimate the percentage of the improvement actually related to a particular consulting intervention. This question can be asked on the action plan form or on a follow-up questionnaire.

Require Action Plans to Be Presented to the Group, If Possible

There is no better way to secure commitment and ownership of the action planning process than to have a participant describe his or her action plan in front of fellow participants. Presenting the action plan helps ensure that the process is thoroughly developed and will be implemented on the job. If the number of participants is too large for individual presentations, perhaps the group can be divided into teams, with one participant being selected from each team. Under these circumstances, the team will usually select the best action plan for presentation to the group.

Explain the Follow-Up Mechanism

Participants must have a clear understanding of the timing of the action plan, implementation, and follow-up. The method by which data will be collected, analyzed, and reported should be openly discussed. Five options are common:

1. The group is convened to discuss progress on the plans.
2. Participants meet with their immediate managers and discuss the success of the plan. A copy is forwarded to the consultants.
3. A meeting is held with the evaluator, the participant, and the participant's manager to discuss the plan and the information it contains.
4. Participants send the plan to the evaluator and it is discussed in a conference call.
5. Participants send the plan directly to the consulting staff with no meetings or discussions. This is the most common option.

While there are other ways to collect the data, it is important to select a mechanism that fits the culture and constraints of the organization.

Collect Action Plans at Predetermined Follow-Up Times

Because it is critical to have an excellent response rate, several steps may be necessary to ensure that action plans are completed and that data are returned to the appropriate individual or group for analysis. Some organizations send follow-up reminders by mail or e-mail, others call participants to check progress, and still others offer assistance in developing the final plan. These steps may require additional resources, which must be weighed against the importance of having more data. When the action plan process is implemented as outlined in this chapter, the response rates will normally be very high—in the 50 to 80 percent range. Usually, participants will see the importance of the process and will develop their plans in detail during the consulting intervention.

Summarize and Report the Data

If developed properly, each action plan should result in improvements. Also, each individual has indicated the percentage of improvement directly related to the consulting intervention either on the action plan or the questionnaire. The data must be tabulated, summarized, and reported in a way that shows success with application and implementation.

Advantages/Disadvantages of Action Plans

Although there are many advantages to using action plans, there are at least two concerns:

1. The process relies on direct input from the participant, usually with no assurance of anonymity. As such, the information can sometimes be biased and unreliable.
2. Action plans can be time consuming for the participant and, if the participant's manager is not involved in the process, there may be a tendency for the participant not to complete the assignment.

As this section has illustrated, the action plan approach has many inherent advantages. Action plans are simple and easy to administer; are easily understood by participants; are suitable in a wide variety of consulting interventions; are appropriate for all types of data; are able to measure reaction, learning, behavior changes, and results; and may be used with or without other evaluation methods.

Because of the tremendous flexibility and versatility of the process and the conservative adjustments that can be made in analysis, action plans have become important data collection tools for the consulting project evaluation.

Using Performance Contracts to Measure Implementation and Application

The performance contract is essentially a slight variation of the action planning process. Based on the principle of mutual goal setting, a performance contract is a written agreement between a participant and the participant's manager. The participant agrees to improve performance in an area of mutual concern related to the consulting project. The agreement is in the form of a project to be completed or a goal to be accomplished soon after the consulting intervention is complete. The agreement spells out what is to be accomplished, at what time, and with what results.

Although the steps can vary according to the specific kind of contract and the organization, a common sequence of events follows:

1. The employee (consulting participant) becomes involved in the consulting intervention.
2. The participant and manager mutually agree on a subject for improvement related to the consulting intervention. (What's in it for me?)
3. Specific, measurable goals are set.
4. The participant is involved in the intervention when the contract is discussed, and plans are developed to accomplish the goals.
5. After the consulting intervention, the participant works on the contract against a specific deadline.
6. The participant reports the results of the effort to the manager.
7. The manager and participant document the results and forward a copy to the consultant along with appropriate comments.
8. The individuals mutually select the subject or action to be taken or performance to be improved prior to the intervention.

The procedure for selecting the area of improvement is similar to that used in the action planning process. The topic can cover one or more of the following areas:

- *Routine performance:* includes specific improvements in routine performance measures, such as production, efficiency, and error rates
- *Problem solving:* focuses on specific problems, such as an unexpected increase in accidents, a decrease in efficiency, or a loss of morale
- *Innovative or creative applications:* includes initiating changes or improvements in work practices, methods, procedures, techniques, and processes
- *Personal development:* involves learning new information or acquiring new skills to increase individual effectiveness

The topic selected should be stated in terms of one or more objectives. The objectives should state what is to be accomplished when the contract is complete. The objectives should be:

- Written
- Understandable by all involved
- Challenging (requiring an unusual effort to achieve)
- Achievable (able to be accomplished)
- Largely under the control of the participant
- Measurable and dated

The details required to accomplish the contract objectives are developed following the guidelines for action plans presented earlier. Also, the methods for analyzing data and reporting progress are essentially the same, as with the action planning process.

Shortcut Ways to Measure Application and Implementation

Measuring application and implementation is a critical issue for most consulting projects. It would be hard to understand the success of the consulting project unless there was some indication of how well the stakeholders are using the process. While this chapter presents a variety of techniques for measuring application and implementation, ranging from questionnaires to observation to action plans, a simplified approach for low-key, inexpensive projects is to use a basic questionnaire. The questionnaire presented in Figure 6.1 is very detailed around a complex project. A much more simplified questionnaire addressing five or six key issues would be sufficient for small-scale projects. The areas that should be targeted are actual changes in:

- Work and skills applied
- Specific implementation issues
- Degree of success of implementation
- Problems encountered in implementation
- Issues that supported the project

These are the core issues that must be addressed.

Another option is to combine data collected on reaction and satisfaction with the data on application and implementation. These are related issues, and a questionnaire combining the key issues on topics presented in this chapter and in Chapter 4 may be sufficient. The important point is to collect data in the simplest way to see how well the project worked.

Final Thoughts

This chapter has outlined techniques for measuring application and implementation—a critical issue in determining the success of the project. This essential measure determines not only the success achieved, but areas where improvement is needed and areas where the success can be replicated in the future. A variety of techniques are available, ranging from observation to questionnaires to action plans, but the method chosen must match the scope of the project. Complicated projects require a comprehensive approach that measures all of the issues involved in application and implementation. Simple projects can take a less formal approach and collect data only from a questionnaire.

Further Reading

Boyce, Bert R., Charles T. Meadow, and Donald H. Kraft. *Measurement in Information Science*. San Diego: Academic, 1994.

Dixon, Nancy M. *Evaluation: A Tool for Improving HRD Quality*. San Diego: University Associates/American Society for Training and Development, 1990.

Fitz-enz, Jac. *How to Measure Human Resources Management* (2d ed.). New York: McGraw-Hill, 1995.

Gummesson, Evert. *Qualitative Methods in Management Research* (revised ed.). Newbury Park, CA: Sage Publications, 1991.

Kirkpatrick, Donald L. *Evaluating Training Programs: The Four Levels* (2d ed.). San Francisco: Berrett-Koehler, 1998.

Krueger, Richard A. *Focus Groups: A Practical Guide for Applied Research* (2d ed.). Thousand Oaks, CA: Sage, 1994.

Kvale, Steinar. *InterViews: An Introduction to Qualitative Research Interviewing*. Thousand Oaks, CA: Sage, 1996.

Langdon, Danny, G. *The New Language of Work*. Amherst, MA: HRD, 1995.

McClelland, Samuel B. *Organizational Needs Assessments: Design, Facilitation, and Analysis*. Westport, CT: Quorum, 1995.

Phillips, Jack J. *Accountability in Human Resource Management*. Houston, TX: Gulf, 1996.

Phillips, Jack J. *Handbook of Training Evaluation and Measurement Methods* (3d ed.). Houston, TX: Gulf, 1997.

Rea, Louis M., and Richard A. Parker. *Designing and Conducting Survey Research: A Comprehensive Guide* (2d ed.). San Francisco: Jossey-Bass, 1997.

Renzetti, Claire M., and Raymond M. Lee (eds.). *Researching Sensitive Topics*. Newbury Park, CA: Sage, 1993.

Schwartz, Norbert, and Seymour Sudman (eds.). *Answering Questions: Methodology for Determining Cognitive and Communicative Processes in Survey Research*. San Francisco: Jossey-Bass, 1996.

CHAPTER

7

What Was the Impact?

How to Capture Business Impact Data

THIS CHAPTER FOCUSES directly on tracking business performance measures and is the last chapter on collecting data. Some consultants—and clients—regard business impact data as the most important type because of the connection of this type of data with business unit success. Also, less-than-desired results in business measures are what translate into the types of business needs that ultimately initiate consulting projects. This chapter covers the types of business impact data and the specific processes needed to generate the measures within a consulting project. Coverage begins with monitoring the record-keeping systems, then moves on to action plans and the use of questionnaires. These three processes account for most of the opportunities for collecting these important and critical data.

Why Measure Business Impact?

Although there are several obvious reasons for measuring impact, four particular issues support the rationale for collecting business impact data related to a consulting project.

Higher-Level Data

Following the assumption that higher-level data create more value for the client, the business impact measures in a five-level framework offer more valuable data that are considered to be the consequence of the application and implementation of a consulting project. These data often represent the bottom-line measures that are positively influenced when a project is successful.

A Business Driver for Projects

For most consulting projects, the business impact data represent the initial drivers for the project. It is the problem of deteriorating or less-than-desired performance or the opportunity for improvement of a business measure that often leads to a consulting project. If the business needs defined by business measures are the drivers for a project, then the key measure for evaluating the project is the business impact. The extent to which measures have actually changed is the key determinant of the success of the project.

Payoff with Clients

Business impact data often reflect key payoff measures from the perspective of the client. These are the measures that are often desired by the client and that the client wants to see changed or improved. These data often represent hard, indisputable facts that reflect performance critical to the business and operating unit level of the organization.

Easy to Measure

One unique feature about business impact data is that they are often very easy to measure. Hard and soft data measures at this level often reflect key measures that are found in plentiful numbers throughout an organization. It is not unusual for an organization to have hundreds or even thousands of measures reflecting specific business impact items. The challenge is to connect the consulting objectives of the project to the appropriate business measures. This is more easily accomplished at the beginning of the consulting intervention due to the availability and ease of location of many of the data items.

Types of Data

The fundamental premise for evaluating a consulting project is to collect data directly related to the objectives of the project. Consultants are sometimes concerned that appropriate data are not available in the organization. Fortunately, this is not the case. The data needed to evaluate consulting have already been collected in a vast majority of settings. The confusion sometimes stems from the types of outcomes planned for interventions. Often, an intervention focuses on skill and behavioral outcomes reflecting what participants will be able to do after the project is completed. The outcomes of some interventions are easy to observe and evaluate: it is easy to measure the speed and quality of a new team-based assembly line, for instance. However, behavioral outcomes associated with change management are not nearly as obvious or measurable. Demonstrating that a manager is an effective change agent is much more difficult than demonstrating that an assembly line operation is maintaining quality and quantity standards.

To help clients focus on the desired measures, a distinction is made between two general categories of data: hard and soft. Hard data are the primary measurements of improvement, presented through rational, undisputed facts that are easily gathered. This is the most desirable type of data to collect. The ultimate criteria for measuring the effectiveness of management rest on hard data items such as productivity, profitability, cost control, and quality control.

Hard data are:

• Easy to measure and quantify
• Relatively easy to convert to monetary values
• Objectively based
• Common measures of organizational performance
• Credible with management

Because changes in these data may lag behind changes in the organization by many months, it is highly recommended that these measures be supplemented with interim assessments of measures of soft data such as attitude, motivation, satisfaction, and skill usage. Although a consulting project designed to enhance competencies or manage change should have an ultimate impact on hard data items, it may be more efficiently measured by soft data items. Soft data are more difficult to collect and analyze, but are used when hard data are unavailable. Soft data are:

- Sometimes difficult to measure or quantify directly
- Difficult to convert to monetary values
- Subjectively based, in many cases
- Less credible as a performance measurement
- Usually behaviorally oriented

Hard Data

Hard data can be grouped into four categories (or subdivisions), as shown in Figure 7.1. These categories—output, quality, cost, and time—are typical performance measures in almost every organization.

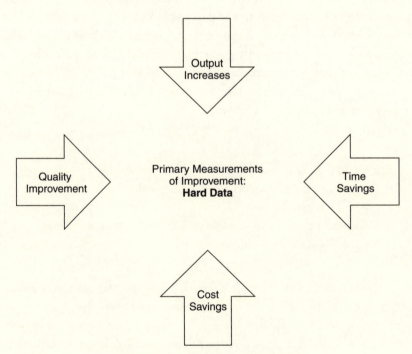

Figure 7.1 The four major categories of hard data.

When these are unavailable, the basic approach is to convert soft data to one of the four basic categories.

Output
Probably the most visible hard data results achieved from consulting are those involving improvements in the output of the work unit. Every organization, regardless of type, has basic measurements of work output, appearing in various forms as outlined in Table 7.1. Since these fac-

Table 7.1 Examples of Hard Data

Output	Time	Costs	Quality
Units produced	Cycle time	Budget variances	Scrap
Tons manufactured	Response time for complaint	Unit costs	Waste
Items assembled		Cost by account	Rejects
Items sold	Equipment downtime	Variable costs	Error rates
Sales	Overtime	Fixed costs	Rework
Forms processed		Overhead costs	Shortages
Loans approved	Average delay time	Operating costs	Product defects
Inventory turnover		Delay costs	Deviation from standard
Patients visited	Time to project Completion	Penalties/fines	
Applications processed	Processing time	Project cost savings	Product failures
Students graduated	Supervisory time	Accident costs	Inventory adjustments
Tasks completed	Training time	Program costs	Percentage of tasks completed properly
Productivity	Meeting time	Sales expense	Number of accidents
Work backlog	Repair time	Administrative costs	
Incentive bonus	Efficiency (time based)	Average cost reduction	Customer complaints
Shipments	Work stoppages		
New accounts generated	Order response time		
	Late reporting		
	Lost time days		

tors are monitored by organizations, changes can be easily measured by comparing work output before and after an intervention.

Quality

One of the most significant hard data results is quality. Every organization is concerned with quality, and processes are usually in place to measure and monitor it. Many consulting projects are designed to improve quality, and the results can be easily documented using a variety of quality improvement measurements as illustrated in Table 7.1.

Cost

Another significant hard data results area is improvement in costs. Many consulting projects that produce a direct cost savings can easily show a bottom-line contribution. A few examples of the types of costs are shown in Table 7.1. There can be as many cost items as there are accounts in a cost accounting system. In addition, costs can be combined to develop any number of combinations needed for evaluation.

Time

The fourth hard data category area is time. Easy to measure and just as critical as cost and quality, time savings may mean a project is completed faster than was planned, a new product was introduced earlier, or the time to repair equipment was reduced. The savings translate into additional output or lower operating costs. Examples of time savings generated by consulting projects are shown in Table 7.1.

The distinction between these four groups of hard data is sometimes unclear, since there are overlap factors to consider. For example, accident costs may be listed under the cost category, the number of accidents under quality, and lost days due to an accident under the time category. The rationale? Accidents represent a cost that can easily be determined. Accidents are usually caused by someone making a mistake and are often a reflection of the quality of employee efforts. Days lost represent time lost to the organization. An incentive bonus may be listed as output, since the amount of bonus is usually tied directly to the output of an employee or group of employees. However, the bonus is usually presented in cash, which represents a cost to the organization. The distinction between the different subdivisions is not as important as the awareness of the vast number of measurements in these four areas.

Soft Data

There are times when hard, rational numbers just do not exist. When this is the case, soft data may be meaningful in evaluating consulting projects. Table 7.2 shows common types of soft data categorized or subdivided into six areas: work habits, climate, new skills, development, satisfaction, and initiative. There may be other ways to divide soft data into categories. Due to the many types of soft data, the possibilities are almost limitless.

Table 7.2 Examples of Soft Data

Work Habits	Customer Service
Absenteeism	Customer complaints
Tardiness	Customer satisfaction
Visits to the dispensary	Customer dissatisfaction
First aid treatments	Customer impressions
Violations of safety rules	Customer loyalty
Number of communication breakdowns	Customer retention
	Customer value
Excessive breaks	Lost customers

Work Climate/Satisfaction	Employee Development
Number of grievances	Number of promotions
Number of discrimination charges	Number of pay increases
Employee complaints	Number of training programs attended
Litigation	
Job satisfaction	Requests for transfer
Organizational commitment	Performance appraisal ratings
Employee turnover	Increases in job effectiveness
Attitude Shifts	Initiative/Innovation
Employee loyalty	Implementation of new ideas
Increased confidence	Successful completion of projects
	Number of suggestions implemented
	Setting goals and objectives
	New products and services developed
	New patents and copyrights

Work Habits

Employee work habits are critical to the success of a work group. Dysfunctional work habits can lead to an unproductive and ineffective work group, while productive work habits can boost the output and morale of the group. The most common and easily documented unproductive work habits include absenteeism and tardiness. These can be tied to cost much more easily than other types of soft data. Some consulting projects, such as absenteeism reduction interventions, are designed to improve the work habits of employees. In most organizations, measurement systems are in place to record employee work habit problems such as absenteeism, tardiness, and visits to the infirmary. In other situations, the work habits may have to be documented by supervisors.

Work Climate/Satisfaction

The climate of the work group is important in team effectiveness. Grievances, discrimination charges, complaints, and job dissatisfaction are often linked to the work climate. The result: lower efficiency, less output, unionization drives, and possibly employee resignations. Many consulting projects are designed to improve work climate.

Consulting projects are also frequently designed to improve satisfaction with work, environment, or customers. Reactions to these measures provide additional evidence of the success of an intervention.

Customer Service

One of the most important soft data areas is the customer service category. Measuring the extent of customer satisfaction and dissatisfaction is critical to developing the desired customer loyalty and retention.

Employee Development

Another important type of soft data is employee development. Promotions, transfers, pay increases, and performance ratings are typical types of data that indicate improvement in this area. In the case of managers/supervisors, measures focus on the extent to which these people provide developmental opportunities for their employees.

Initiative and Innovation

The final category of soft data is initiative. In some consulting projects, participants are encouraged to try new ideas and techniques. The extent to which employees accomplish their goals is additional evidence of the success of the project. Also, the employees' initiative to generate ideas and submit suggestions is further indication that improvement has occurred. New product and service developments and new inventions, patents, and copyrights are important innovation measures.

As with hard data, these subdivisions have some overlap. Some items listed under one category could appropriately be listed in another. For instance, consider employee loyalty. Loyalty is related both to the feelings and attitudes of an employee and to work habits. An employee exhibits loyalty through attitudes and feelings in the following situations:

- Balancing the organization's goals with personal goals
- Purchasing the company's products rather than those of a competitor

On the other hand, loyalty may surface in these work habits of an employee:

- Returning to work promptly after breaks
- Studying job information on his or her own time
- Taking work home when necessary to finish the job

Soft Data Versus Hard Data

The preference for hard data in consulting evaluations does not decrease the value of soft data. Soft data are essential for a complete evaluation of a consulting intervention. A project's total success may rest on soft data measurements. For example, in a project to reduce turnover at a fast-food restaurant, four key measures of success were identified: employee turnover, interview-to-hire ratios, participants' performance evaluations, and reduced litigation.

Most interventions use a combination of hard and soft data items in the evaluation. A comprehensive evaluation uses several hard data and soft data measurements. For example, a maintenance consulting project had the following measures of success:

- Reduction of costs associated with specific maintenance activities
- Improvement in production equipment and processes

- Changes in maintenance responsibilities and procedures
- Improvement in intervention of maintenance employees
- Changes in organization and personnel

These changes included both hard data (production and costs) and soft data (increased intervention, changes in procedures, and changes in the organization).

Soft data are usually best used when evaluating behavior and skill outcomes. For example, in building core competencies, which has proven to be a very effective strategy for many organizations, the evaluation of behavioral and skill outcomes relies almost entirely on soft data.

The important point is that there is a place for both hard and soft data intervention evaluation. A comprehensive intervention will use both types of data. Some interventions will rely on soft data as primary measures, while others will rely on hard data. Hard data are preferred because of their distinct advantages and level of credibility.

Other Data Categories

In addition to classifying data as hard and soft, it is sometimes helpful to explain other ways to classify or categorize data. As shown in Figure 7.2, data can be categorized at several different levels. As the figure illustrates, some data are considered strategic and are linked to the corporate level of an organization. Other data are more operational at the business unit level. Still other data are considered more tactical in nature and scope and are utilized at the operating level.

Examples of data categorized at the strategic level include financial, people oriented, or internal versus external. At the business unit level, classifications such as output, quality, time, cost, job satisfaction, and customer satisfaction are critical categories. At the tactical level, the categories are more plentiful and include items such as productivity, efficiency, cost control, quality, time, attitudes, and individual and team performance. The important point is not concern about the classification of data but awareness of the vast array of data available. Regardless of what label they are given, these data are a consequence measure of consulting project success. These measures are captured throughout an organization and used for a variety of purposes. The challenge is to find the data items connected directly to the consulting project. Ideally, this

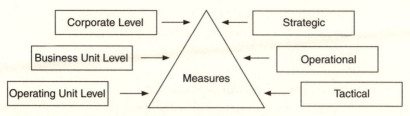

Figure 7.2   Measures at different levels.

would be accomplished on the front end of the process so that the data are linked with the initial analysis. If not, it would be a process of trying to identify the appropriate measures for the output of the consulting process.

Monitoring Business Performance Data

Data are available in every organization to measure business performance. Monitoring performance data enables management to measure performance in terms of output, quality, costs, time, job satisfaction, and customer satisfaction. In determining the source of data in the evaluation, the first consideration should be existing databases and reports. In most organizations, performance data suitable for measuring improvement resulting from a consulting intervention are available. If not, additional record-keeping systems will have to be developed for measurement and analysis. At this point, the question of economics surfaces. Is it economical to develop the record-keeping systems necessary to evaluate a consulting intervention? If the costs are greater than the expected return for the entire intervention, then it is pointless to develop these systems.

Using Current Measures

If existing performance measures are available, specific guidelines are recommended to ensure that the measurement system is easily developed.

Identify Appropriate Measures
Existing performance measures should be thoroughly researched to identify those related to the proposed objectives of the intervention. Frequently, an organization will have several performance measures

related to the same item. For example, the efficiency of a production unit can be measured in several ways, some of which are outlined in the following list:

- Number of units produced per hour
- Number of on-schedule production units
- Percentage of utilization of equipment
- Percentage of equipment downtime
- Labor cost per unit of production
- Overtime required per unit of production
- Total unit cost

Each of these, in its own way, measures the efficiency of the production unit. All related measures should be reviewed to determine those most relevant to the consulting intervention.

Convert Current Measures to Usable Ones

Occasionally, existing performance measures are integrated with other data, and it may be difficult to keep them isolated from unrelated data. In this situation, all existing related measures should be extracted and tabulated again to be more appropriate for comparison in the evaluation. At times, conversion factors may be necessary. For example, the average number of new sales orders per month may be presented regularly in the performance measures for the sales department. In addition, the sales costs per sales representative are also presented. However, in the evaluation of a consulting project, the average cost per new sale is needed. The average number of new sales orders and the sales lost per sales representative are required to develop the data necessary for comparison.

Developing New Measures

In some cases, data are not available for the information needed to measure the effectiveness of a consulting intervention. The consulting staff must work with the client organization to develop record-keeping systems, if economically feasible. In one organization, a turnover problem with new professional staff prompted a consulting intervention. To help ensure the success of the project, several measures were planned, including early turnover defined as the percentage of employees who left the company in the first six months of employment. Initially this measure was not available. Once the intervention was implemented, the organization began collecting early turnover figures for comparison. Several questions regarding this issue should be addressed:

- Which department will develop the measurement system?
- Who will record and monitor the data?
- Where will the data be recorded?
- Will forms be used?

These questions will usually involve other departments or a management decision that extends beyond the scope of the consultants. Often the administration department, the operations department, or the information technology unit will be instrumental in helping to determine whether new measures are needed and, if so, how they will be developed.

Using Action Plans to Develop Business Impact Data

Chapter 6 showed how action plans can capture Level 3 data to measure application and implementation. The action plan can also be a very useful tool for capturing business impact data. The basic design principles and the issues involved in developing and administering action plans are the same for business impact data as they are for application and implementation. However, a few issues unique to business impact and ROI are presented here. The following steps are recommended when an action plan is developed and implemented to capture business impact data and convert the data to monetary values.

Have Each Participant Set Goals and Targets

As shown in Figure 7.3, an action plan can be developed with a direct focus on business impact data. The plan presented in this figure requires participants to develop an overall objective, which is usually the primary objective of the consulting solution. In some cases, there may be more than one objective, which requires additional action plans. In addition to the objective, the improvement measure and the current levels of performance are identified. This information requires the par-

Name: _____ Consultant Signature: _____ Follow-Up Date: _____

Objective: _____ Evaluation Period: _____ to _____

Improvement Measure: _____ Current Performance: _____ Target Performance: _____

Action Steps	Analysis
1. _____	A. What is the unit of measure? _____
_____	B. What is the value (cost) of one unit? $ _____
2. _____	C. How did you arrive at this value? _____
_____	_____
3. _____	_____
_____	_____
4. _____	_____
_____	_____
5. _____	D. How much did the measure change during
_____	the evaluation period? (monthly value) _____
6. _____	E. What percent of this change was actually
_____	caused by this program? _____ %
7. _____	F. What level of confidence do you place on the
_____	above information? (100% = certainty,
Intangible benefits: _____	0% = no confidence) _____ %

Comments: _____

Figure 7.3 Action plan.

ticipant to anticipate the application and implementation of the consulting project and to set goals for specific performances that can be realized.

The action plan is completed during the consulting intervention, often with the input, assistance, and facilitation of the consultant. The consultant actually approves the plan, indicating that it meets the particular requirements of being very **S**pecific, **M**easurable, **A**chievable, **R**ealistic, and **T**ime-based (SMART). The plan can actually be developed in a one- to two-hour time frame and often begins with action steps related to the implementation of the consulting solution. These action steps are actually Level 3 activities that detail the application and implementation of the consulting intervention. All of these steps build support for, and are linked to, business impact measures.

Define the Unit of Measure

The next important issue is defining the actual unit of measure. In some cases, more than one measure may be used and will subsequently be contained in additional action plans. The unit of measure is necessary to break the process down into the simplest steps so that the ultimate value of the intervention can be determined. The unit can be output data, such as an additional unit manufactured or additional hotel room rented, or it can be sales and marketing data such as additional sales units, dollars earned, or percentage of increase in market share. In terms of quality, the unit can be one reject, error, or defect. Time-based units are usually measured in minutes, hours, days, or weeks. Other units are specific to their particular type of data, such as one grievance, complaint, or absence. The important point is to break units down into the simplest terms possible.

Require Participants to Assign Monetary Values for Each Improvement

During the consulting intervention, participants are asked to determine, calculate, or estimate the monetary value for each improvement outlined in the plan. The unit value is determined using standard values, expert input, external databases, or estimates. The process used in arriving at the value is described in the action plan. When the actual improvement occurs, participants will use these values to capture the annual monetary benefits of the plan. For this step to be effective, it is helpful to see examples of common ways in which values can be assigned to the actual data.

Require Participants to Implement the Action Plan

Participants implement the action plan during the consulting intervention; the action plan often lasts for weeks or months following the intervention. Upon completion, a major portion if not all of the consulting project is slated for implementation. The consulting participants implement action plan steps and the subsequent results are achieved.

Ask Participants to Estimate Improvements

At the end of the specified follow-up period—usually three months, six months, nine months, or one year—the participants indicate the specific improvements made, sometimes expressed as a monthly amount. This determines the actual amount of change that has been observed, measured, or recorded. It is important for the participants to understand the necessity for accuracy as data are recorded. In most cases only changes are recorded, as those amounts are needed to calculate the actual value of the intervention. In other cases, before and after data may be recorded, allowing the researchers to calculate the actual differences.

Ask Participants to Isolate the Effects of the Intervention

Although the action plan is initiated because of the intervention, the actual improvements reported on the action plan may be influenced by other factors. Thus, the action planning process initiated in the consulting intervention should not be given full credit for the improvement. For example, an action plan for reducing employee turnover in a division could receive only partial credit for an improvement because of the other variables that affect the turnover rate. While there are several ways to isolate the effects of a consulting intervention, participant estimation is usually most appropriate in the action planning process. Consequently, participants are asked to estimate the percentage of the improvement actually related to this particular intervention. This question can be asked on the action plan form or in a follow-up questionnaire.

Ask Participants to Provide a Confidence Level for Estimates

Since the process for converting data to monetary values may not be exact and the amount of the improvement actually related to the intervention may not be precise, participants are asked to indicate their level of confidence in those two values collectively. On a scale of 0 to 100 percent, where 0 percent means the values are completely false and 100 percent means the estimates represent certainty, this value provides participants a mechanism for expressing their uneasiness with their ability to be exact with the process.

Collect Action Plans at Specified Time Intervals

An excellent response rate is essential, so several steps may be necessary to ensure that the action plans are completed and returned. Usually participants will see the importance of the process and will develop their plans in detail before leaving the intervention. Some organizations use follow-up reminders by mail or e-mail. Others call participants to check progress. Still others offer assistance in developing the final plan. These steps may require additional resources, which must be weighed against the importance of having more data.

Summarize the Data and Calculate the ROI

If developed properly, each action plan should have annualized monetary values associated with improvements. Also, each individual should have indicated the percentage of the improvement directly related to the intervention. Finally, participants should have provided a confidence percentage to reflect their uncertainty with the process and the subjective nature of some of the data that may be provided.

Because this process involves estimates, it may not appear to be accurate. Several adjustments during the analysis make the process very credible and more accurate. The following adjustments are made:

Step 1: It is assumed that those participants who do not provide data have no improvement to report. This is a very conservative approach.

Step 2: Each value is checked for realism, usability, and feasibility. Extreme values are discarded and omitted from the analysis.

Step 3: Because the improvement is annualized, it is assumed that the intervention caused no improvement after the first year for short-term projects. Some interventions add value in years two and three.

Step 4: The improvement from Step 3 is then adjusted with the confidence level, multiplying it by the confidence percentage. The confidence level is actually an error percentage suggested by the participants. For example, a participant indicating 80 percent confidence with the process is reflecting a 20 percent error possibility. In a $10,000 estimate with an 80 percent confidence factor, the participant is suggesting that the value can be in the range of $8,000 to $12,000. To be conservative, the lower number is used. Thus, the confidence factor is multiplied by the amount of improvement.

Step 5: The new values are then adjusted by the percentage of the improvement related directly to the intervention using straight multiplication. This isolates the effects of the consulting intervention.

The monetary values determined in these five steps are totaled to arrive at a total intervention benefit. Since these values are already annualized, their total becomes the annual benefit for the intervention. This value is placed in the numerator of the ROI formula to calculate the ROI.

Case Application

The impact of the action plan process is impressive. In a medium-size manufacturing facility of a metals company, a consulting intervention was implemented for an operations division. Some of the areas addressed were productivity improvement, scrap reduction, absenteeism, turnover, grievances, and safety. These areas were analyzed thoroughly, and supervisors implemented improvements in each area. Supervisors were required to develop action plans for improvement and report the results in a follow-up six months after the intervention. In this situation, the improvement measures were predetermined by the needs assessment. The following results were documented from a pilot group:

- The department unit hour was increased from 65 to 75. This is a basic measure of productivity, where a unit hour of 60 is considered to be average and acceptable work.
- Scrap was reduced from 11 percent to 7.4 percent.
- Absenteeism was reduced from 7 percent to 3.25 percent.
- The annual turnover rate was drastically reduced from 30 percent to 5 percent.
- Grievances were reduced by 80 percent.
- Lost time accidents were reduced by 95 percent.

These results were achieved by supervisors applying and implementing consulting solutions and reporting the results of action plans. Although results like these are impressive, three additional steps are needed to develop the ultimate evaluation—the return on investment. First, the amount of improvement actually linked to the intervention must be determined. In this situation, supervisors estimated the percentage of the improvement directly linked to the intervention. For example, while the absenteeism improvement showed an overall decrease of 3.75 percent, the supervisors collectively estimated that only 46 percent of the absenteeism reduction was actually linked to the intervention. Thus, a 3.75 percent absenteeism reduction actually becomes 1.725 percent. This figure can be adjusted further by factoring in a confidence level (provided by supervisors when they supplied the estimate). In this example, supervisors were 84 percent confident in their allocation of the absenteeism improvement. This adjustment means that 1.725 percent then becomes 1.45 percent when adjusted for the 84 percent confidence level. These two adjustments isolate the effects of the intervention on the output variable and are fully described in a later chapter.

The second step in developing the ROI is to convert the data to monetary values. In the same example, the value for a single absence must be determined and used to calculate the annual benefit of the improvement. There are at least 10 ways to place values on data, which are fully described in Chapter 11. In this example, supervisors developed an estimated value of one absence, a value that was used previously in several applications in which the cost of absenteeism was needed. Thus, the total number of absences avoided was calculated and multiplied by the value of one absence to obtain the intervention's annual impact on absenteeism reduction. This process shows clearly the economic value of the intervention on that specific output variable. These two steps—isolating the effects of consulting and converting data to monetary values—are performed for each of the six improvement variables, and the total value represents the annual economic benefit of the intervention.

The third step necessary to move to ROI is to develop the fully loaded costs of the intervention. In this step, the costs related to the needs assessment and intervention development are prorated. All direct intervention costs are captured, along with the cost of participants' salaries and benefits while they were actually involved in the consulting intervention. The fully loaded cost for all participants reflects the total investment in this intervention for the group. This process is fully explained in Chapter 12. With these three additional steps, the ROI can be calculated using formulas described in Chapter 2 (net benefits divided by costs). In this example, total annual benefits directly attributed to the intervention after conversion of all six improvement items to monetary units were $775,000. The fully loaded costs for the intervention came out to $65,000. Thus, the ROI becomes:

$$\text{ROI} = \frac{\text{Net Intervention Benefits}}{\text{Intervention Costs}} = \frac{\$775,000 - \$65,000}{\$65,000} \times 100 = 1092\%$$

This impressive ROI has credibility because of the conservative adjustments made to the data. Without these three additional steps, the target audience may be left wondering how much the results were actually linked to the intervention and if the benefits exceeded the costs to the degree reflected in the ROI.

The action planning process is an extremely useful way to collect business impact data. Use of the process has several inherent advantages. Most of the data are taken directly from participants and often have the credibility needed in the analysis. Also, much of the responsibility for the analysis and evaluation is shifted to the participants as they tackle three of the most critical parts of the process. In effect, they collect data, show improvements, isolate the effects of the consulting intervention, and convert data to monetary values. This enables the evaluation to be conducted with limited resources and shifts much of the actual involvement to those who are actually applying and implementing the consulting project.

Using Questionnaires to Collect Business Impact Measures

As described in the previous chapters, the questionnaire is one of the most versatile data collection tools and can be appropriate for Level 1, 2, 3, and 4 data. In Chapter 6, a questionnaire example is presented in which Level 3 application and implementation data are collected and business impact data are developed as well. Some of the issues discussed there apply equally to collecting business impact data. Essentially, the design principles and the content issues are the same except that questionnaires developed for a business impact evaluation will contain additional questions to capture those data items.

Key Impact Questions

Figure 7.4 shows a series of key impact questions that can be added to a questionnaire to capture business impact data. While there are a variety of ways to collect this category of data, these simple questions can be very powerful if participants are committed to providing this type of information.

To ensure an appropriate response, the strategies outlined in Chapter 4 apply equally to follow-up questionnaires where business impact data are collected. These questions must be thoroughly explained and if possible even reviewed prior to actually achieving the accomplishments outlined in the questionnaire. The first impact question provides participants with the opportunity to detail specifically what has changed about their work as a result of the consulting project. These are actually application data, but they set the stage for collecting the business impact data.

Question 2 focuses directly on business impact data but is expressed in general terms to allow flexibility for participant responses. If the responses need to follow a narrowly focused set of possibilities, the question can be more narrowly worded.

Question 3 focuses on the actual monetary values. While this may only be necessary if an ROI analysis is planned, it is sometimes helpful to see the impact of the particular change in business measures expressed in monetary terms. Participants are asked not only to supply the values, but to provide an annual improvement as well. Most importantly, they are asked to provide an explanation of how they arrived at

1. What has changed about you or your work as a result of your participation in this consulting project? (Specific behavior change, action items, new projects, etc.)

   _____

   _____

   _____

2. Please identify any specific accomplishments/improvements that you can link to the project. (Job performance, project completion, response times, etc.)

   _____

   _____

   _____

3. What specific annualized value in U.S. dollars can be attributed to the above accomplishments/improvements? Use first-year values only. While this is a difficult question, try to think of specific ways in which the above improvements can be converted to monetary units. Along with the monetary value, please indicate the basis of your calculation. $ _____ . Basis:

   _____

   _____

   _____

4. Other factors often influence improvements in performance. Please indicate the percentage of the above improvement that is related directly to this project. _____ %. Please explain.

   _____

   _____

   _____

5. Do you think this program represented a good investment for the company?

   ☐ Yes   ☐ No   Please explain.

   _____

   _____

   _____

6. What level of confidence do you place on the above estimations? (0% = no confidence, 100% = certainty) _____ %

   _____

   _____

   _____

Figure 7.4   Key impact questions.

these values. This brings additional credibility to the responses and is important in making the decision to use the data.

Question 4 focuses on isolating the effects of the consulting project on business impact measures. In almost every setting, other factors will influence the output measures, so it is important to try to determine how much of the improvement is actually related to the consulting assignment. This question attempts to do that by asking participants to provide a percentage of the improvement related to the consulting project.

Question 5 simply asks participants their opinion as to whether or not the program was a good investment for the company. While this information cannot be used in the analysis, it provides supporting evidence of success—or the lack thereof.

Finally, in question 6, the level of confidence is captured using the scale of 0 to 100 percent. This confidence is spread over all of the questions and can be used to provide additional supporting evidence around the data gathered in the previous question. Also, the confidence value can be used to adjust the data. This will be explored later.

These simple questions can make the data collection instrument very powerful and can identify significant improvements in the business impact area.

There are different approaches and different ways to explore the issues surrounding data collection. The most important issue is that the proper climate be established for participants to provide the data.

ROI Analysis

While there are several approaches to data analysis, the recommended steps for calculating ROI are briefly described here. The calculations are based on the responses to the series of impact questions. The following five adjustments are made to the data to ensure that they are credible and accurate:

1. The participants who do not complete the questionnaire or provide usable data on the impact questions are assumed to have no improvement.
2. Extreme and unrealistic data items are omitted.
3. Only annualized values are used, as requested in the responses.

4. The values are adjusted to reflect the confidence level of participants.
5. The values are adjusted for the amount of the improvement
related directly to the intervention.

These five adjustments create a very credible value that is usually
considered to be an understatement of the benefits.

Selecting the Appropriate Method for Each Level

This chapter and the previous three present several methods to capture
business impact data. Collectively, they offer a wide range of opportunities for collecting data in a variety of situations. Eight specific issues
should be considered when deciding which method is appropriate for a
situation. These should be considered when selecting data collection
methods for other evaluation levels as well.

Type of Data

Perhaps one of the most important issues to consider when selecting
the method is the type of data to be collected. Some methods are more
appropriate for Level 4, while others are best for Level 3. Table 7.3
shows the most appropriate types of data for specific methods of Level
3 and 4 data collection. Follow-up surveys, observations, interviews,
and focus groups are best—sometimes exclusively—suited for Level 3
data. Performance monitoring, action planning, and questionnaires can
easily capture Level 4 data.

Table 7.3 Collecting Postintervention Data

Data Collection Method	Level 3	Level 4
Follow-up surveys	✔	
Follow-up questionnaires	✔	✔
Observation on the job	✔	
Interviews with participants	✔	
Follow-up focus groups	✔	
Action planning	✔	✔
Performance contracting	✔	✔
Business performance monitoring		✔

Participants' Time for Data Input

Another important factor in selecting the data collection method is the amount of time participants must spend with data collection and evaluation systems. Time requirements should always be minimized, and the method should be positioned so that it is a value-added activity (i.e., the participants understand that this activity is something valuable so they will not resist). This requirement often means that sampling is used to keep the total participant time to a minimum. Some methods, such as performance monitoring, require no participant time, while others, such as interviews and focus groups, require a significant time investment.

Supervisory Time for Data Input

The amount of time that a participant's direct supervisor must allocate to data collection is another important issue in method selection. This time requirement should always be minimized. Some methods, such as performance contracting, may require much involvement from the supervisor before and after the intervention. Other methods, such as questionnaires administered directly to participants, may not require any supervisor time.

Cost of Method

Cost is always a consideration when selecting the method. Some data collection methods are more expensive than others. For example, interviews and observations are very expensive. Surveys, questionnaires, and performance monitoring are usually inexpensive.

Disruption of Normal Work Activities

Another key issue in selecting the appropriate method—and perhaps the one that generates the most concern with managers—is the amount of disruption the data collection will create. Routine work processes should be disrupted as little as possible. Some data collection techniques, such as performance monitoring, require very little time and distraction from normal activities. Questionnaires generally do not disrupt the work environment and can often be completed in only a few minutes, or even after normal work hours. On the other extreme, some items such as observations and interviews may be overly disruptive to the work unit.

Accuracy of Method

The accuracy of the technique is another factor to consider when selecting the method. Some data collection methods are more accurate than others. For example, performance monitoring is usually very accurate, whereas questionnaires can be distorted and unreliable. If actual on-the-job behavior must be captured, observation is clearly one of the most accurate methods.

Utility of an Additional Method

Because there are many different methods of collecting data, it is tempting to use too many data collection methods. Multiple data collection methods add to the time and costs of the evaluation and may result in very little additional value. *Utility* refers to the added value of the use of an additional data collection method. As more than one method is used, this question should always be addressed. Does the value obtained from the additional data warrant the extra time and expense of the method? If the answer is no, the additional method should not be implemented.

Cultural Bias for Data Collection Method

The culture or philosophy of the organization can dictate which data collection methods are used. For example, some organizations are accustomed to using questionnaires and find that the process fits in well with their cultures. Some organizations will not use observation because their cultures do not support the potential invasion of privacy often associated with it.

How the Credibility of Data Is Influenced

When impact data are collected and presented to selected target audiences, credibility will be an issue. The degree to which the target audience will believe the data is influenced by the following factors.

Reputation of the Data Source

The actual source of the data represents the first credibility issue. How credible are the individuals or groups providing the data? Do they understand the issues? Are they knowledgeable about all the processes? The target audience will often place more credibility on data obtained from those who are closest to the source of the actual improvement or change.

Reputation of the Source of the Study

The target audience scrutinizes the reputation of the individuals, groups, or organizations presenting the data. Do they have a history of providing accurate reports? Are they unbiased in their analyses? Are they fair in their presentation? Answers to these and other questions will form an impression about the reputations behind the report.

Motives of the Evaluators

Do the individuals presenting the data have an ax to grind? Do they have a personal interest in creating a favorable or unfavorable result? These issues will cause the target audience to closely examine the motives of those who conducted the study.

The perspective of the target audience can make a difference as well. If audience members are biased for or against a particular project or consulting intervention, they may react favorably or unfavorably based on their predisposition, attitude, or previous knowledge of the issue. Consequently, the expected bias of the target audience is identified as the data are prepared, and the counterargument is fully explained so as to dilute the audience's predetermined position.

Methodology of the Study

The target audience will want to know specifically how the research was conducted. How were the calculations made? What steps were followed? What processes were used? A lack of information on the methodology will cause the audience to become wary and suspicious of the results.

Assumptions Made in the Analysis

In many impact studies, calculations and conclusions are based on certain assumptions made. What are the assumptions? Are they standard? How do they compare with other assumptions in other studies? When assumptions are omitted, the audience will substitute its own, often unfavorable, assumptions.

Realism of Outcome Data

Impressive values and high ROI numbers could cause problems. When outcomes appear to be unrealistic, it may be difficult for the target audience to believe them. Huge claims often fall on deaf ears, causing reports to be thrown away before they are reviewed.

Types of Data

The target audience usually has a preference for hard data, as it is seeking business performance data tied to output, quality, costs, and time. These measures are usually easily understood and closely related to organizational performance. Conversely, soft data are sometimes viewed suspiciously from the outset, as many senior executives are concerned about their soft nature and the limitations they may impose on the analysis.

Scope of Analysis

Is the scope of the analysis very narrow? Does it involve just one group, or all of the employees in the organization? Limiting the study to a small group of employees or a series of groups makes the process more accurate.

Collectively, these factors will influence the credibility of an impact study and provide a framework with which the final report may be developed. Thus, when considering each of the issues, the following key points are suggested for an impact study:

- Use the most credible and reliable source for estimates.
- Present the material in an unbiased, objective way.

- Fully explain the methodology used throughout the process, preferably on a step-by-step basis.
- Define the assumptions made in the analysis and compare them to assumptions made in similar studies.
- Consider factoring or adjusting output values when they appear to be unrealistic.
- Use hard data whenever possible and combine with soft data if available.
- Keep the scope of the analysis very narrow. Conduct the impact study with one or more groups of participants, instead of all participants or all employees.

Shortcut Ways to Capture Business Impact Data

While this chapter explores several different ways to capture business impact data, there are some ways the process can be simplified when the projects are small in scope or inexpensive to develop and deliver.

Revisit Initial Needs

In the ideal situation, the business needs are the drivers for the project. If possible, the initial needs will be revisited to see which specific measures need to change as a result of the consulting intervention. These are the measures that should be examined for changes. This can be an extremely simple process if the project is developed as it should be. If not, other approaches may be necessary.

Monitor Business Performance Measures

For most consulting projects, even those that are small in scope, it is possible to monitor the business measures that are linked or perceived to be linked to the projects. These are usually well known, discussed in conjunction with the project, and readily available in operating units and business units throughout the organization. Only those measures perceived to be directly linked to the intervention should be examined, and some caution should be taken not to overextend the project by examining measures that may be only casually linked to the consulting project.

Build It into the Process

As described in one of the examples in this chapter, it is a relatively easy task to build data collection and part of the analysis into the project. With this approach, the participants provide the data, isolate the effects of the consulting project on those data, and covert the data to monetary values. The remaining steps for a consulting ROI process are simply the additional steps for capturing the costs, detailing the intangibles, actually developing the ROI calculations, and, of course, presenting the entire report. By building data collection and some analysis into the process and gaining the necessary commitments from participants, it is possible for a consulting team to generate with very little cost and effort the required business data that are directly connected to the project.

If Questionnaires Are Used, Consider Business Impact Data

If a detailed follow-up questionnaire is used to capture data for application and implementation, a few additional questions can be added to capture business impact. The key impact questions contained in Figure 7.4 are very simple and can usually be addressed by many professional employees. They can be included in the questionnaire with little additional effort, and the analysis is not very time consuming. The results can be very eye-opening and far-reaching data that show not only value, but also identify several issues pertinent to the consulting project. Collectively, these are shortcut ways to ensure that business impact data are collected with minimum effort. It is important and almost essential that business data be collected if they are linked to the consulting project. After all, this is the type of data that most clients desire and are expecting from the project.

Final Thoughts

After describing the types of data that reflect business impact, this chapter provides an overview of several data collection approaches that can be used to capture business data. A variety of options are available. Some methods are gaining more acceptance for use in developing ROI calculations. In addition to performance monitoring, follow-up questionnaires and action plans are used regularly to collect data for an impact analysis. The credibility of data will always be an issue when data at this level are collected and analyzed. Several strategies are offered to enhance the credibility of data analysis.

Further Reading

Brown, Mark Graham. *Keeping Score: Using the Right Metrics to Drive World-Class Performance.* New York: Quality Resources, 1996.

Campanella, Jack. *Principles of Quality Costs: Principles, Implementation, and Use* (3d ed.). Milwaukee: ASQ Quality, 1999.

Lynch, Richard L., and Kelvin F. Cross. *Measure Up! Yardsticks for Continuous Improvement.* Blackwell Business, 1991.

Naumann, Earl, and Kathleen Giel. *Customer Satisfaction Measurement and Management: Using the Voice of the Customer.* Thomson, 1995.

Price Waterhouse Financial & Cost Management Team. *CFO: Architect of the Corporation's Future.* New York: Wiley, 1997.

How to Calculate and Interpret ROI

... and Other Measures of Financial Payoff

THE MONETARY VALUES for the benefits of a consulting intervention, explained in Chapter 11, are combined with program cost data, discussed in Chapter 12, in order to calculate the return on investment. This chapter explores the various techniques, processes, and issues involved in calculating the return on investment.

Why Measure ROI?

As discussed in earlier parts of the book, ROI is becoming a critical measure demanded by many stakeholders, including clients and senior executives. It is the ultimate level of evaluation, showing the actual payoff of the consulting project expressed as a percentage and based on the same formula as the evaluation of other types of investment. Because of its perceived value and senior management's familiarity with it, ROI is now becoming a common requirement for consulting interventions. When ROI is required, it must be developed; otherwise it may be optional unless there is some compelling reason to take the evaluation to this level.

Basic Issues

Before formulas for calculating ROI are presented, a few basic issues will be described and explored. An adequate understanding of these issues is necessary to complete this major step in the ROI process.

Definitions

The phrase *return on investment in consulting* is occasionally misused—sometimes intentionally. In these situations, a very broad definition for ROI is offered to include any benefit of the consulting intervention. ROI is thus defined as a vague concept in which even subjective data linked to a program are included. In this book, *return on investment* is used more precisely and is meant to represent an actual value arrived at by comparing consulting costs to benefits. The two most common measures are the benefit-cost ratio and the ROI formula. Both of these are presented, along with other approaches to calculate the return or payback.

For many years, consultants sought to calculate return on investment for consulting interventions. If a consulting intervention is considered an investment and not an expense, then it is appropriate to place consulting in the same funding category as other investments, such as those in equipment and facilities. Although the other investments are quite different, they are often viewed by management in the same way. Thus, it is critical to the success of the consulting intervention to develop specific values that reflect the return on the investment.

Annualized Values: A Fundamental Concept

All of the formulas presented in this chapter use annualized values so that the first-year impact of the program investment can be calculated. Using annualized values is becoming a generally accepted practice for developing ROI in many organizations. This approach is a conservative way to develop ROI, since many short-term consulting interventions accumulate added value in the second or third year. For long-term consulting interventions, first-year values are inappropriate and longer time frames need to be used. For example, in an ROI analysis of a consulting project involving self-directed teams at Litton Industries, a seven-year time frame was utilized. However, for most short-term consulting interventions that last only a few weeks, first-year values are appropriate.

When selecting the approach to be used in measuring ROI, it is important to communicate to the target audience the formula used and the assumptions made in arriving at the decision to use it. This helps avoid misunderstandings and confusion surrounding how the ROI value is actually developed. Although several approaches are described in this chapter, two stand out as the preferred methods: the benefit-cost ratio and the basic ROI formula. These two approaches are described next, along with brief coverage of the others.

Benefit-Cost Ratio

One of the earliest methods for evaluating consulting interventions was the benefit-cost ratio. This method compares the benefits of the consulting intervention to the costs using a ratio. In formula form, the ratio is:

$$BCR = \frac{\text{Consulting Benefits}}{\text{Consulting Costs}}$$

In simple terms, the BCR compares the annual economic benefits of the consulting intervention to the cost of the consulting. A BCR of 1 means that the benefits equal the costs. A BCR of 2, usually written as 2:1, indicates that for each dollar spent on consulting, \$2 are returned in benefits.

The following example illustrates the use of the benefit-cost ratio. A behavior management consulting intervention designed for managers and supervisors was implemented at an electric and gas utility. In a follow-up evaluation, action planning and business performance monitoring were used to capture benefits. The first-year payoff for the program was \$1,077,750. The total fully loaded implementation cost was \$215,500. Thus, the ratio was:

$$BCR = \frac{\$1,077,750}{\$215,500} = 5:1$$

For every dollar invested in the consulting intervention, \$5 in benefits were returned.

The principal advantage of using this approach is that it does not use traditional financial measures, so there is no confusion when comparing consulting investments with other investments in the company. Investments in plants, equipment, or subsidiaries, for example, are not usually evaluated by the benefit-cost method. Some consulting firm executives prefer not to use the same method to compare the return on consulting investments with the return on other investments. In these situations, the ROI for consulting interventions stands alone as a unique type of evaluation.

Unfortunately, there are no standards that constitute an acceptable benefit-cost ratio from the client perspective. A standard should be established within the organization, perhaps even for a specific type of consulting intervention. However, a 1:1 ratio (break-even status) is unacceptable for many consulting interventions. In others, a 1.25:1 ratio is required, meaning the benefits of the consulting are 1.25 times the cost.

ROI Formula

Perhaps the most appropriate formula for evaluating consulting investments is net program benefits divided by cost. The ratio is usually expressed as a percentage when the fractional values are multiplied by 100. In formula form, the ROI becomes:

$$\text{ROI (\%)} = \frac{\text{Net Consulting Benefits}}{\text{Consulting Costs}} \times 100$$

Net benefits are consulting benefits minus costs. The ROI value is related to the BCR by a factor of 1. For example, a BCR of 2.45 is the same as an ROI value of 145 percent (1.45 × 100%). This formula is essentially the same as that for ROI in other types of investments. For example, when a firm builds a new plant, the ROI is developed by dividing annual earnings by the investment. The annual earnings are comparable to net benefits (annual benefits minus the cost). The investment is comparable to fully loaded consulting intervention costs, which represent the investment in the consulting.

An ROI of 50 percent on a consulting intervention means that the costs are recovered and an additional 50 percent of the costs are reported as earnings. A consulting intervention ROI of 150 percent indicates that the costs have been recovered and an additional 1.5 times the costs are captured as earnings. An example illustrates the ROI calculation. Magnavox Electronics Systems Company was involved in a consulting intervention for entry-level electrical and mechanical assemblers. The results of the program were impressive. Productivity and quality alone yielded an annual value of $321,600. The total fully loaded costs for the project were $38,233. Thus, the return on investment becomes:

$$ROI\ (\%) = \frac{\$321,600 - \$38,233}{\$38,233} \times 100 = 741\%$$

For each dollar invested, Magnavox received $7.40 in return after the costs of the consulting project had been recovered.

Using the ROI formula essentially places consulting investments on a level playing field with other investments that utilize the same formula and similar concepts. The ROI calculation is easily understood by key management and financial executives who regularly use ROI with other investments.

While there are no generally accepted standards, some organizations establish a minimum requirement or *hurdle rate* for the ROI. This rate is based on the expected ROI for other investments, which is determined by the cost of capital and other factors. An ROI minimum of 25 percent is set by many organizations. In North America, Western Europe, and the Asia Pacific regions, this target value is usually greater than the percentage required for other types of investments. The rationale? The ROI process for consulting is still relatively new and sometimes involves subjective input, including estimations. Because of this, a higher standard is required or suggested, with 25 percent being the desired figure for most organizations.

BCR/ROI Case Application

Global Computer Company (GCC), a large national software chain located in most major U.S. markets, attempted to boost revenues by changing the point-of-sale automation system used by its sales associates. The system, developed and implemented by a consulting firm, was a response to a clearly defined need to increase the quality of information obtained from customers and to reduce customer response time by speeding up transactions. With a successful system, sales per associate would increase because each associate would have more time to take care of more customers. Also, the customer marketing information would provide data to drive a new telemarketing program. The system was designed during the first 4 weeks of the consulting intervention; 3 weeks of implementation at each of 10 pilot stores followed. The third part of the project addressed operations and maintenance issues.

The management team was willing to experiment with the application to see if it added enough value to overcome the investment costs. If not, the system could be modified to add value. Realistically, this was a good bet, because there was a definite need and the system showed great promise.

ROI Analysis

Postprogram data collection was accomplished using four methods. First, the average number of weekly sales per associate for each store was monitored (business performance monitoring of output data). Second, a follow-up questionnaire was distributed to all sales associates three months after the implementation was completed to determine the success of the implementation. Third, routine customer survey data were examined to spot changes in customer satisfaction. Finally, telemarketing records were analyzed to track the success of the telemarketing program. Techniques for overcoming the barriers to program implementation were also discussed.

The method used to isolate the effects of the consulting intervention was a control group arrangement. Ten store locations were identified for the control group and compared with 10 stores in the pilot group. The variables of store size, store location, customer traffic levels, previous store performance, and experience levels were used to match the two groups so that they could be as identical as possible.

The method used to convert data to monetary values was a direct profit contribution of the increased output (sales). The profit obtained from each additional $1 of sales was readily available and was used in the calculation. Sales increases in the stores were converted, as well as the sales generated by the telemarketing program.

BCR and ROI Calculations

Although the consulting intervention was evaluated at all five levels, the emphasis of this study was on the Level 5 calculation. Level 1, 2, and 3 data either met or exceeded expectations. Table 8.1 shows the Level 4 data, which is the average weekly sales of both store groups after the consulting intervention. For convenience and at the request of management, a three-month follow-up period was used. A longer period of review was recommended, but management wanted to make the decision to implement the project at other locations quickly if it appeared to be successful in the first three months of operation. Three months may be premature to determine the total impact of the new system, but it often becomes a mandated time period for evaluation based on a constraint dictated by management. Data for the first three weeks after implementation are shown in Table 8.1 along with data for the last three weeks of the evaluation period (weeks 13, 14, and 15). The data show what appears to be a significant difference in the values for the pilot groups and the control group.

Two steps are required to move from Level 4 to Level 5 data. In the first step, Level 4 data must be converted to monetary values. In the second step, the cost of the program must be tabulated. Table 8.2 shows the annualized benefits from the consulting assignment. The total benefit was $2,000,960. The profit contribution at the store level, obtained directly from the accounting department, was 8 percent. For every dol-

Table 8.1 Level 4 Data: Average Weekly Sales

	Post–Consulting Intervention Data	
Weeks After Implementation	**Ten Stores with New System (Thousands)**	**Ten Stores Without New System (Thousands)**
1	$2241	$2203
2	2549	2305
3	2694	2412
13	3143	2711
14	3210	2690
15	3295	2805
Average for weeks 13, 14, 15	$3216	$2735

lar of additional sales attributed to the new system, only 8 cents would be considered to be the added value. At the corporate level, the number was even smaller—about 5 percent. First-year values were used to reflect the total impact of the consulting. Ideally, if the new system was effective, as indicated in the Level 3 evaluation, there should have been some value for its use in year two or three, or perhaps even year five. However, for short-term consulting interventions, only first-year values are used, requiring the investment to have an acceptable return in a one-year time period. The total benefit was rounded off to $2 million.

Table 8.3 shows the cost summary for this program. Costs are fully loaded, including data for all 10 stores. Since the system is installed by the consulting firm, there are no direct costs. With another contractor, the costs included prorated development costs as well as equipment and software costs. Client time included estimated salaries plus a 35 percent factor for employee benefits. Meeting facility costs were included in client expenses, although the company does not normally capture the costs when internal facilities are used, as was the case with this project. The estimated costs for maintenance and monitoring, overhead, and evaluation were also included. The total cost was rounded off to $977,000. Thus, the benefit-cost ratio becomes:

$$BCR = \frac{\$2,000,000}{\$977,000} = 2.05:1$$

and the return on investment becomes:

$$ROI\ (\%) = \frac{\$2,000,000 - \$977,000}{\$977,000} \times 100 = 105\%$$

Thus, the consulting project had an excellent return on investment in its initial trial run after three months of on-the-job application of the new system.

Table 8.2 Annualized Implementation Benefits

Average weekly sales (last 3 weeks), 10 stores with system	$3,216,000
Average weekly sales (last 3 weeks), 10 stores without system	2,735,300
Increase	481,000
Profit contribution (8% of stores' sales)	38,480
Total annual benefits ($38,480 × 52 weeks)	$2,000,960

Table 8.3 Cost Summary

New System in Ten Stores

Initial analysis	$ 45,000
Development costs (prorated)	52,000
Equipment costs (prorated)	88,000
Consulting fees	370,000
Expenses for consultants	49,000
Software	17,000
Client time (training/meetings)	112,000
Client expenses (1 year)	29,000
Maintenance and monitoring (client and consultants; 1 year)	120,000
Overhead/support (1 year)	25,000
Evaluation and reporting	70,000
Total costs	$977,000

Other ROI Measures

In addition to the traditional ROI formula previously described, several other measures are occasionally used under the general heading of return on investment. These measures are designed primarily for evaluating other types of financial measures but sometimes work their way into consulting intervention evaluations.

Payback Period

The payback period is another common method for evaluating capital expenditures. With this approach, the annual cash proceeds (savings) produced by an investment are equated to the original cash outlay required by the investment to arrive at some multiple of cash proceeds equal to the original investment. Measurement is usually in terms of years and months. For example, if the cost savings generated from a consulting intervention are constant each year, the payback period is determined by dividing the total original cash investment (development costs, expenses, etc.) by the amount of the expected annual or actual savings. The savings represent the net savings after the program expenses are subtracted.

To illustrate this calculation, assume that an initial program cost is $100,000 with a three-year useful life. The annual net savings from the program is expected to be $40,000. Thus, the payback period becomes:

$$\text{Payback period} = \frac{\text{Total Investment}}{\text{Annual Savings}} = \frac{\$100,000}{\$40,000} = 2.5 \text{ years}$$

The program will pay back the original investment in 2.5 years.

The payback period is simple to use but has the limitation of ignoring the time value of money. It has not enjoyed widespread use in evaluating consulting intervention investments.

Discounted Cash Flow

Discounted cash flow is a method of evaluating investment opportunities in which certain values are assigned to the timing of the proceeds from the investment. The assumption, based on interest rates, is that a dollar earned today is more valuable than a dollar earned a year from now.

There are several ways of using the discounted cash flow concept to evaluate a consulting investment. The most common approach is the net present value of an investment. This approach compares the savings year by year with the outflow of cash required by the investment. The expected savings received each year is discounted by selected interest rates. The outflow of cash is also discounted by the same interest rate. If the present value of the savings should exceed the present value of the outlays after discounting at a common interest rate, the investment is usually considered acceptable by management. The discounted cash flow method has the advantage of ranking investments, but it becomes difficult to calculate.

Internal Rate of Return

The internal rate of return (IRR) method determines the interest rate required to make the present value of the cash flow equal to zero. It represents the maximum rate of interest that could be paid if all project funds were borrowed and the organization had to break even on the projects. The IRR considers the time value of money and is unaffected by the scale of the project. It can be used to rank alternatives and can be used to determine whether to accept or reject decisions when a minimum rate of return is specified. A major weakness of the IRR method is that it assumes all returns are reinvested at the same internal rate of return. This can make an investment alternative with a high rate of return look even better than it really is and a project with a low rate of return look even worse. In practice, IRR is rarely used to evaluate consulting intervention investments.

Consequences of Not Engaging in an Intervention

For some organizations, the consequences of not engaging in an intervention can be very serious. A company's inability to perform adequately in a particular area might mean that it is unable to take on additional business or that it may lose existing business because of a persistent problem or missed opportunity. Also, a consulting intervention can help prevent serious operational problems (such as production efficiencies) or noncompliance issues (such as EEOC violations). This method of calculating the return on consulting interventions has received recent attention and involves the following steps:

- Establish that there is a potential problem, loss, or opportunity.
- Isolate the problems created by this situation, such as noncompliance issues, loss of business, or inability to take on additional business.
- Develop an estimate of the potential value of the problem, loss, or opportunity.
- If other factors are involved, determine the impact of each factor on the loss of income or costs.
- Estimate the total cost of the consulting intervention using the techniques outlined in Chapter 12.
- Compare benefits with costs.

This approach has some disadvantages. Because estimates are used, the potential loss of income can be highly subjective and difficult to measure. Also, it may be difficult to isolate the factors involved and to determine their weight relative to lost income. Because of these concerns, this approach to evaluating the return on consulting intervention investments is limited to certain types of programs and situations.

ROI Issues

The ROI process can become quite complex, raising several issues that will need additional coverage. The most important issues are covered next.

Benefits of the ROI Process

Although the benefits of adopting the ROI evaluation may appear to be obvious, the following distinct and important benefits can be derived from the implementation of ROI for consulting interventions. They represent a brief summary of the advantages of the ROI process.

Measures the Contribution
The consulting staff will know the contribution of a specific consulting intervention. The ROI will show how the benefits, expressed in monetary values, overshadow the costs. It will determine if the program made a contribution to the organization and if it was indeed a good investment.

Develops Priorities for Consulting Projects
Calculating the ROI for different types of consulting interventions will determine which projects contribute the most to the organization, allowing priorities to be established for high-impact projects.

Improves the Consulting Process
As with any evaluation technique, an ROI impact study provides a variety of data that can be used to make adjustments and changes to the consulting process. Because different data are collected at different levels, from different sources, the opportunity for improvement is significant. This allows for a complete analysis.

Focuses on Results
The ROI process is a results-based process that focuses on the results of all consulting interventions, even for those not targeted for ROI calculation. The process requires consultants and support groups to concentrate on measurable objectives (i.e., what the consulting intervention is attempting to accomplish). Thus, this process has the added benefit of improving the effectiveness of all consulting interventions.

Builds Management Support for the Consulting Process

The ROI process, when applied consistently and comprehensively, can convince the management group that consulting is an investment and not an expense. Managers will see consulting as making a viable contribution to their objectives, and thus their respect and support for the process will increase. ROI development is an important step in building a partnership with management and increasing the commitment to consulting.

Alters Perceptions of Consulting

Routine ROI impact data, when communicated to a variety of target audiences, will alter perceptions of consulting. Consulting participants, their leaders, and other client staff will view consulting as a legitimate function in the organization that adds value to work units, departments, and divisions. They will have a better understanding of the connection between consulting and results.

These key benefits, inherent in almost any type of impact evaluation process, make the ROI process an attractive challenge for the consulting field.

Simplifies a Complex Issue

As discussed in Chapter 2, developing the return on investment for a consulting intervention is a complex issue. The approach presented in this book is to take a complex process and simplify it by breaking it into small steps so it is understandable and acceptable to a variety of audiences. Figure 8.1 illustrates the complexity of this process.

This book presents the 10 most common ways to collect postimplementation data, 10 ways to isolate the effects of a consulting intervention on business performance measures, and 10 ways to convert business impact data into monetary values. In essence, therefore, there are 1000 possible ways to evaluate a consulting intervention. This situation alone is enough to cause even some of the most eager individuals to avoid the ROI process. However, when each step is taken separately and issues are addressed for a particular topic, the decisions are made incrementally all the way through the process. This helps reduce a complex process to a more simplified and manageable effort. Figure 8.1 underscores an important advantage of this process. With so many dif-

The Number of Possibilities Makes the Process Complex

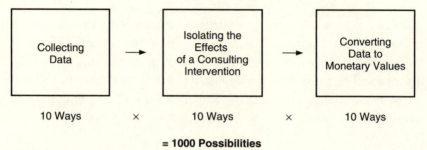

Collecting
Data

Isolating the
Effects
of a Consulting
Intervention

Converting
Data to
Monetary Values

| 10 Ways | × | 10 Ways | × | 10 Ways |

= 1000 Possibilities

Figure 8.1   ROI complexity.

ferent ways to manage these three issues, the ROI process can be applied to almost any type of consulting intervention.

Cautions When Using ROI: Potential Shortcuts

Because of the complexity and sensitivity of the ROI process, caution is needed when developing, calculating, and communicating the return on investment. The ROI process is a very important issue, and achieving a positive ROI is the goal of many consulting interventions. A few issues, described next, should be addressed to keep the process from going astray.

> *The ROI process should be developed for projects where needs assessments have been conducted.* Because of the evaluation problems that can develop when there is not a clear needs assessment, it is recommended that the ROI be conducted only for interventions in which comprehensive needs assessments, preferably with Level 3 and 4 data, have been performed. However, practical considerations and management requests may prohibit this.
>
> *The ROI analysis should always include one or more strategies for isolating the effects of the consulting intervention.* Because of the importance of accounting for the influence of other factors, this step in the process must not be ignored. Too often, an excellent study derived from what appears to be a very successful consulting intervention is considered worthless because there was no attempt to account for other factors. Omission of this step seriously diminishes the credibility of the study.

When making estimates, use the most reliable and credible sources. Because estimates are critical to any type of analysis, they will usually be an important part of the ROI process. When estimates are used, they should be developed properly and obtained from the most reliable and credible sources, the individuals who best understand the overall situation and can provide the most accurate estimation.

Take a conservative approach when developing both benefits and costs. Conservatism in ROI analysis builds accuracy and credibility. What matters most is how the target audience perceives the value of the data. A conservative approach is always recommended for both the numerator of the ROI formula (benefits) and the denominator (program costs).

Use caution when comparing the ROI for consulting interventions with other financial returns. There are many ways to calculate the return on funds invested or assets employed; ROI is just one of them. Although the calculation of ROI for a consulting intervention uses the same basic formula as in other investment evaluations, it may not be fully understood by the target group. Therefore, the calculation method and its meaning should be clearly communicated. More importantly, it should be an item accepted by management as an appropriate measure for a consulting intervention evaluation.

Involve management in developing the return. Management ultimately decides whether an ROI value is acceptable. To the extent possible, management should be involved in setting the parameters for calculations and establishing targets by which programs are considered acceptable within the organization.

Approach sensitive and controversial issues with caution. Occasionally, sensitive and controversial issues will be generated when discussing an ROI value. It is best to avoid debates over what is measurable and what is not unless there is clear evidence for the issue in question. Also, some consulting projects are so fundamental to the survival of the organization that any attempt to measure them is unnecessary. For example, a project designed to improve customer service in a customer-focused company may escape the scrutiny of an ROI evaluation on the assumption that if the program is well designed, it will improve customer service.

Teach others the methods for calculating the return. Each time an ROI is calculated, the appropriate executive should use the opportunity to educate other managers and colleagues in the organization. Even if this is not in their area of responsibility, they will be able to see the value of this approach to the consulting intervention and evaluation. Also, when possible, each project should serve as a case study to educate the consulting staff on specific techniques and methods.

Do not boast about a high return. It is not unusual to generate what appears to be a very high return on investment for a consulting intervention. Several examples in this book have illustrated the possibilities. A consultant who boasts about a high rate of return will be open to potential criticism from others unless the calculation is based on indisputable facts.

Do not try to use ROI on every consulting assignment. Some programs are difficult to quantify, and an ROI calculation may not be feasible. Other methods of presenting the benefits may be more appropriate. As discussed in Chapter 2, consulting executives are encouraged to set targets for the percent of programs in which the ROI is developed. Also, specific criteria should be established that select programs for ROI analysis.

Final Thoughts

After the benefits are collected and converted to monetary values and the consulting costs are tabulated, the ROI calculation becomes a very easy step. It is just a matter of plugging the values into the appropriate formula. This chapter has presented the two basic approaches for calculating the return: the ROI formula and the benefit-cost ratio. Each has its own advantages and disadvantages. Alternatives to ROI development have also been briefly discussed. Several examples have been presented along with key issues that must be addressed in ROI calculations.

Further Reading

Dauphinais, G. William, and Colin Price (eds.). *Straight from the CEO: The World's Top Business Leaders Reveal Ideas that Every Manager Can Use.* London: Brealey, 1998.

Epstein, Marc J., and Bill Birchard. *Counting What Counts: Turning Corporate Accountability to Competitive Advantage*. Reading, MA: Perseus, 1999.

Friedlob, George T., and Franklin J. Plewa Jr. *Understanding Return on Investment*. New York: Wiley, 1991.

Gates, Bill, with Collins Hemingway. *Business @ the Speed of Thought: Using a Digital Nervous System*. New York: Warner, 1999.

Hiebeler, Robert, Thomas B. Kelly, and Charles Ketteman. *Best Practices: Building Your Business with Customer-Focused Solutions*. New York: Arthur Andersen/Simon & Schuster, 1998.

Mitchell, Donald, Carol Coles, and Robert Metz. *The 2,000 Percent Solution: Free Your Organization From "Stalled" Thinking to Achieve Exponential Success*. New York: AMACOM/American Management Association, 1999.

Phillips, Jack J. *Return on Investment in Training and Performance Improvement Programs*. Houston, TX: Gulf, 1997.

Price Waterhouse Financial & Cost Management Team. *CFO: Architect of the Corporation's Future*. New York: Wiley, 1997.

Weddle, Peter D. *ROI: A Tale of American Business*. McLean, VA: ProAction, 1989.

How to Capture and Report the Nonfinancial Benefits of a Consulting Intervention

Identifying Intangible Measures

CONSULTING PROJECT RESULTS include both tangible and intangible measures. Intangible measures are the benefits or detriments directly linked to a consulting project that cannot or should not be converted to monetary values. These measures are often monitored after the consulting project has been completed. Although they are not converted to monetary values, they are still an important part of the evaluation process. The range of intangible measures is almost limitless; however, this chapter describes some common variables linked with consulting. Table 9.1 lists common examples of these measures.

This listing is not meant to imply that these measures cannot be converted to monetary values. In one study or another, each item has been monetarily quantified. However, in typical impact studies, these variables are considered intangible benefits.

Table 9.1 Common Intangible Variables Linked with Consulting
Interventions

• Knowledge base	• Request for transfers
• Job satisfaction	• Customer satisfaction/dissatisfaction
• Organizational commitment	• Community image
• Work climate	• Investor image
• Employee complaints	• Customer complaints
• Employee grievances	• Customer response time
• Employee stress reduction	• Customer loyalty
• Employee tenure	• Teamwork
• Employee absenteeism	• Cooperation
• Employee turnover	• Conflict
• Employee lateness	• Decisiveness
• Innovation	• Communication

Why Identify Intangibles?

Not all measures can or should be converted to monetary values. By
design, some are captured and reported as intangibles. Although they
may not be perceived as being as valuable as the quantifiable measures,
intangibles are critical to the overall evaluation process. In some consulting interventions, team development, job satisfaction, communications, and customer satisfaction are more important than monetary
measures. Consequently, these measures should be monitored and
reported as part of the overall evaluation. In practice, every intervention, regardless of its nature, scope, or content, will produce intangible
measures. The challenge is to identify these measures effectively and
report them appropriately.

Where Do They Come From?

Intangible measures can be taken from different sources and at different
times in the process, as depicted in Figure 9.1. They can be uncovered
early in the process during the needs assessment and planned for collection as part of the overall data collection strategy. For example, one
consulting project has several hard data measures linked to it. An intangible measure, employee satisfaction, is identified and monitored with

no plans to convert it to a monetary value. Thus, this measure is destined from the beginning to be a nonmonetary benefit reported along with the ROI results.

A second opportunity to identify intangible benefits comes through discussion with clients or sponsors of the consulting intervention. Clients can usually identify the intangible measures they expect to be influenced by the intervention. For example, a consulting project in a large multinational company was conducted, and an ROI analysis was planned. Consultants, participants, participants' managers, and senior executives identified potential intangible measures that were perceived to be influenced by the intervention.

The third opportunity to identify intangible measures presents itself during data collection. Although a measure may not be anticipated in the initial project design, it may surface on a questionnaire, in an interview, or during a focus group. Questions are often asked about other improvements linked to a consulting project, and participants usually provide several intangible measures for which there are no plans to assign a value. For example, in the evaluation of a customer service consulting project, participants were asked what specifically had improved about their work area and relationships with customers as a result of the project. Participants provided more than a dozen intangible measures that managers attributed to the intervention.

The fourth opportunity to identify intangible measures is during data analysis and reporting, while attempting to convert data to monetary values. If the conversion loses credibility, the measure should be reported as an intangible benefit. For example, in a sales improvement consulting project, customer satisfaction was identified early in the

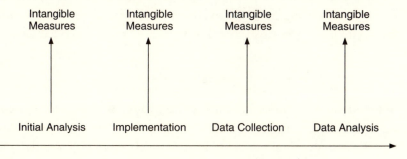

Figure 9.1   Identifying intangible measures: timing and score.

process as a measure of the consulting success. A conversion to monetary values was attempted, but it lacked accuracy and credibility. Consequently, customer satisfaction was reported as an intangible benefit.

How Are Intangibles Analyzed?

For each intangible measure identified, there must be some evidence of its connection to the consulting project. However, in many cases no specific analysis is planned beyond tabulating responses. Early attempts to quantify intangible data sometimes result in aborting the entire process; thus, no further data analysis is conducted. In some cases, isolating the effects of the consulting project may be undertaken using one or more of the methods outlined in Chapter 10. This step is necessary when there is a need to know the specific amount of change in the intangible measure linked to the intervention. Intangible data often reflect improvement. However, neither the precise amount of improvement nor the amount of improvement directly related to consulting is usually identified. Since the value of these data is not included in the ROI calculation, intangible measures are not normally used to justify additional consulting or continuing an existing intervention. A detailed analysis is not necessary. Intangible benefits are viewed as additional evidence of the intervention's success and are presented as supportive qualitative data.

Are They Satisfied? Measuring Employee Satisfaction

Employee satisfaction is one of the most important intangible measures. Many consulting projects improve job satisfaction if they are perceived to be successful by the participants or managers. A few of the most important employee satisfaction measures are briefly described here.

Job Satisfaction

Many organizations conduct surveys that gauge how satisfied employees are with their organizations, jobs, supervisors, coworkers, and a host of other issues. Employee job satisfaction is closely correlated with absenteeism and turnover, both of which are sometimes linked with consulting interventions. Some survey items focus on issues directly related to consulting, such as satisfaction with job design changes, reengineered processes, or compensation adjustments. Attitude survey data are usually linked to consulting when specific issues in the survey address the consulting intervention. For example, in a reengineering consulting project involving all employees, the annual job satisfaction survey contained four questions regarding perceptions of the consulting project.

Because attitude surveys are usually taken annually, the results may not be in sync with the timing of the consulting intervention. When job satisfaction is one of the objectives, some organizations conduct surveys after the consulting project and design the survey instrument around consulting issues.

Organizational Commitment

Organizational commitment is perhaps a more important measure for understanding employees' motivational state. Similar to attitude surveys, organizational commitment instruments gauge to what degree employees are aligned with company goals, values, philosophies, and practices. Organizational commitment measures often correlate with productivity and performance; therefore, organizational commitment is an important intangible measure. Changes in organizational commitment in survey data may indicate the success of a consulting project if the project is designed to change employee motivation. The difficulty with this intangible measure is that it is not routinely tracked in organizations.

Work Climate

Some organizations conduct climate surveys, which reflect work climate changes in communication, openness, trust, feedback, and other areas. Climate surveys are similar to attitude surveys but are more general and often focus on a range of workplace issues and environmental enablers and inhibitors. Conducting climate surveys before and after a consulting project aids in determining how much the intervention changed these intangible measures.

Employee Complaints

Some organizations record and report specific employee complaints. Because a reduction in employee complaints is sometimes directly related to consulting projects, such as team-building interventions, the level of complaints is reported as an intangible and is used to measure the success of the intervention.

Grievances

In both union and nonunion organizations, grievances often reflect levels of dissatisfaction or disenchantment in a variety of areas. Certain consulting projects, such as those focusing on labor-management cooperation, are designed to reduce excessive numbers of grievances. An improvement in the grievance level reflects the success of the intervention. This measure can be converted to a monetary value or reported as an intangible.

Discrimination Complaints

Employee dissatisfaction can appear in different types of discrimination complaints, ranging from informal complaints to external charges—even litigation. Consulting interventions such as sexual harassment prevention projects may be designed to prevent complaints or reduce current levels of complaints. The measured success of a project may not be converted to a monetary value because of the various assumptions and estimations involved in the process. In such cases, these measures are reported as intangible benefits.

Employee Stress Reduction

Occasionally, consulting interventions reduce work-related stress by focusing on job and technology improvements that allow employees to be more efficient. The reduction in tension and anxiety, and the subsequent reduction in stress, may be directly linked to the intervention.

Will They Leave? Measuring Employee Withdrawal

When employee satisfaction deteriorates to the point that employees withdraw from work or the organization, either permanently or temporarily, the results can be disastrous. Several employee withdrawal measures are often linked to consulting projects.

Employee Turnover

Perhaps the most serious employee withdrawal measure is employee turnover. Turnover is an extremely costly variable and, when excessive, can have devastating consequences on organizations. Many consulting projects are designed to reduce employee turnover in specific work units, and turnover is often converted to a monetary value using one of the methods described in Chapter 10. However, because of the multitude of costs and assumptions involved in calculating the value, some organizations prefer not to do so. In these cases, a reduction in turnover is reported as an intangible benefit, reflecting the success of the intervention.

Employee Tenure

The opposite of employee turnover is tenure. This represents an important objective for many organizations. Knowledge-based industries are especially interested in maintaining long-tenured employees who are often exposed to a variety of job situations. Tenure is usually tracked as a human capital measure and is sometimes a by-product of consulting projects. The average tenure can be converted to a monetary value but is frequently reported as an important intangible benefit.

Employee Absenteeism

Unplanned or unscheduled absenteeism is another costly variable. Excessive absenteeism disrupts customer service and customer contact functions and jeopardizes customer loyalty. Some consulting projects are aimed at reducing absenteeism, and the impact of an intervention on absenteeism can usually be pinpointed. Although the cost of absenteeism can be calculated, the conversion process is not credible enough for some audiences. In those situations, absenteeism changes are reported as intangible effects.

Employee Lateness

Many organizations, particularly those that use electronic and computerized time reporting, monitor employee lateness (tardiness). Lateness is an irritating and problematic work habit that can cause inefficiencies and delays. Some consulting interventions are designed to reduce this phenomenon, but it is difficult to quantify lateness. Consequently, when a consulting project demonstrates success in reducing employee lateness, it is usually presented as an intangible benefit.

Requests for Employee Transfers

Another way employees withdraw is by requesting a transfer to another section, department, or division within the organization. Requests for transfers often reflect dissatisfaction with a variety of issues, including management, policies, and workplace practices. Consulting projects are sometimes designed to reduce or remove these unpleasant environmental influences. In these situations, requests for transfers are monitored and reported as an intangible consulting measurement, and there is no attempt to assign a monetary value.

How About the Customers? Measuring Customer Service

Because of the importance of building and improving customer service, a number of related measures are typically monitored and reported to track the payoff of consulting. Several types of customer service consulting projects have a direct influence on these measures, but since it is so difficult to place values on the changes, the outcomes are sometimes reported as intangible benefits. Some of these customer measures are described in the following text.

Customer Satisfaction/Dissatisfaction/Impression

One of the most important measures is surveys of satisfied or dissatisfied customers. These survey values, reported as absolute data or as an index, represent important data that can be used to determine the success of a customer service consulting intervention. Techniques to convert survey data to monetary values are available, but in most cases a conversion is not attempted, and improvements are reported as intangible benefits.

Customer Complaints

Most organizations monitor customer complaints. Each complaint is recorded, along with the disposition, the time required to resolve the complaint, and specific costs associated with complaint resolution. Consulting projects are often designed to reduce or prevent an increase in the number of customer complaints. Because it is difficult to assign accurate monetary values to complaints, the measure is usually reported as an important intangible.

Customer Response Time

Providing prompt customer service is a critical issue for most organizations. Therefore, organizations monitor the time it takes to respond to specific customer service requests or problems. Although reducing response time is often an objective of a consulting intervention, the measure is not usually converted to a monetary value. Thus, customer response time is reported as an important intangible measure.

Other Customer Responses

Many other types of customer responses can be tracked, such as creativity with customer responses, sensitivity to cost and pricing issues, and customer loyalty. Monitoring these variables can provide more evidence of consulting results when the intervention influences specific variables. Because of the difficulty in assigning values to these items, they are usually reported as intangible measures.

How About Teams? Measuring Team Effectiveness

To evaluate the success of teams within an organization, several key measures are monitored. Although the output and quality of the teams' work are often measured as hard data and converted to monetary values, other interpersonal measures may be tracked and reported separately. A few of these measures are represented here.

Teamwork

Cross-functional, high-performance, and virtual teams are important assets for organizations striving to improve performance. Sometimes team members are surveyed before and after a consulting project to see if the level of teamwork has increased. The monetary value of increased teamwork is rarely developed as a measure; rather, it is usually reported as an intangible benefit.

Cooperation/Conflict

The success of a team often depends on the cooperative spirit of team members. Some instruments measure the level of cooperation before and after a consulting project, but since it is so difficult to convert the findings to a monetary value, this measure is always reported as an intangible.

In some team environments, the level of conflict is measured. A decrease in conflict may reflect the success of the consulting intervention. In most situations, a monetary value is not placed on such a reduction, and it is reported as an intangible benefit.

Decisiveness/Decision Making

Teams make decisions, and the expedience and quality of the decision-making process often become important issues. Decisiveness is usually measured by how quickly decisions are made. Survey measures may reflect the perception of the team or, in some cases, monitor precisely how quickly decisions are made. The quality of the decisions reflects value as well. Some consulting projects are expected to influence this process, with improvements usually reported as intangible benefits.

Team Communication

Communication is critical in every team. Several instruments are available for qualifying and quantifying communication within a team. Positive changes in communication skills or perceptions of skills driven by a consulting project are not usually converted to monetary values but rather are reported as intangible benefits.

Final Thoughts

Get the picture? Intangible measures are crucial to reflecting the success of a consulting project. While they may not carry the weight of measures expressed in dollars and cents, they are nevertheless an important part of the overall evaluation. Intangible measures should be identified, explored, examined, and monitored for changes linked to the consulting intervention. Collectively, they add a unique dimension to the consulting report since most, if not all, interventions involve intangible variables. Although some of the most common intangible measures have been explored in this chapter, the coverage is not meant to be complete. The range of intangible measures is practically limitless.

Further Reading

Bacon, Frank R. Jr., and Thomas W. Butler Jr. *Achieving Planned Innovation: A Proven System for Creating Successful New Products and Services.* New York: The Free Press, 1998.

Campanella, Jack (ed.). *Principles of Quality Costs: Principles, Implementation and Use.* Milwaukee: ASQ Quality, 1999.

Denton, Keith D. *Quality Service: How America's Top Companies Are Competing in the Customer-Service Revolution . . . and How You Can Too.* Houston, TX: Gulf, 1989.

Heskett, James L., W. Earl Sasser Jr., and Leonard A. Schlesinger. *The Service Profit Chain: How Leading Companies Link Profit and Growth to Loyalty, Satisfaction, and Value.* New York: The Free Press, 1997.

Howe, Roger J., Dee Gaeddert, and Maynard A. Howe. *Quality on Trial: Bringing Bottom-Line Accountability to the Quality Effort* (2d ed.). New York: McGraw-Hill, 1995.

Keen, Peter G. W. *The Process Edge: Creating Value Where It Counts.* Boston: Harvard Business School, 1997.

Naumann, Earl, and Kathleen Giel. *Customer Satisfaction Measurement and Management: Using the Voice of the Customer.* Cincinnati: Thomson, 1995.

Silverman, Lori L., and Annabeth L. Propst. *Critical Shift: The Future of Quality in Organizational Performance.* Milwaukee: ASQ Quality, 1999.

Slaikeu, Karl A., and Ralph H. Hasson. *Controlling the Costs of Conflict: How to Design a System for Your Organization.* San Francisco: Jossey-Bass, 1998.

PART
III

Key Issues with the Measures

Separating the Consulting Impact from Other Factors

How to Isolate the Effects of the Consulting Intervention

WHEN A SIGNIFICANT increase in performance is noted after a consulting project has been conducted, the two events appear to be linked. A key manager may ask, "How much of this improvement was caused by the consulting project?" When this potentially embarrassing question is posed, it is rarely answered with any degree of accuracy and credibility. While the change in performance may be linked to the consulting project, other nonconsulting factors usually contribute to the improvement as well. This chapter explores useful techniques for isolating the effects of consulting. These techniques are utilized in some of the most successful organizations as they attempt to measure the return on investment in consulting.

Why the Concern over This Issue?

In almost every consulting intervention there are multiple influences that drive the success of the business measures targeted for the intervention. With multiple influences it is imperative to measure the actual effect of each of the different factors, or at least the extent to which the effect can be attributed to the consulting intervention. Without this isolation of factors, the success of the intervention will be in question. The results will be inappropriate and overstated if it is suggested that all of the change in the business impact measure is attributed to the consulting project. When this issue is ignored, the impact study is considered to be invalid and inconclusive, which places tremendous pressure on consultants to show the actual value of their interventions when compared to other factors.

Preliminary Issues

The cause-and-effect relationship between consulting and performance can be very confusing and difficult to prove, but can be shown with an acceptable degree of accuracy. The challenge is to develop one or more specific techniques to isolate the effects of consulting early in the process, usually as part of an evaluation plan. Up-front attention ensures that appropriate techniques will be used with minimum costs and time commitments. The most important issues in isolating the effects of a consulting intervention are covered in the following text.

Chain of Impact

Before presenting the techniques, it is helpful to examine the chain of impact implied in the different levels of evaluation. Measurable results achieved via a consulting project should be derived from the application of recommendations in a business over a specified period of time after the intervention has been completed. This application of a consulting intervention is referred to as Level 3 in the five evaluation levels described in Chapter 4. Continuing with this logic, successful application of the intervention on the job should stem from participants learning new skills or acquiring new knowledge from the consulting project, which is measured as a Level 2 evaluation. Therefore, for a business impact improvement (Level 4 evaluation), this chain of impact implies that measurable, on-the-job application and implementation are realized (Level 3 evaluation) and new knowledge and skills are learned (Level 2 evaluation). Without this preliminary evidence, it is difficult to isolate the effects of a consulting intervention. In other words, if there is no learning or application on the job, it is virtually impossible to conclude that any performance improvements were caused by the consulting intervention. From a practical standpoint, this issue requires data collection at four levels for an ROI calculation. If data are collected on business impact, they should also be collected for other levels of evaluation to ensure that the consulting project helped produce the business results. While this requirement is a prerequisite for isolating the effects of a consulting intervention, it does not prove that there was a direct connection between intervention and effects, nor does it pinpoint how much of the improvement was caused by the intervention. It merely shows that without improvements at previous levels, it is difficult to make a connection between the ultimate outcome and the consulting project.

Identifying Other Factors: A First Step

As a first step in isolating the impact of a consulting project on performance, all key factors that may have contributed to the performance improvement should be identified. This step communicates to interested parties that other factors may have influenced the results, underscoring that the consulting project is not the sole source of improvement. Consequently, the credit for improvement is shared with several possible variables and sources—an approach that is likely to gain the respect of the client.

There are several potential sources of information available to assist in identification of major influencing variables. If the intervention is implemented on request, the client may be able to identify factors that will influence the output variable. The client will usually be aware of other initiatives or factors that may influence the output.

Participants in the consulting process are usually aware of other influences that may have caused performance improvement. After all, it is the impact of their collective efforts that is being monitored and measured. In many situations, they have witnessed previous movements in the performance measures and can pinpoint reasons for changes.

The consultants involved in the process are another source of information for identifying variables that impact results. Although the needs analysis will usually uncover these influencing variables, consultants usually analyze these variables while addressing the issues in the consulting intervention.

In some situations, immediate managers of participants (work unit managers) may be able to identify variables that influence the performance improvement. This is particularly useful when participants are nonexempt employees (operatives) who may not be fully aware of the variables that can influence performance.

Finally, members of middle and top management may be able to identify other influences based on their experience and knowledge of the situation. Perhaps they have monitored, examined, and analyzed the variables previously. The authority of these individuals often increases the data's credibility.

Taking time to focus attention on variables that may influence performance brings additional accuracy and credibility to the process. It moves beyond presenting results with no mention of other influences— a situation that often destroys the credibility of a consulting impact study. It also provides a foundation for some of the techniques described in this book by identifying the variables that must be isolated to show the effects of a consulting project. A word of caution is appropriate here. Halting the process after this step would leave many unknowns about the consulting impact and might create a negative impression with management, since the process may have identified variables not previously considered. Therefore, it is recommended that consultants go beyond this initial step and utilize one or more of the available techniques to isolate the impact of a consulting intervention.

Use of Control Groups

The most accurate approach for isolating the impact of a consulting intervention is the use of control groups in an experimental design process. This approach involves the use of an experimental group that experiences the consulting intervention and a control group that does not. The composition of both groups should be as identical as possible, and if feasible, participants for each group should be selected randomly. When this is achieved, and both groups are subjected to the same environmental influences, the difference in the performance of the two groups can be attributed to the consulting project.

As illustrated in Figure 10.1, the control group and experimental groups do not necessarily undergo preintervention measurements. Measurements can be taken after the intervention, and the difference between the performances of the two groups shows the amount of improvement that is directly related to the consulting intervention.

One caution to keep in mind is that the use of control groups may make it appear that the consultants are producing a laboratory setting, which can cause a problem for some executives. To avoid this stigma, some organizations conduct a pilot project using participants as the experimental group. A similarly matched nonparticipating control group is selected but does not receive any communication about the project.

For example, in a consulting project for Dell Computer Corporation, a control group arrangement was used.[1] The consulting process included a variety of consulting interventions involving regional and other sales managers, account managers, account executives, account representatives, and sales representatives. The output measures involved profit quota attainment, total revenue attainment, profit margin, and various sales volumes. An experimental group was involved in the consulting intervention and was carefully matched with a control group that was not involved. The equivalent number of participants for the control group was selected at random using the company database. This effort ensured that the control group and the consulting group had equivalent job positions, job levels, and experience. This project provided evidence of the distinct difference between the two groups.

The control group approach does have some inherent problems that may make it difficult to apply in practice. The first major problem is the selection of the groups. From a theoretical perspective, it is virtually

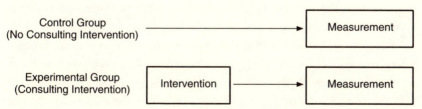

Figure 10.1 Postmeasure only, control group design.

impossible to have identical control and experimental groups. Dozens of factors—some of them individual, others contextual—can affect employee performance. To address this issue on a practical basis, it is best to select four to six variables that will have the greatest influence on performance. For example, in a consulting project designed to boost direct sales in a large retail store chain, three stores were selected and their performance was compared to that of three similar stores that constituted the control group. The selection of these particular groups of stores was based on four variables store executives thought would have the greatest influence on sales performance: market area, store size, customer traffic, and previous store performance. Although there are other factors that could have influenced performance, these four variables were used to make the selection.

Another problem is contamination, which can develop when participants in the consulting group (experimental group) communicate with others who are in the control group. Sometimes the reverse situation occurs when members of the control group model the behavior of the consulting group. In either case, the experiment becomes contaminated as the influence of the consulting intervention is passed on to the control group. This can be minimized by ensuring that control groups and consulting groups work different shifts or are located in different buildings or on different floors in the same building. When this is not possible, it may be helpful to explain to both groups that one group will be involved in the consulting intervention now, and the other will be involved at a later date. Also, it may be helpful to appeal to the sense of responsibility of those involved in the consulting project and ask them not to share information with others.

Another problem occurs when the different groups function under different environmental influences. This is usually the case when groups are at different locations. Sometimes the selection of the groups can help prevent this problem from occurring. Another tactic is to use more groups than necessary and discard those with some environmental differences.

Because the use of control groups is an effective technique for isolating the impact of consulting, it should be considered when a major ROI impact study is planned. In these situations, when it is important that the consulting impact be isolated with a high level of accuracy, the primary advantage of the control group process is accuracy.

Trend Line Analysis

Another useful technique for approximating the impact of consulting is trend line analysis. With this approach, a trend line is drawn to project the future, using previous performance as a base. When the consulting intervention is conducted, actual performance is compared to the trend line projection. Any improvement of performance over the levels predicted by the trend line can then be reasonably attributed to the consulting intervention. While this is not an exact process, it provides a reasonable estimation of the impact of the consulting intervention.

Figure 10.2 shows an example of trend line analysis taken from a shipping department of a large book distribution company. The percentage reflects the level of actual shipments compared to scheduled shipments. Data are presented before and after a consulting project was conducted in July. As shown in the figure, there was an upward trend in the data prior to the intervention. Although the intervention apparently had a dramatic effect on shipment productivity, the trend line shows that some improvement would have continued anyway, based on the trend that had previously been established. It is tempting to measure the improvement by comparing the average of the six months of shipments prior to the intervention (87.3 percent) to the average for the six months after the intervention (94.4 percent), yielding a 7.1 percent difference. However, a more accurate comparison is the average for the six months after the intervention compared to the trend line (92.3 percent). In this example, the difference is 2.1 percent. Using this more conservative measure increases the accuracy and credibility of the process of isolating the impact of the intervention.

A primary disadvantage of the trend line approach is that it is not always accurate. This approach assumes that the events that influenced the performance variable prior to the intervention are still in place after it, except for the implementation of the consulting project (i.e., the trends that were established prior to consulting will continue in the same relative direction.) Also, it assumes that no new influences entered the situation during the time consulting was conducted—which may not always be the case.

The primary advantage of this approach is that it is simple and inexpensive. If historical data are available, a trend line can quickly be drawn

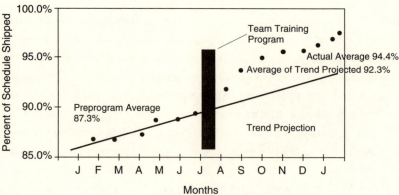

Figure 10.2 Example of trend line analysis.

and differences can be estimated. While not exact, trend line analysis does provide a quick assessment of the consulting impact.

Forecasting Methods

A more analytical approach to trend line analysis is the use of forecasting methods that predict a change in performance variables. This approach represents a mathematical interpretation of the trend line analysis when other variables enter a situation during the time of the consulting intervention. With this approach, the output measure targeted by the consulting assignment is forecasted based on the influence of other variables that have changed during the implementation or evaluation period of the consulting assignment. The actual value of the measure is compared to the forecasted value. The difference reflects the contribution of consulting.

An example will help explain the application of this process. A large retail computer store chain routinely develops a revised sales forecast. The sales forecasting model has a reputation for being accurate and is based on several inputs such as staffing levels, advertising, economic indicators, and a competition index. The model has the flexibility to add new variables or remove variables that no longer influence the output measure. The sales forecast is usually revised each month, and the previous month's result is used in the model. However, it is possible to omit the influence of the previous month.

A consulting project was initiated to improve sales. The project involved changes in order processing systems and communication training, as well as many job aids. An important measure of the success of the consulting intervention was the unit sales per sales associate. The average sales per associate prior to the consulting intervention was projected using a trend line analysis. Six months after the intervention, the average daily sales per employee was $1500. Two related questions must be answered: is the difference between these two values attributable to the intervention program? Did other factors influence the sales level?

As illustrated in Figure 10.3, the consulting project was completed and changes were implemented in January. When potential influencing factors were reviewed with several store executives, two factors—the level of advertising and competitor pricing—appeared to have changed significantly during the period of evaluation. The trend line projection using the previous sales per associate data was not appropriate since a direct relationship no longer existed. As expected, when advertising expenditures and competitor pricing increased, the sales per associate increased proportionately. The forecasting model was used to predict sales with the two changes incorporated: Figure 10.3 shows the forecasted value. The influence of the previous month was omitted to isolate the effect of the consulting project.

The values in Figure 10.3 need further explanation. In the key on the right side of this figure, A represents the preintervention value that would be achieved if sales remained flat or constant. B represents the

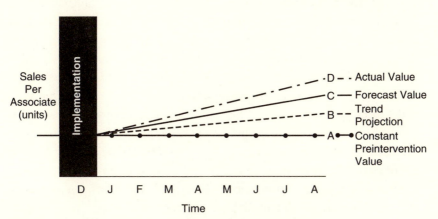

Figure 10.3   Forecasted and actual values for sales of computers.

trend value that would have been achieved if the preintervention influences had remained constant. C represents the forecasted value with the changes in the two influences (advertising and competitor pricing), and D represents the actual value. The difference between the actual value and the forecasted values (D – C) represents the monthly impact of the consulting project. This 6-month snapshot is annualized to develop the 1st-year impact (the monthly difference times 12). Assuming that the other factors possibly influencing sales were constant, this value represents the impact of the consulting intervention.

With the forecasting approach, a major disadvantage occurs when several variables enter the process. The complexity multiplies, and the use of sophisticated statistical packages for multiple-variable analysis is necessary. Even then, a good fit of the data to the model may not be possible. Unfortunately, some organizations have not developed mathematical relationships for output variables as a function of one or more inputs, and without these, the forecasting method is difficult to use.

The primary advantage of this process is that it can accurately predict business performance measures without the consulting intervention if appropriate data and models are available. The presentation of specific methods is beyond the scope of this book.[2]

Participants' Estimate of Impact

An easily implemented method for isolating the impact of consulting is obtaining information directly from participants during the process. The effectiveness of this approach rests on the assumption that participants are capable of determining or estimating what proportion of a performance improvement is related to a consulting intervention. Because their actions have produced the improvement, participants may have highly accurate input on the issue. They should know how much of the change was caused by implementing the consulting solution. Although an estimate, this value will usually have considerable credibility with management personnel because they know participants are at the center of the change or improvement. Participant estimation is obtained by asking participants the series of questions in Table 10.1 after describing the improvement. Table 10.2 illustrates this approach with an example of one participant's estimations.

Table 10.1 Questions for Participant Estimation

What percentage of this improvement can be attributed to the implementation of the consulting project?

What is the basis for this estimation?

What other factors contributed to this improvement in performance?

What confidence do you have in this estimate, expressed as a percentage? (0% = no confidence; 100% = complete confidence)

What other individuals or groups could estimate this percentage to determine the amount?

Participants who do not provide information on these questions are excluded from the analysis; as well, erroneous, incomplete, and extreme information should be discarded before analysis. To be conservative, the confidence percentage can be factored into the values. The confidence percentage is actually a reflection of the error in the estimate. Thus, an 80 percent confidence level equates to a potential error range of ±20 percent. With this approach, the level of confidence is multiplied by the estimate using the lower side of the range. In the example, the participant allocates 60 percent of the improvement to the consulting project and is 80 percent confident in the estimate. The confidence percentage is multiplied by the estimate to develop a usable consulting factor value of 48 percent. This adjusted percentage is then multiplied

Table 10.2 Example of a Participant's Estimation

Factor That Influenced Improvement	Percent of Improvement Caused By	Confidence Expressed as a Percent	Adjusted Percent of Improvement Caused By
Consulting project	60%	80%	48%
System changes	15%	70%	10.5%
Environmental changes	5%	60%	3%
Compensation changes	20%	80%	16%
Other	%	%	%
Total	100%		

by the actual amount of the improvement (postintervention minus preintervention value) to isolate the portion attributed to consulting. The adjusted improvement is now ready for conversion to monetary values and, ultimately, for use in the return on investment calculation.

Although an estimate, this method does provide considerable accuracy and credibility. Five adjustments are effectively applied to the participant estimation to reflect a conservative approach:

1. Participants who do not provide usable data are assumed to have experienced no improvements.
2. Extreme data and incomplete, unrealistic, or unsupported claims are omitted from the analysis, although they may be included in the intangible benefits.
3. For short-term consulting projects, it is assumed that no benefits are realized from the consulting intervention after the first year of implementation. For long-term projects, it may be several years after the consulting intervention before a benefit is realized.
4. The improvement level is adjusted by the amount directly related to consulting intervention, expressed as a percentage.
5. The confidence level, expressed as a percentage, is multiplied by the improvement value to reduce the amount of the improvement by the potential error.

When presented to senior management, the result of an impact study is perceived to be an understatement of an intervention's success. The data and the process are considered to be credible and accurate. As an added enhancement to this method, the next level of management above the participants may be asked to review and approve the participants' estimates.

An example will illustrate the process for participant estimates. A restaurant chain initiated a consulting project on performance improvement. The intervention was designed to improve the operating performance of the restaurants using a variety of tools to establish measurable goals for employees, provide performance feedback, measure progress toward goals, and take action to ensure that goals were met. As part of the intervention, each store manager developed an action plan for improvement. Managers also learned how to convert measurable improvements to an economic value for the restaurant. Their action plans could focus on any improvement area as long as they considered the content in the intervention and converted the improvements to either cost savings or restaurant profits. Some of the improvement areas were inventory, food spoilage, cash shortages, employee turnover, absenteeism, and productivity.

As part of the follow-up evaluation, each action plan was thoroughly documented, showing results in quantitative terms that were converted to monetary values. The annual monetary value for each improvement for each participant was calculated from action plans. Realizing that other factors could have influenced the improvement, managers were asked to estimate the percentage of the improvement that resulted directly from the consulting project (the contribution estimate). Restaurant managers are aware of factors that influence costs and profits and usually know how much of an improvement is traceable to the intervention. Each manager was asked to be conservative and to provide a confidence estimate for the contribution estimate (100 percent = certainty, 0 percent = no confidence). The results are shown in Table 10.3.

Estimation of the impact of the consulting intervention can be calculated using the conservative approach of adjusting for the contribution of the project and adjusting for the error of the contribution estimate. For example, the $5500 annual value for labor savings is adjusted to consider the consulting contribution ($5500 × 60% = $3300). Next, the resulting figure is adjusted for confidence ($3300 × 80% = $2640). The conservative approach yields an overall improvement of $68,386. Participant 5 did not submit a completed action plan and was discarded from the analysis, although the costs are still included in the ROI calculation.

Another interesting observation emerges from this type of analysis. When the average of the three largest improvements is compared with the average of the three smallest values, important information is revealed about the potential for return on investment. If all the participants in the consulting project had focused on high-impact improvements, a substantially higher ROI could have been achieved. This information can be helpful to the management group, whose support is often critical to the success of interventions. While an impressive ROI is refreshing, a potentially greater ROI is outstanding.

Table 10.3 Estimates of Consulting Intervention Impact from Participants

Participant	Total Annual Improvement (Dollar Value)	Basis	Contribution Estimate from Managers (Participants)	Confidence Estimate from Store Managers (Participants)	Conservative Value Reported
1	$ 5,500	Labor savings	60%	80%	$ 2,640
2	$ 15,000	Turnover	50%	80%	$ 6,000
3	$ 9,300	Absenteeism	65%	80%	$ 4,836
4	$ 2,100	Shortages	90%	90%	$ 1,701
5	0				
6	$ 29,000	Turnover	40%	75%	$ 8,700
7	$ 2,241	Inventory	70%	95%	$ 1,490
8	$ 3,621	Procedures	100%	80%	$ 2,897
9	$ 21,000	Turnover	75%	80%	$12,600
10	$ 1,500	Food spoilage	100%	100%	$ 1,500
11	$ 15,000	Labor savings	80%	85%	$10,200
12	$ 6,310	Accidents	70%	100%	$ 4,417
13	$ 14,500	Absenteeism	80%	70%	$ 8,120
14	$ 3,650	Productivity	100%	90%	$ 3,285
Total	$128,722				$68,386

This process has some disadvantages. It is an estimate and consequently does not have the accuracy desired by some consultants and clients. Also, the input data may be unreliable since some participants are incapable of providing these types of estimates because they may not be aware of exactly which factors contributed to the results.

Several advantages make this technique attractive. It is a simple process, easily understood by most participants and by others who review evaluation data. It is inexpensive, takes very little time and analysis, and thus results in an efficient addition to the evaluation process. Also, these estimates originate from a credible source—the consulting participants who produced the improvement.

The advantages of this approach seem to offset the disadvantages. It will never be possible to precisely isolate the effects of a consulting intervention, but this type of estimate may be accurate enough for most clients and management groups. The process is appropriate when the participants are managers, supervisors, team leaders, sales associates, engineers, and other professional or technical employees.

Managers' Estimate of Impact

In lieu of, or in addition to, participant estimates, the participants' manager may be asked to provide input as to the extent to which the consulting intervention produced improved performance. In some settings, the participants' manager may be more familiar with the other factors influencing performance. Consequently, the manager may be better equipped to provide estimates of impact. The recommended questions to ask managers, after describing the improvement caused by the participants, are provided in Table 10.4.

These questions are essentially the same ones described in the participant's questionnaire. Manager estimates should be analyzed in the same manner as participant estimates. To be more conservative, actual estimates may be adjusted by the confidence percentage. When participants' estimates have also been collected, the decision of which estimate to use becomes an issue. If there is some compelling reason to think that one estimate is more credible than the other, then the one deemed more credible should be used. The most conservative approach is to use the lowest value and include an appropriate explanation. Another potential option is to recognize that each source has its own

Table 10.4   Questions for Manager's Estimate

What percentage of the improvement in performance measures of the participant resulted from the intervention program?

What is the basis for this estimate?

What other factors could have contributed to this success?

What is your confidence in this estimate, expressed as a percentage?
(0% = no confidence; 100% = complete confidence)

What other individuals or groups would know about this improvement and could estimate this percentage?

---

unique perspective and that an average of the two is appropriate, placing an equal weight on each input. If feasible, it is recommended that input be obtained both from participants and their managers.

In some cases, upper management may estimate the percent of improvement that should be attributed to an intervention. After considering additional factors that could contribute to an improvement, such as technology, procedures, and process changes, management applies a subjective factor to represent the portion of the results that should be attributed to the consulting intervention. While this is quite subjective, the input is usually accepted by the individuals who provide or approve funding for the intervention. Sometimes the comfort level of these people with the process is the most important consideration.

This approach of using management estimates has the same disadvantages as the use of participant estimates. It is subjective, and consequently it may be viewed with skepticism by senior management. Also, managers may be reluctant to participate or may be incapable of providing accurate impact estimates. In some cases, they may not know about other factors that contributed to the improvement.

The advantages of this approach are similar to the advantages of participant estimation. It is simple and inexpensive, and it enjoys an acceptable degree of credibility because it comes directly from the managers of individuals who are involved in the consulting project. When manager estimates are combined with participant estimates, credibility is enhanced considerably. Also, when this type of estimate is factored by the level of confidence, its value increases further.

Customer Input on Consulting Impact

Another helpful approach in some narrowly focused situations is to solicit input directly from customers on the impact of consulting. In these situations, customers are asked why they chose a particular product or service or are asked to explain how their reaction to the product or service has been influenced by individuals or systems involved in the consulting project. This technique often focuses directly on what the intervention is designed to improve. For example, after a customer service consulting project involving customer response was conducted in an electric utility, market research data showed that the percentage of customers who were dissatisfied with response time was reduced by 5 percent compared to market survey data gathered before the consulting intervention. Since response time was reduced by the consulting intervention and no other factor contributed to the reduction, the 5 percent reduction in dissatisfied customers was directly attributable to the consulting intervention.

Routine customer surveys provide an excellent opportunity to collect input directly from customers concerning their reaction to an assessment of a new or improved product, service, process, or procedure. Pre- and postproject data can pinpoint the changes related to an improvement driven by a consulting intervention.

When collecting customer input, it is important to link it with the current data collection methods and avoid creating surveys or feedback mechanisms if at all possible. This measurement process should not add to the data collection systems.

Customer input could perhaps be the most powerful and convincing data if it is complete, accurate, and valid.

Expert Estimation of Consulting Impact

External or internal experts can sometimes estimate the portion of results that can be attributed to a consulting intervention. When using this technique, experts must be carefully selected based on their knowledge of the process, program, and situation. For example, an expert in quality might be able to provide estimates of how much change in a quality measure can be attributed to a consulting intervention and how much can be attributed to other factors.

An example will illustrate this process. Omega Consultants provides consulting services to the banking industry and implements sales consulting programs in a variety of settings. Utilizing control group arrangements, Omega determines that a typical intervention will generate a 30 percent increase in sales volume three months after implementation. Given this value, implementation should result in a 30 percent improvement in another financial institution with a similar target audience and a similar need. Although the situations may vary considerably, this is an approximate value that can be used in comparisons. If more than 30 percent improvement is achieved, the additional amount could be due to a factor other than the consulting intervention. Experts, consultants, or researchers are usually available for almost any field. They bring their experience with similar situations into the analysis.

This approach does have disadvantages. It can be inaccurate unless the program and setting the estimate is based on are quite similar to the situation in question. Also, this approach may lose credibility because the estimates come from external sources and may not necessarily involve those who are close to the process.

This process has an advantage in that its credibility often reflects the reputation of the expert or independent consultant. It is a quick source of input from a reputable expert or independent consultant. Sometimes top management will place more confidence in external experts than in its own internal staff.

Calculating the Impact of Other Factors

Although it is not appropriate in all cases, sometimes it is possible to calculate the impact of factors (other than consulting) that influence a portion of the improvement and to credit the consulting intervention with the remaining portion. In this approach, the consulting intervention takes credit for improvement that cannot be attributed to other factors.

An example will help explain the approach. In a consumer lending consulting project for a large bank, a significant increase in consumer loan volume was generated after the consulting intervention was completed. Part of the increase in volume was attributed to the consulting intervention, with the remainder due to the influence of other factors in place during the same time period. Two other factors were identified:

an increase in marketing and sales promotion and falling interest rates, which caused an increase in consumer volume.

With regard to the first factor, as marketing and sales promotion increased, so did consumer loan volume. The amount of this factor was estimated using input from several internal experts in the marketing department. For the second factor, industry sources were used to estimate the relationship between increased consumer loan volume and falling interest rates. These two estimates together accounted for a modest percentage of increased consumer loan volume. The remaining improvement was attributed to the consulting intervention.

This method is appropriate when the other factors are easily identified and the appropriate mechanisms are in place to calculate their impact on the improvement. In some cases it is just as difficult to estimate the impact of other factors as it is to estimate the impact of the consulting, leaving this approach less advantageous. This process can be very credible if the method used to isolate the impact of other factors is credible.

Using the Techniques

With all these techniques available to isolate the impact of consulting, selecting the one that is most appropriate for a specific project can be difficult. Some techniques are simple and inexpensive, while others are more time consuming and costly. When attempting to make the selection decision, the following factors should be considered:

- Feasibility of the technique
- Accuracy provided by the technique
- Credibility of the technique with the target audience
- Specific cost to implement the technique
- Amount of disruption in normal work activities as the technique is implemented
- Participant, staff, and management time needed for the particular technique

Multiple techniques or multiple sources for data input should be considered since two sources are usually better than one. When multiple sources are utilized, a conservative method is recommended for combining the inputs. The reason is that a conservative approach builds acceptance. The target audience should always be provided with explanations of the process and the various subjective factors involved. Multiple sources allow an organization to experiment with different strategies and build confidence with a particular technique. For example, if management is concerned about the accuracy of participants' estimates, a combination of a control group arrangement and participants' estimates could be attempted to check the accuracy of the estimation process.

It is not unusual for the ROI of a consulting project to be extremely large. Even when a portion of the improvement is allocated to other factors, the numbers are still impressive in many situations. The audience should understand that although every effort is made to isolate the impact, the figure arrived at is still not precise and may contain error. It represents the best estimate of the impact given the constraints, conditions, and resources available. Chances are it is more accurate than other types of analysis regularly used in other functions within the organization.

Shortcut Ways to Isolate the Effects of the Consulting Intervention

Because of the importance of this issue, it cannot be ignored, omitted, or disregarded in a consulting project. At least one technique must be used to isolate the effects of the consulting intervention. However, for smaller, low-cost projects, estimates will have to be used and will normally be acceptable under these circumstances. The challenge is to collect the estimates in the most credible and accurate way, using many of the techniques described in this chapter. If the client desires a more sophisticated method, then one of the other techniques may be applicable. Obviously, this would take more time and effort and perhaps cost the client additional funds.

Final Thoughts

This chapter presents a variety of techniques for isolating the effects of consulting. The techniques represent the most effective approaches to address this issue and are used by some of the most progressive organizations. Too often, results are reported and linked with the consulting intervention without any attempt to isolate the exact portion of the results that can be attributed to consulting. If professionals in the consulting field are committed to improving their image, as well as to meeting their responsibility for obtaining results, this issue must be addressed early in the process for all major projects.

References

1. Tesoro, Ferdinand. "Implementing an ROI Measurement Process," in *In Action: Implementing Evaluation Systems and Processes.* Alexandria, VA: American Society for Training and Development, 1998, pp. 179–192.
2. Makridakis, S. *Forecasting Methods for Management* (5th ed.). New York: Wiley, 1989.

Further Reading

Fetterman, David M., Shakeh J. Kaftarian, and Abraham Wandersman (eds.). *Empowerment Evaluation: Knowledge and Tools for Self-Assessment & Accountability.* Thousand Oaks, CA: Sage, 1996.

Gummesson, Evert. *Qualitative Methods in Management Research.* Newbury Park, CA: Sage, 1991.

Hronec, Steven M., and Arthur Anderson & Co. *Vital Signs: Using Quality, Time, and Cost Performance Measurements to Chart Your Company's Future.* New York: AMACOM/American Management Association, 1993.

Langdon, Danny G., Kathleen S. Whiteside, and Monica M. McKenna (eds.). *Intervention Resource Guide: 50 Performance Improvement Tools.* San Francisco: Jossey-Bass/Pfeiffer, 1999.

Phillips, Jack J. *Handbook of Training Evaluation and Measurement Methods* (3d ed.). Houston, TX: Gulf, 1997.

Rea, Louis M., and Richard A. Parker. *Designing and Conducting Survey Research: A Comprehensive Guide* (2d ed.). San Francisco: Jossey-Bass, 1997.

CHAPTER

11

How to Convert Business Measures to Monetary Values

TRANSFORMING OR CONVERTING data into monetary values is an essential step in calculating the return on investment for a consulting assignment. Many consulting reports stop with a tabulation of business results. While these results are important, it is even more valuable to convert the positive outcomes into dollar figures and weigh them against the cost of consulting. This exercise is the ultimate level in the five-level evaluation framework presented in Chapter 2. This chapter explains how leading consultants are moving beyond simply tabulating business results to developing monetary values used in calculating ROI.

Why Convert Data to Monetary Values?

The answer to this question is not always clearly understood by some consultants. A consulting intervention could be labeled a success without conversion to monetary values, just by using business impact data showing the amount of change directly attributed to the project. For example, a change in quality, cycle time, market share, or customer satisfaction could represent a significant improvement linked directly to consulting. For some projects this may be sufficient. However, if the client desires a return on investment calculation with monetary benefits compared to costs, then this extra step of converting data to monetary values will be necessary. Also, the client may need additional information about the value of the business impact data. Sometimes the monetary value has more impact on the client than just the change in the number itself. For example, consulting intervention success in terms of a reduction of 10 customer complaints per month may not seem significant. However, if the value of a customer complaint had been determined to be $3,000, this turns converts to a monthly improvement of at least $30,000, a more impressive figure.

The Five Key Steps in Converting Data to Dollars

Before describing specific techniques to convert both hard and soft data to monetary values, there are five general steps that should be completed for each data item.

1. *Focus on a unit of measure.* First, define a unit of measure. For output data, the unit of measure is the item produced, service provided, or sale consummated. Time measures might include the time to complete a project, cycle time, or customer response time, and are usually expressed in minutes, hours, or days. Quality is a common measure, with a unit being defined as one error, reject, defect, or reworked item. Soft data measures vary, with a unit of improvement representing such things as an absence, a turnover statistic, or a one-point change in the customer satisfaction index.

2. *Determine the value of each unit.* Place a value (V) on the unit identified in the first step. For measures of production, quality, cost, and time, the process is relatively easy. Most organizations maintain records or reports that can pinpoint the cost of one unit of production or one defect. Soft data are more difficult to convert to dollars. For example, the value of one customer complaint or a one-point change in an employee attitude value is often difficult to determine. The techniques described in this chapter provide an array of approaches for making this conversion. When more than one value is available, usually the most credible or the lowest is used in the calculation.

3. *Calculate the change in performance data.* Calculate the change in output data after the effects of the consulting project have been isolated from other influences. The change (Δ) is the performance improvement, measured as hard or soft data, that is directly attributed to the consulting project. The value may represent the performance improvement for an individual, a team, a group of participants, or several groups of participants.

4. *Determine an annual amount for the change.* Annualize the Δ value to develop a total change in the performance data for at least one year (ΔP). Using annual values has become a standard approach for organizations seeking to capture the benefits of a consulting project, although the benefits may not remain constant through the entire year. First-year benefits are used even when the consulting project produces benefits beyond one year. This approach is considered conservative.

5. *Calculate the annual value of the improvement.* Arrive at the total value of improvement by multiplying the annual performance change (ΔP) by the unit value (V) for the complete group in question. For example, if one group of participants is involved in the consulting project being evaluated, the total value will include total improvement for all participants in the group. This value for annual intervention benefits is then compared to the cost of consulting, usually with the ROI formula presented in Chapter 1.

How Does It Work?

An example taken from a team-building consulting project at a manufacturing plant describes the five-step process of converting data to monetary values. This intervention was developed and implemented after initial needs assessment and analysis revealed that a lack of teamwork was causing an excessive number of labor grievances. Thus, the actual number of grievances resolved at step 2 in the four-step grievance process was selected as an output measure. Table 11.1 shows the steps taken in assigning a monetary value to the data, arriving at a total consulting impact of $546,000.

Several strategies for converting data to monetary values are available. Some are appropriate for a specific type of data or data category, while others may be used with virtually any type of data. The consul-

Table 11.1   An Example Illustrating the Steps for Converting Data to Monetary Values

Setting:	Team-Building Consulting Project in a Manufacturing Plant
Step 1	*Focus on a unit of measure.* One grievance reaching step 2 in the four-step grievance resolution process.
Step 2	*Determine the value of each unit.* Using internal experts (i.e., the labor relations staff), the cost of an average grievance was estimated to be $6500 when time and direct costs are considered ($V = \$6500$).
Step 3	*Calculate the change in performance data.* Six months after the intervention was completed, total grievances per month reaching step 2 declined by 10. Seven of the 10 reductions were related to the consulting intervention, as determined by supervisors (isolating the effects of the consulting project).
Step 4	*Determine an annual amount for the change.* Using the 6-month value of 7 grievances per month yields an annual improvement of 84 ($\Delta P = 84$).
Step 5	*Calculate the annual value of the improvement.* Annual value $= \Delta P \times V$ $= 84 \times \$6{,}500$ $= \$546{,}000$

tant's challenge is to select the strategy that best suits the situation. These strategies are presented next, beginning with the most credible approach.

How Much Is a Widget Worth? Converting Output Data

When a consulting project produces a change in output, the value of the increased output can usually be determined from the organization's accounting or operating records. For organizations operating on a profit basis, this value is typically the marginal profit contribution of an additional unit of production or service provided. For example, a team within a major appliance manufacturer is able to boost the production of small refrigerators after a comprehensive consulting project. The unit of improvement is the profit margin of one refrigerator. For organizations that are performance driven rather than profit driven, this value is usually reflected in the savings accumulated when an additional unit of output is realized for the same input. For example, in the visa section of a government office, an additional visa application is processed at no additional cost. Thus, an increase in output translates into a cost savings equal to the unit cost of processing a visa application.

The formulas and calculations used to measure this contribution depend on the type of the organization and the status of its record keeping. Most organizations have standard values readily available for performance monitoring and setting goals. Managers often use marginal cost statements and sensitivity analyses to pinpoint values associated with changes in output. If the data are not available, the consulting staff must initiate or coordinate the development of appropriate values.

In one case involving a commercial bank, a consulting project in the consumer lending department produced increased consumer loan volume. To measure the ROI for the project, it was necessary to calculate the value (profit contribution) of one additional consumer loan. This was relatively easy to calculate from the bank's records. As shown in Table 11.2, the calculation involved several components.

The first step was to determine the yield, which was available from bank records. Next, the average spread between the cost of funds and the yield realized on the loan was calculated. For example, the bank could obtain funds from depositors at 5.5 percent on average, including the cost of operating the branches. The direct costs of making the loan—such as advertising expenditures and salaries of employees directly involved in consumer lending—were subtracted from this difference. Historically, these direct costs amounted to 0.82 percent of the

Table 11.2 Loan Profitability Analysis

Profit Component	Unit Value
Average loan size	$15,500
Average loan yield	9.75%
Average cost of funds (including branch costs)	5.50%
Direct costs for consumer lending	0.82%
Corporate overhead	1.61%
Net profit per loan	1.82%

loan value. To cover overhead costs for other corporate functions, an additional 1.61 percent was subtracted from the value. The remaining 1.82 percent of the average loan value represented the bank's profit margin on a loan. The good news in this situation and with this approach is that these calculations are already completed for the most important data items and are reported as standard values.

What Does Quality Cost? Calculating the Standard Cost of Quality

Quality and the cost of quality are important issues in most manufacturing and service firms. Since many consulting projects are designed to increase quality, the consulting staff must place a value on improvement in certain quality measures. For some quality measures, this task is easy. For example, if quality is measured via defect rate, the value of the improvement is the cost to repair or replace the product. The most obvious cost of poor quality is the scrap or waste generated by mistakes. Defective products, spoiled raw materials, and discarded paperwork are all results of poor quality. Scrap and waste translate directly into a monetary value. In a production environment, for example, the cost of a defective product is the total cost incurred to the point at which the mistake is identified, minus the salvage value.

Employee mistakes and errors can cause expensive rework. The most costly rework occurs when a product is delivered to a customer and must be returned for correction. The cost of rework includes both labor and direct costs. In some organizations, rework costs can be as much as 35 percent of operating expenses.

In one example, a consulting project focused on customer service provided by dispatchers in an oil company. The dispatchers processed orders and scheduled deliveries of fuel to service stations. A measure of quality that was considered to need improvement was the number of pullouts experienced. (A pullout occurs when a delivery truck cannot fill an order for fuel at a service station and must then return to the terminal for an adjustment to the order.) This is essentially a rework item. The average cost of a pullout was developed by tabulating the cost from a sampling of actual pullouts. The elements in the tabulation included driver time, the cost of using the truck for adjusting the load, the cost of terminal use, and estimated administrative expenses. This value became the accepted standard following completion of the consulting intervention.

Organizations have made great progress in developing standard values for the cost of quality. Quality costs can be grouped into four major categories: internal failure, external failure, appraisal, and prevention.[1]

1. *Internal failure* represents costs associated with problems detected prior to product shipment or service delivery. Typical costs are reworking and retesting.
2. *External failure* refers to problems detected after product shipment or service delivery. Typical items are technical support, complaint investigation, remedial upgrades, and fixes.
3. *Appraisal costs* are expenses involved in determining the condition of a particular product or service. Typical costs are testing and related activities, such as product quality audits.
4. *Prevention costs* include efforts undertaken to avoid unacceptable product or service quality. These efforts include service quality administration, inspections, process studies, and improvements.

Perhaps the costliest element of inadequate quality is customer and client dissatisfaction. In some cases, serious mistakes result in lost business. Customer dissatisfaction is difficult to quantify, and arriving at a monetary value may be impossible using direct methods. The judgment and expertise of sales, marketing, or quality managers are usually the best resources to draw upon when measuring the impact of dissatisfaction. More and more quality experts are measuring customer and client dissatisfaction with market surveys.[2] However, other strategies discussed in this chapter may be more appropriate for the task.

Another useful technique is finding a correlation between a customer satisfaction measure and another measure that can easily be converted to a monetary value. Figure 11.1 shows a relationship between customer satisfaction and customer loyalty that ultimately relates to profits.[3] As the figure illustrates, there is a strong correlation between customer satisfaction and customer loyalty. Many organizations are able to show a strong connection between these two measures. Furthermore, there is often a strong correlation between customer loyalty—which may be defined in terms of customer retention or defection—and the actual profit per customer. By connecting these two variables, it becomes possible to estimate the actual value of customer satisfaction by linking it to other measures. This technique is explored in greater detail later in this book.

How Much Is Time Worth? Converting Employee Time Using Compensation

Decreasing workforce or employee time is a common objective for consulting projects. In a team environment, an intervention may enable the team to complete tasks in less time or with fewer people. A major consulting project could effect a reduction of several hundred employees. On an individual basis, consulting may be designed to help professional, sales, supervisory, and managerial employees save time in performing daily tasks. The value of the time saved is an important measure, and determining the monetary value is a relatively easy process.

The most obvious time savings are from reduced labor costs for performing the same amount of work. The monetary savings are found by multiplying the hours saved by the labor cost per hour. For example, after participating in personal time management consulting, participants estimated that they saved an average of 74 minutes per day, worth

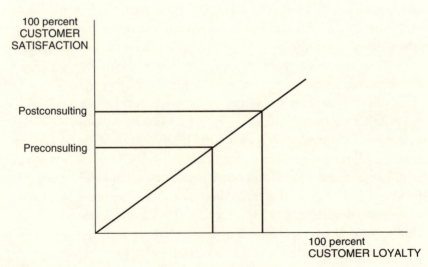

Figure 11.1   Direct correlation of measures.

$31.25 per day or $7500 per year. The time savings were based on the average salary plus benefits for the typical participant.

The average wage, with a percent added for employee benefits, will suffice for most calculations. However, employee time may be worth more. For example, additional costs of maintaining employees (office space, furniture, telephones, utilities, computers, secretarial support, and other overhead expenses) could be included in calculating the average labor cost. Thus, the average wage rate may escalate quickly. In a large-scale employee reduction effort, calculating additional employee costs may be more appropriate for showing the value. However, for most projects the conservative approach of using salary plus employee benefits is recommended.

Beyond reducing the labor cost per hour, time savings can produce benefits such as improved service, avoidance of penalties for late projects, and additional profit opportunities. These values can be estimated using other methods discussed in this chapter.

A word of caution is in order when developing time savings. Savings are only realized when the amount of time saved translates into a cost reduction or profit contribution. Even if a consulting project produces savings in manager time, a monetary value is not realized unless the manager puts the additional time to productive use. If a team-based project sparks a new process that eliminates several hours of work each day, the actual savings will be based on a reduction in staff or overtime pay. Therefore, an important preliminary step in developing time savings is determining whether the expected savings will be genuine.

How About Cost Savings? Using Historical Costs from Records

Sometimes historical records contain the value of a measure and reflect the cost (or value) of a unit of improvement. This strategy relies on identifying the appropriate records and tabulating the cost components for the item in question. For example, a large construction firm initiated a consulting project to improve safety. The intervention improved several safety-related performance measures, ranging from government fines to total workers' compensation costs. By examining the company's records using one year of data, the average cost for each safety measure was developed.

Historical cost data are usually available for most hard data. Unfortunately, this is generally not true for soft data, so other techniques explained in this chapter must be employed to convert those data to monetary values.

Is There an Expert in the House? Using Input from Internal and External Experts

When faced with converting soft data items for which historical cost data are not available, it might be feasible to consider input from experts on the processes. Internal experts provide the cost (or value) of one unit of improvement. Individuals with knowledge of the situation and the respect of management are often the best prospects for expert input. They must understand the processes and be willing to provide estimates—as well as the assumptions made in arriving at those estimates. Most experts have their own methodologies for developing these values, so when requesting their input it is important to explain the full scope of what is needed, providing as many specifics as possible.

In the example described earlier of the team building intervention designed to reduce grievances, the company had no records, other than settlement costs and direct external expenses, reflecting the total cost of grievances (i.e., there were no data for the time required to resolve a grievance). Therefore, an educated estimate was needed. The manager of labor relations, who had credibility with senior management and thorough knowledge of the grievance process, provided a cost estimate based on the average settlement when a grievance was lost, the direct costs related to grievances (arbitration, legal fees, printing, research), the estimated amount of supervisor and employee time expended, and a factor for reduced morale. This internal estimate, although not a precise figure, was appropriate for the analysis and had credibility with management.

When internal experts are not available, external experts are sought. External experts must be selected based on their experience with the unit of measure. Fortunately, there are many available experts working directly with important measures such as employee attitudes, customer satisfaction, turnover, absenteeism, and grievances. They are often willing to provide estimates of the cost (or value) of these intangibles.

Because the accuracy and credibility of the estimates are directly related to the expert's reputation, his or her reputation is critical.

Are There Data Available? Using Values from External Databases

For some soft data, it may be appropriate to use cost (or value) estimates based on the research of others. This technique taps external databases that contain studies and research projects focusing on the cost of data items. Fortunately, there are many databases that include cost studies of many data items related to consulting interventions, and most are accessible through the Internet. Data are available on the costs of turnover, absenteeism, grievances, accidents, and even customer satisfaction. The difficulty is in finding a database with studies or research appropriate to the current intervention. Ideally, the data should come from a similar setting in the same industry, but that is not always possible. Sometimes data on all industries or organizations are sufficient, perhaps with some adjustments to suit the project at hand.

An example illustrates the use of this process. A consulting project was designed to reduce turnover of branch managers in a financial services company. To complete the evaluation and calculate the ROI, the cost of turnover was needed. To develop the turnover value internally, several costs were identified, including the expenses of recruiting, employment processing, orientation, training new managers, lost productivity during the training of new managers, quality problems, scheduling difficulties, and customer satisfaction problems. Additional costs could include the time regional managers spend working with turnover issues and, in some cases, the costs of litigation, severance, and unemployment. Obviously, these expenses are significant. Most consulting staff members do not have time to calculate the cost of turnover, particularly if this figure is only needed for a one-time event, such as evaluating a consulting intervention. In this example, turnover cost studies in the same industry placed the value at about one and a half times the average annual salary of employees. Most turnover cost studies report the cost of turnover as a multiple of annual base salaries. In this example, management decided to be conservative and adjust the value downward to equal the average base salary of branch managers.

Is There a Connection with Other Data?
Linking with Other Measures

When standard values, records, experts, and external studies are not available, a feasible approach might be developing a relationship between the measure in question and some other measure that may be easily converted to a monetary value. This involves identifying, if possible, existing relationships that show a strong correlation between one measure and another with a standard value.

For example, the classical relationship depicted in Figure 11.2 shows a correlation between increasing job satisfaction and employee turnover. In a consulting project designed to improve job satisfaction, a value is needed for changes in the job satisfaction index. A predetermined relationship showing the correlation between improvements in job satisfaction and reductions in turnover can link the changes directly to turnover. Using standard data or external studies, the cost of turnover can easily be developed as described earlier. Thus, a change in job satisfaction is converted to a monetary value, or at least an approximate value. It is not always exact because of the potential for error and other factors, but the estimate is sufficient for converting the data to monetary values.

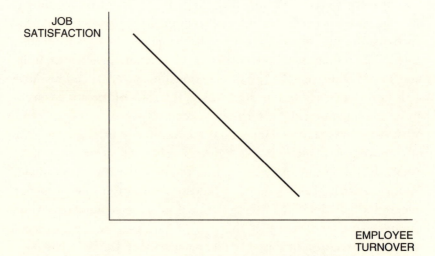

Figure 11.2   Relationship between job satisfaction and turnover.

In some situations, a chain of relationships may be established to show the connection between two or more variables. In this approach, a measure that may be difficult to convert to a monetary value is linked to other measures that, in turn, are linked to measures on which a value can be placed. Ultimately these measures are traced to a monetary value that is often based on profits. Figure 11.3 shows the model used by Sears, one of the world's largest retail chains.[4] The model connects job attitudes (collected directly from the employees) with customer service, which is directly related to revenue growth. The rectangles in the chart represent survey information, while the ovals represent hard data. The shaded measurements are collected and distributed in the form of Sears total performance indicators.

As the model shows, a 5-point improvement in employee attitudes will drive a 1.3-point improvement in customer satisfaction. This, in turn, drives a 0.5 percent increase in revenue growth. Thus, if employee attitudes at a local store improved by five points, and previous revenue growth was 5 percent, the new revenue growth would be 5.5 percent.

These links between measures, often called the *service-profit chain*, create a promising way to place monetary values on hard-to-quantify

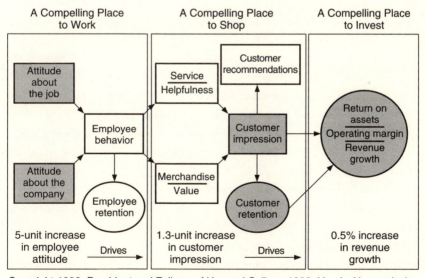

Figure 11.3   Linkage of job satisfaction and revenue.

measures. This research practice is significant, and the opportunity for customized work is tremendous.

Who Can Estimate This Value? Using Estimates from Participants

In some cases, participants in a consulting project should estimate the value of soft data improvement. This technique is appropriate when participants are capable of providing estimates of the cost (or value) of the unit of measure improved through consulting solutions. When using this approach, participants should be provided clear instructions, along with examples of the type of information needed. The advantage of this approach is that the individuals closest to the improvement are often capable of providing the most reliable estimates of its value.

An example illustrates this process. A group of supervisors was involved in a major absenteeism reduction project. Successful application of the project would produce a reduction in absenteeism. To calculate the ROI for the intervention, it was necessary to determine the average value of one absence in the company. As is the case with most organizations, historical records for the cost of absenteeism were not available. Experts were not available, and external studies were sparse for this particular industry. Consequently, supervisors (intervention participants) were asked to estimate the cost of an absence. In a focus group format, each participant was asked to recall the last time an employee in his or her work group was unexpectedly absent and to describe what was necessary to adjust for the absence. Because the impact of an absence varies considerably from one employee to another within the same work unit, the group listened to all explanations. After reflecting on what actions to take when an employee was absent, each supervisor was asked to provide an estimate of the average cost of an absence in the company.

Although some supervisors are reluctant to provide estimates, with prodding and encouragement they usually will. The group's values are averaged, and the result is the cost of an absence that may be used in evaluating the project. Although this is an estimate, it is probably more accurate than data from external studies, calculations using internal records, or estimates from experts. And, because it comes from supervisors who wrestle with the issue daily, it will carry weight with senior management.

Can the Managers Estimate the Value? Using Estimates from the Management Team

In some situations, participants in a consulting project may be incapable of placing a value on the improvement. Their work may be so far removed from the output of the process that they cannot reliably provide estimates. In these cases, the team leaders, supervisors, or managers of participants may be capable of providing estimates. Consequently, they may be asked to provide a value for a unit of improvement linked to the intervention.

For example, an intervention involving customer service representatives was designed to reduce customer complaints. While the intervention resulted in a reduction of complaints, the value of a single customer complaint was still needed to determine the value of improvement. Although customer service representatives had knowledge of some issues surrounding customer complaints, they could not gauge the full impact, so their managers were asked to provide a value. In other situations, managers are asked to review and approve participants' estimates and confirm, adjust, or discard the values.

In some cases, senior management provides estimates of the value of data. With this approach, senior managers interested in the consulting intervention are asked to place a value on the improvement based on their perception of its worth. This approach is used when it is difficult to calculate the value or when other sources of estimation are unavailable or unreliable. An example illustrating this strategy is a hospital chain that was attempting to improve patient satisfaction with a consulting intervention. Patient satisfaction was measured by an external customer satisfaction index. To determine the value of the consulting intervention, the value of a unit of improvement (one point on the index) was needed. Because senior managers were interested in improving the index, they were asked to provide input on the value of a unit before the project was completed. In a regular executive meeting, each senior manager and hospital administrator was asked to describe what it means for a hospital when the index increases. After some discussion, each individual was asked to provide an estimate of the monetary value gained when the index moves one point. Although the senior managers were initially reluctant to provide the information, with some encouragement they finally did so. The values were then averaged. The result was a monetary estimate of one unit of improvement, which was used in calculating the benefit of the intervention. Although this process is subjective, it does have the benefit of ownership from senior executives—the same executives who approved the consulting intervention budget.

Should We Estimate This? Using Consulting Staff Estimates

The final strategy for converting data to monetary values is using consulting project staff estimates. Using all the available information and experience, the staff members most familiar with the situation provide estimates of the value. For example, a consulting project for an international oil company was designed to reduce dispatcher absenteeism and improve other performance problems. Unable to identify a value using other strategies, the consulting staff estimated the cost of an absence to be $200. This value was then used in calculating the savings for the reduction in absenteeism that followed the consulting intervention. Although the staff may be capable of providing accurate estimates, this approach is sometimes perceived as being biased. It should therefore be used only when other approaches are unavailable or inappropriate.

Selecting the Techniques and Finalizing the Values

With so many techniques available, the challenge is selecting one or more strategies appropriate for the situation and available resources. It may be helpful to develop a table or list of values or techniques appropriate for the situation. Table 11.3 shows the common conversion process for a group of output measures in a manufacturing firm. This process could be expanded to other categories and tailored specifically to the organization. The following guidelines may help determine the proper selection and finalize the values.

Use the Technique Appropriate for the Type of Data

Some strategies are designed specifically for hard data, while others are more appropriate for soft data. Consequently, the type of data often dictates the strategy. Hard data, while always preferred, are not always

Table 11.3 Common Measures and the Methods to Convert to Monetary Values

Output Measures	Example	Strategy	Comments
Production unit	One unit assembled	Standard value	Available in almost every manufacturing unit
Service unit	Parts delivered on time	Standard value	Developed for most service providers when it is a typical service delivery unit
Sales	Monetary increase in revenue	Margin (profit)	The profit from 1 additional dollar of sales is a standard item.
Market share	10% increase in market share in 1 year	Margin of increased sales	Standard for most units
Productivity measure	10% change in productivity index	Standard value	This measure is very specific to the type of production or productivity measured. It may include per unit of time.

available. Soft data are often required and thus must be addressed using appropriate strategies.

Move from Most Accurate to Least Accurate

The strategies are presented in order of accuracy, beginning with the most accurate. Working down the list, each strategy should be considered for its feasibility in a given situation. The strategy with the most accuracy is always recommended if it is feasible in the situation.

Consider Availability and Convenience

Sometimes the availability of a particular source of data will drive the selection. In other situations, the convenience of a technique may be an important selection factor.

When Estimates Are Sought, Use the Source with the Broadest Perspective on the Issue

The individual providing the estimate must be knowledgeable of the processes and the issues surrounding the value of the data.

Use Multiple Techniques When Feasible

Sometimes it is helpful to have more than one technique for obtaining values for the data. When multiple sources are feasible, they should be used to serve as comparisons or to provide additional perspectives. The data must be integrated using a convenient decision rule, such as the lowest value. A conservative approach must be taken.

Minimize the Amount of Time to Use a Technique

As with other processes, it is important to keep the time invested in this phase to a minimum, so that the total effort for the ROI study does not become excessive. Some techniques can be implemented in less time than others. Spending too much time on this step may dampen otherwise enthusiastic attitudes about the process.

Apply the Credibility Test

The techniques presented in this chapter assume that each data item collected and linked with consulting interventions can be converted to a monetary value. Although estimates can be developed using one or more strategies, the process of converting data to monetary values may lose credibility with the target audience, which may question its use in analysis. Highly subjective data, such as changes in employee attitudes or reductions in the number of employee conflicts, are difficult to convert. The key question in making this determination is: "Could these results be presented to senior management with confidence?" If the process does not meet this credibility test, the data should not be converted to monetary values but rather listed as intangibles. Other data, particularly hard data items, may be used in the ROI calculation, leaving the highly subjective data expressed in intangible terms.

Review the Client's Needs

The accuracy of data and the credibility of the conversion process are important concerns. Consultants sometimes avoid converting data because of these issues. They are more comfortable reporting that an intervention reduced absenteeism from 6 percent to 4 percent, without attempting to place a value on the improvement. They may assume that the client will place a value on the absenteeism reduction. Unfortunately, the target audience may know little about the cost of absenteeism and will usually underestimate the actual value of the improvement. Consequently, there should be some attempt to include this conversion in the ROI analysis.

Consider a Potential Management Adjustment

In organizations where soft data are used and values are derived with imprecise methods, senior management is sometimes offered the opportunity to review and approve the data. Because of the subjective nature of this process, management may factor (reduce) the data so that the final results are more credible. In one example, senior managers at Litton Industries adjusted the value for the benefits derived from implementing self-directed teams.[5]

Consider an Adjustment for the Time Value of Money

Since an intervention investment is made in one time period and the return is realized at a later time, some organizations adjust intervention benefits to reflect the time value of money using discounted cash flow techniques. The actual monetary benefits of the intervention are adjusted for this time period. The amount of adjustment, however, is usually small when compared with the typical benefits of consulting programs.

Shortcut Ways to Convert Data to Monetary Values

This step is essential only if the ROI process is being developed or if the client needs to know the actual value of the data. Otherwise, it may be optional for every consulting intervention. If monetary values of data are required and the project is small, or if resources are scarce, some of the techniques outlined in this chapter may be appropriate. Some of the options are (1) locating a standard value internally, (2) finding someone internally to estimate the value, or (3) identifying an external expert to provide a value. The individual providing the estimate must have credibility and must be considered an expert on the issue. This is usually a reasonable task in most organizations, as there are individuals or departments with expertise on the particular issue in question.

Final Thoughts

In consulting interventions, money is an important value. Consultants are striving to be more aggressive in defining the monetary benefits of a consulting project. Progressive consultants are no longer satisfied with simply reporting the business performance results from interventions. Instead, they are taking additional steps to convert impact data to monetary values and weigh them against the consulting cost. In doing so, these consultants achieve the ultimate level of evaluation: return on investment. This chapter has presented several strategies used to convert business results to monetary values, offering an array of techniques to fit any situation and consulting project.

References

1. Campanella, Jack (ed.). *Principles of Quality Costs* (3d ed.). Milwaukee: American Society for Quality, 1999.
2. Rust, Roland T., Anthony J. Zahorik, and Timothy L. Keiningham. *Return on Quality: Measuring the Financial Impact of Your Company's Quest for Quality.* Chicago: Probus, 1994.
3. Bhote, Keki R. *Beyond Customer Satisfaction to Customer Loyalty: The Key to General Profitability.* New York: American Management Association, 1996.
4. Ulrich, Dave (ed.). *Delivering Results.* Boston: Harvard Business School, 1998.
5. Graham, Morris, Ken Bishop, and Ron Birdsong. "Self-Directed Work Teams," in *In Action: Measuring Return on Investment* (vol. 1), Jack J. Phillips (ed.). Alexandria, VA: American Society for Training and Development, 1994, pp. 105–122.

Further Reading

Anton, Jon. *CallCenter Management: By the Numbers.* West Lafayette, IN: Purdue University, 1997.

Heskett, James L., Earl Sasser Jr., and Leonard A. Schlesinger. *The Service Profit Chain.* New York: The Free Press, 1997.

Hronec, Steven M./Arthur Anderson & Co. *Vital Signs: Using Quality, Time, and Cost Performance Measurements to Chart Your Company's Future.* New York: AMACOM/American Management Association, 1993.

Jones, Steve (ed.). *Doing Internet Research.* Thousand Oaks, CA: Sage, 1999.

Kaplan, Robert S., and Robin Cooper. *Cost and Effect: Using Integrated Cost Systems to Drive Profitability and Performance.* Boston: Harvard Business School, 1997.

Phillips, Jack J. *Return on Investment in Training and Performance Improvement Programs.* Houston, TX: Gulf, 1997.

Stalk, George Jr., and Thomas M. Hout. *Competing Against Time: How Time-Based Competition Is Reshaping Global Markets.* New York: The Free Press, 1990.

How Much Did It Cost?

Monitoring the True Costs of the Consulting Intervention

THIS CHAPTER EXPLORES cost accumulation and tabulation steps, outlining the specific costs that should be captured and some economical ways in which they can be developed. One of the important challenges addressed in this chapter is deciding which costs should be tabulated or estimated. In consulting, some costs are hidden and never counted. The conservative philosophy presented here is to account for all costs, direct and indirect. Several checklists and guidelines are also included in the chapter.

Why Monitor Costs?

Monitoring the consulting costs is an essential step in developing the ROI calculation because it represents the denominator in the ROI formula. It is just as important to pay attention to costs as it is to benefits. In practice, however, costs are often more easily captured than benefits.

Costs should be monitored in an ongoing effort to control expenditures and keep the project within budget. Monitoring cost activities not only reveals the status of expenditures, but also gives visibility to expenditures and influences the entire project team to spend wisely. And of course, monitoring costs in an ongoing fashion is much easier, more accurate, and more efficient than trying to reconstruct events to capture costs retrospectively.

How to Develop Costs

The first step in monitoring costs is to define and discuss several issues regarding a cost control system. The key issues are presented here.

Costs Are Critical

Capturing costs is challenging because the figures must be accurate, reliable, and realistic. Although most organizations develop costs with much more ease than the monetary value of the benefits, the true cost of consulting is often an elusive figure even in some of the easiest projects. While the direct charges are usually easily developed, it is more difficult to determine the indirect costs of a project. Fortunately, for most consulting projects, the major costs are known up front in the project proposal. However, the hidden and indirect costs to the organization that are linked to the project are not usually detailed. To develop a realistic ROI, cost figures must be accurate, complete, and credible. Otherwise, the painstaking difficulty and attention to the monetary benefits will be wasted because of inadequate or inaccurate costs.

Why Disclose All Costs?

Today, there is more pressure than ever before to report all consulting costs, or what are referred to as *fully loaded costs*. This takes the cost profile beyond the direct cost of consulting fees and encompasses the time participants spend on the intervention, including their benefits and other overhead. For years, management has realized that there are many indirect costs of consulting. Now managers are asking for an accounting of these costs.

Perhaps this point is best illustrated in a situation that recently developed in a state government, in which the management controls of a large state agency were examined by the state auditor. (The agency prefers not to be identified.) A portion of the audit focused on internal consulting costs. Cost tracking for an intervention usually focuses on

direct or "hard" costs and largely ignores the cost of time spent participating in or supporting the consulting project. The costs of participant
time to prepare for and attend consulting meetings are not tracked. For
one series of consulting interventions, including such costs raised the
total consulting costs dramatically. The agency stated that the total
two-year costs for the specific project were about $600,000. This figure
included only direct, out-of-pocket costs to the consulting firm and, as
such, is substantially less than the cost of the time spent by staff in
preparing for and attending the various meetings and sessions. With
prework and attendance accounted for, the figure came to $1.39 mil-
lion. If the statewide average of 45.5 percent for employee benefits is
considered, the total indirect cost of staff time to prepare for and attend
meetings related to the project was $2 million. Finally, if the agency's
direct costs of $600,000 are added to the $2 million total indirect cost
just noted, the total becomes more than $2.6 million.

Among other factors that drive actual costs higher in this example are:

- Cost of travel, meals, and lodging for participants involved in the
  consulting intervention
- Allocated salaries and benefits of staff providing administrative
  and logistic support
- Opportunity costs of productivity lost by staff while doing prework and attending consulting meetings

Failure to consider all indirect or "soft" costs may expose the agency
to noncompliance with the Fair Labor Standards Act (FLSA), particularly as the consulting intervention spreads through the rank and file.
Since the FLSA requires that such staff be directly compensated for
overtime, it is no longer appropriate for the agency to ask employees to
complete consulting assignments and prework on their own time. Continuing to handle such overtime work this way may encourage false
overtime reporting, skew overtime data, and/or increase the amount of
uncompensated overtime.

Numerous barriers exist to agency efforts to determine how much a
consulting project costs:

- Cost systems tend to hide administrative, support, internal, and
  other indirect or "soft" costs.

- Costs generally are monitored at the division level rather than at the level of individual interventions or activities.
- Cost information required by activity-based cost systems is not being generated.

While this case may be an extreme, it vividly demonstrates that the cost of consulting is much more than direct expenditures, and the consultants are expected to report fully loaded costs in their projects.

Fully Loaded Costs

When using a conservative approach to calculating the ROI, it is recommended that consulting costs be fully loaded. Using this approach, all costs that can be identified and linked to a particular consulting assignment are included. The philosophy is simple: for the denominator, when in doubt include it (i.e., if it is questionable whether a cost should be included, it is recommended that it be included, even if the cost guidelines for the organization do not require it). When an ROI is calculated and reported to target audiences, the process should withstand even the closest scrutiny in terms of its accuracy and credibility. The only way to meet this test is to ensure that all costs are included. Of course, from a realistic viewpoint, if the controller or chief financial officer insists on not using certain costs, then it is best to leave them out.

The Danger of Reporting Costs Without the Benefits

It is dangerous to communicate the costs of a consulting intervention without presenting benefits. Unfortunately, many organizations have fallen into this trap for years. Because costs can easily be collected, they are presented to management in all types of ingenious ways, such as cost of the intervention, cost per employee, and cost per unit of product or service. While these may be helpful for efficiency comparisons, it may be troublesome to present them without benefits. When most executives review consulting intervention costs, a logical question comes to mind: "What benefit was received from the consulting project?" This is a typical management reaction, particularly when costs are perceived to be very high. For example, in one organization, all of the costs associated with a major transformation consulting project were tabulated and reported to the senior management team to let team members know the total investment in the intervention. The total figure exceeded the perceived value of the project, and the executive group's immediate reaction was to request a summary of monetary and nonmonetary benefits derived from the complete transformation. The conclusion was that few, if any, economic benefits had been produced by the intervention. Consequently, future consulting projects were drastically reduced. While this may be an extreme example, it shows the danger of presenting only half of the equation. Because of this, some organizations have developed a policy of not communicating consulting cost data unless the benefits can be captured and presented along with the costs. Even if the benefits are subjective and intangible, they are included with the cost data. This helps to maintain a balance between the two issues.

Developing and Using Cost Guidelines

For most consulting groups, it may be helpful to detail the philosophy and policy on costs in guidelines for the consultants or others who monitor and report costs. Cost guidelines detail specifically which cost categories are included with consulting projects and how the data are captured, analyzed, and reported. Standards, unit cost guiding principles, and generally accepted values are included in the guidelines. Cost guidelines can range from a one-page brief to a hundred-page document in a large, complex organization. The simpler approach is better. When fully developed, cost guidelines should be reviewed and approved by the finance and accounting staff. The final document serves as the guiding force in collecting, monitoring, and reporting costs. When the ROI is calculated and reported, costs are included in a summary form or table, and the cost guidelines are referenced in a footnote or attached as an appendix.

Cost-Tracking Issues

The most important task is to define which specific costs are included in consulting project costs. This task involves decisions that will be made by the consulting staff and usually approved by the client. If appropriate, the client's finance and accounting staff may need to approve the list.

Sources of Costs

It is sometimes helpful to first consider the sources of consulting cost. There are three major categories of sources, as illustrated in Table 12.1. The charges and expenses from the consulting firm represent the greatest segment of costs and are transferred directly to the client for payment. These are often placed in categories under fees and expenses. The second major cost category is those expenses—both direct and indirect—borne by the client organization. In many consulting interventions, these costs are not identified but nevertheless reflect the cost of the consulting project. The third cost is the cost of payments made to other organizations as a result of the consulting intervention. These include payments directly to suppliers for equipment and services prescribed in the consulting project. The finance and accounting records should be able to track and reflect the costs from these three different sources, and the process presented in this chapter has the capability of tracking these costs as well.

Consulting Process Steps and Cost

Another important way to consider consulting costs is in the characteristics of how the project unfolds. Figure 12.1 shows the specific functions of a complex consulting assignment, beginning with the initial analysis and assessment and progressing to the evaluation and the reporting of the results. These are the functional process steps that are

Table 12.1 Sources of Costs

Source of Costs	Cost Reporting Issues
1. Consulting firm fees and expenses	A Costs are usually accurate.
	B Variable expenses may be underestimated.
2. Client expenses (direct and indirect)	A Direct expenses are usually not fully loaded.
	B Indirect expenses are rarely included in costs.
3. Other expenses (equipment and services)	A Sometimes understated.
	B May lack accountability.

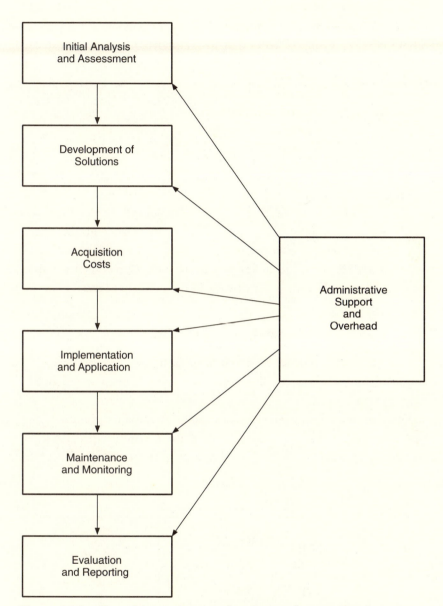

Figure 12.1   Consulting assignment functions and cost categories.

outlined earlier in the book and later in this chapter. They represent the typical flow of work. As a problem is addressed, a solution is developed or acquired and implemented in the organization. There are maintenance and monitoring processes usually put in place that will result in ongoing costs. The entire process is routinely reported to the client, and evaluation is undertaken to show the success of the project. There is also a group of costs that will support the process primarily from the client's perspective, as these represent important administrative support and overhead costs. To be fair, the consulting project should be analyzed in these different categories, as described later in the chapter.

This may be a bit complex for some consulting processes, which are small in scope and involve only a few consultants—in some cases maybe only one consultant. In these situations a more simplistic approach is taken that follows the simplified process flow described in Figure 12.2, which represents the consulting process reflected in fees, the direct cost of the expenses, and the client cost. These occur as the consultant allocates time and generates costs, and the client incurs some recurring or ongoing costs in the project. The important point is to consider costs as they occur naturally and systematically in the consulting intervention.

Prorated Versus Direct Costs

Usually all costs related to a consulting project are captured and expensed to that project. However, some costs are prorated over a longer period of time. Equipment purchases, software development and acquisition, and the construction of facilities are all significant costs with a useful life that may extend beyond the consulting project. Consequently, a portion of these costs should be prorated to the consulting

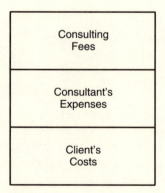

Figure 12.2 Simplified breakdown of consulting costs.

project. Using a conservative approach, the expected life of the consulting project is fixed. Some organizations consider one year of operation for a simple project; others may consider three to five years. In a consulting project involving the implementation of self-directed teams at one organization, a seven-year time frame was used. If there is some question about the specific time period to be used in the proration formula, the finance and accounting staff should be consulted, or appropriate guidelines should be developed and followed.

A brief example will illustrate the proration of development costs. In a large telecommunications company, a consulting project requires the development of a computer-based training program at a cost of $98,000. It is anticipated that the training will have a three-year life cycle before needing a major revision. The revision costs at the end of the three years are estimated to be about half of the original development costs, or $49,000. The consulting project uses a three-year payback period with an ROI calculation planned for benefits extending beyond that period. Since the intervention's computer-based training will have half of its residual value at the end of three years, only half of the costs should be written off for this three-year period. Thus, $49,000, representing half of the software costs, is used.

Employee Benefits Factor

Employee time is valuable, and when time is required on a consulting project, the costs must be fully loaded, representing total compensation. This means that the employee benefits factor should be included. This number is usually well known in the organization and is used in other costing formulas. It represents the cost of all employee benefits expressed as a percentage of payroll. In some organizations this value is as high as 50 to 60 percent. In others, it may be as low as 25 to 30 percent. The average in the United States is 38 percent.[1]

Major Cost Categories

Table 12.2 shows the recommended cost categories for a fully loaded, conservative approach to estimating costs. Each category is described in the following text.

Table 12.2 Consulting Cost Categories

	Cost Item	Prorated	Expensed
A	Initial analysis and assessment		✔
B	Development of solutions		✔
C	Acquisition of solutions		✔
D	Implementation and application		
	Salaries/benefits for consultant time		✔
	Salaries/benefits for coordination time		✔
	Salaries/benefits for participant time		✔
	Consulting materials		✔
	Hardware/software	✔	
	Travel/lodging/meals		✔
	Use of facilities		✔
	Capital expenditures	✔	
E	Maintenance and monitoring		✔
F	Administrative support and overhead	✔	
G	Evaluation and reporting		✔

Initial Analysis and Assessment

One of the most underestimated items is the cost of conducting the initial analysis and assessment. In a comprehensive project, this involves data collection, problem solving, assessment, and analysis. In some consulting projects, this cost is near zero because the intervention is conducted without an appropriate assessment. However, as more consultants give increased attention to needs assessment and analysis, this item will become a significant cost in the future. All costs associated with the analysis and assessment should be captured to the fullest extent possible. These costs include consulting time, direct expenses, and internal services and supplies used in the analysis. The total costs are usually allocated over the life of the consulting project.

Development of Solutions

One of the more significant items is the cost of designing and developing the solutions for a consulting project. These costs include consulting time in both design and development as well as the purchase of supplies, technology, and other materials directly related to the solutions. As with needs assessment costs, design and development costs are usually fully charged to the project. However, in some situations, the major expenditures may be prorated over several projects.

Acquisition Costs

In lieu of development costs, many organizations purchase solutions from other sources to use directly or in a modified format. The acquisition costs for these interventions include purchase price, support materials, and licensing agreements. Many consulting projects have both acquisition costs and solution development costs.

Application and Implementation Costs

Usually the largest cost segment in a consulting project is associated with implementation and delivery. Eight major categories are reviewed in the list that follows.

1. *Salaries and benefits for consulting time.* This includes all of the charges for consultants assigned directly to the staff. This cost represents their specific fees for the time they are involved in the project. These are direct charges only and are usually allocated directly from the consulting organization.
2. *Salaries and benefits for coordinators and organizers.* The salaries of those who implement the consulting project—usually client staff members—should be included. If a coordinator is involved in more than one project, the time should be allocated to the specific project under review. If external facilitators are used, all expenses should be included in the project. The important issue is to capture all of the time of internal employees or external providers who work directly with the intervention. The benefits factor should be included each time direct labor costs are involved. This factor is a widely accepted value, usually generated by the finance and accounting staff and in the 30 to 50 percent range.
3. *Participants' salaries and benefits.* The salaries plus employee benefits of consulting participants represent an expense that should be included. These costs can be estimated using average or mid-

point values for salaries in typical job classifications. When a consulting project is targeted for an ROI calculation, participants can provide their salaries directly in a confidential manner.

4. *Consulting materials.* Consulting materials such as field journals, instructions, reference guides, case studies, surveys, and participant workbooks should be included in the delivery costs, along with license fees, user fees, and royalty payments. Supporting software, CD-ROMs, and videos are also included in this category.

5. *Hardware/software.* This includes all equipment purchased directly for this consulting assignment. If this hardware or software is used in other projects, then a proration per allocation over different projects may be appropriate.

6. *Travel, lodging, and meals.* Direct travel costs for consulting participants, facilitators, coordinators, and originators are included. Lodging and meals during travel and during the intervention are included, as are entertainment and refreshments during the intervention.

7. *Facilities.* The direct cost for the use of facilities for the consulting project should be included. For external meetings, this is the direct charge from the conference center, hotel, or motel. If the meetings are conducted in house, the conference room represents a cost for the organization, and the cost should be estimated and included—even if it is uncommon to include facilities costs in other reports. A commonsense approach should be taken with this issue. Charging excessively for space or charging for small intervals may reflect an unreasonable approach, underscoring the need for formal guidelines.

8. *Capital expenditures.* For expenses that represent significant investment, such as a major remodeling of facilities, the purchase of a building, or the purchase of major equipment, the expenses should be recorded as capital expenditures and allocated over a period of time. If the equipment, building, or facility is used for other projects, then the costs should be allocated over the different projects and only a portion should be captured for a particular assignment.

Maintenance and Monitoring

Maintenance and monitoring involves routine expenses for maintaining and operating the solution implemented in the consulting project.

These represent ongoing expenses to make the new solution continue to work. These may involve staff members and additional expenses, and may be significant for some projects.

Support and Overhead

Another charge is the cost of support and overhead—the additional costs of consulting not directly related to a particular project. The overhead category represents any consulting intervention cost not considered in the preceding calculations. Typical items include the cost of clerical support; telecommunication expenses; office expenses; the salaries of client managers; and other fixed costs. Some organizations obtain an estimate for allocation by estimating the total number of consulting days for the year and then estimating the overhead and support needed each day. This becomes a standard value to use in calculations.

Evaluation and Reporting

Usually the total evaluation cost is included in consulting costs to compute the fully loaded cost. ROI costs include the cost of developing the evaluation strategy, designing instruments, collecting data, analyzing data, preparing and distributing reports, and communicating results. Cost categories include time, materials, purchased instruments, and surveys. A case can be made for prorating the evaluation costs over several consulting projects instead of charging the total amount as an expense in one project. For example, if similar consulting projects are conducted over a three-year period and the next project is selected for an ROI calculation, then some of the ROI costs could logically be prorated over the multiple projects. The initial ROI analysis should reflect some of the costs for the projects (e.g., instructional design, evaluation strategy).

Cost Accumulation and Estimation

There are two basic ways to classify consulting costs. One is with a description of the expenditure, such as labor, materials, supplies, travel, and so on. These are expense account classifications. The other is with categories in the consulting process or function, such as initial analysis and assessment, development of solutions, and implementation and application, as illustrated earlier in Figure 12.1. An effective system monitors costs by account categories according to the description of those accounts but also includes a method for accumulating costs in the process/functional category. Many systems stop short of this second step. While the first grouping sufficiently gives the total intervention cost, it does not allow for a useful comparison with other interventions to provide information on areas where costs might be excessive by relative comparisons.

Cost Classification Matrix

Costs are accumulated under both of the preceding classifications. The two classifications are obviously related, and the relationship depends on the organization. For instance, the specific costs included in the initial analysis and assessment phase of an intervention may vary substantially with the organization.

An important part of the classification process is defining the types of costs in the account classification system that normally apply to the process/functional categories. Table 12.3 is a matrix that represents the categories for accumulating all consulting costs in the organization. Those costs that are normally a part of a process/functional category are checked in the matrix. Each member of the client staff should know how to charge expenses properly (e.g., equipment that is rented to use in the implementation of an intervention). Should all or part of the cost be charged to implementation? Or to maintenance and monitoring? More than likely, the cost will be allocated in proportion to the extent to which the item was used for each category.

Cost Accumulation

With expense account classifications clearly defined and the process/functional categories determined, it is easy to track costs for individual interventions. This is accomplished by using special account numbers and project numbers. An example illustrates the use of these numbers.

A project number is a three-digit number representing a specific consulting intervention. For example:

Reengineering of sales division	112
New team leader job design	315
Statistical quality control project	218
Culture audit	491

Table 12.3 Cost Classification Matrix

Expense Account Classification	Process/Functional Categories					
	Initial Analysis and Assessment	Development of Solutions	Acquisition Costs	Implementation and Application	Maintenance and Monitoring	Evaluation and Reporting
01 Salaries and benefits—consultants	X	X	X	X	X	X
02 Salaries and benefits—client staff	X	X			X	X
03 Meals, travel, and incidentals—consultants	X	X	X	X	X	X
04 Meals, travel, and accommodations—client staff		X	X	X	X	X
05 Office supplies and materials	X	X		X	X	X
06 Intervention materials and supplies	X	X	X	X	X	
07 Printing and copying	X	X	X	X	X	X
08 Software and electronic materials	X	X	X	X	X	
09 External services	X	X	X	X	X	X
10 Hardware/equipment expense allocation	X	X	X	X	X	
11 Hardware/equipment—rental		X	X	X	X	
12 Hardware/equipment—maintenance				X	X	
13 Fees, licenses, and royalties				X	X	
14 Facilities expense allocation				X	X	
15 Facilities rental				X	X	
16 General overhead allocation	X	X	X	X	X	X
17 Other miscellaneous expenses	X	X	X	X	X	X

Numbers are assigned to the process/functional breakdowns. Using the example presented earlier, the following numbers are assigned:

Initial analysis and assessment	1
Development of solutions	2
Acquisition of solutions	3
Implementation and application	4
Maintenance and monitoring	5
Evaluation and reporting	6

Using the two-digit numbers assigned to account classifications in Table 12.3, an accounting system is complete. For example, if CD-ROMs are produced for the reengineering project to be used during implementation, the appropriate charge number is 08-4-112. The first two digits denote the account classification, the next digit the process/functional category, and the last three digits the project number. This system enables rapid accumulation and monitoring of consulting costs. Total costs can be presented:

- By consulting project reengineering the sales division (valuing diversity workshop)
- By process/functional categories (implementation)
- By expense account classification (software and electronic materials)

Cost Estimation

The previous section offered procedures for classifying and monitoring costs related to consulting interventions—which represent historical data. It is important to monitor and compare ongoing costs with the budget or with projected costs. However, an important reason for tracking costs is to predict the cost of future consulting interventions. Usually this goal is accomplished through a formal cost estimation method unique to the organization.

Cost estimating worksheets are sometimes helpful in determining the total cost for a proposed consulting project. Table 12.4 shows an example of a cost estimating worksheet that captures costs by consulting functional areas, such as implementation. The worksheets contain a

Table 12.4 Example of a Cost Estimating Worksheet

	Consulting Firm	Client Firm
Initial analysis and assessment costs		
Salaries and employee benefits—consultants (Number of consultants × average salary × employee benefits factor × number of hours on project)	_____	_____
Salaries and benefits—client staff	_____	_____
Meals, travel, and incidentals—consultants	_____	_____
Office supplies and materials	_____	_____
Printing and copying	_____	_____
Software, electronic materials	_____	_____
External services	_____	_____
Hardware/equipment expense allocation	_____	_____
General overhead allocation	_____	_____
Other miscellaneous expenses	_____	_____
Total initial analysis and assessment cost	_____	_____
Development of solutions		
Salaries and employee benefits—consultants (Number of people × average salary × employee benefits factor × number of hours on project)	_____	_____
Salaries and benefits—client staff	_____	_____
Meals, travel, and incidentals—consultants	_____	_____
Meals, travel, and incidentals—client staff	_____	_____
Office supplies and materials	_____	_____
Intervention materials and supplies	_____	_____
Printing and copying	_____	_____
External services	_____	_____
Hardware/equipment expense allocation	_____	_____
Hardware/equipment—rental	_____	_____
General overhead allocation	_____	_____
Other miscellaneous expenses	_____	_____
Total development of solutions	_____	_____
Acquisition costs		
Salaries and employee benefits—consultants (Number of people × average salary × employee benefits factor × number of hours on project)	_____	_____
Meals, travel, and incidentals—consultants	_____	_____
Intervention materials and supplies	_____	_____
Printing and copying	_____	_____
Software and electronic materials	_____	_____
External services	_____	_____
Hardware/equipment expense allocation	_____	_____
Hardware/equipment—rental	_____	_____

Table 12.4   Example of a Cost Estimating Worksheet (Continued)

	Consulting Firm	Client Firm
General overhead allocation	_____	_____
Other miscellaneous expenses	_____	_____
Total aquisition costs	_____	_____

Implementation and application

	Consulting Firm	Client Firm
Salaries and employee benefits—consultants (Number of people × average salary × employee benefits factor × number of hours on project)	_____	_____
Meals, travel, and incidentals—consultants	_____	_____
Meals, travel, and incidentals—client staff	_____	_____
Office supplies and materials	_____	_____
Intervention materials and supplies	_____	_____
Printing and copying	_____	_____
Software and electronic materials	_____	_____
External services	_____	_____
Hardware/equipment expense allocation	_____	_____
Hardware/equipment—rental	_____	_____
Fees, licenses and royalties	_____	_____
Facilities expense allocation	_____	_____
Facilities rental	_____	_____
General overhead allocation	_____	_____
Other miscellaneous expenses	_____	_____
Total delivery costs	_____	_____

Maintenance and monitoring

	Consulting Firm	Client Firm
Salaries and employee benefits—consultants (Number of people × average salary × employee benefits factor × number of hours on project)	_____	_____
Salaries and benefits—client staff	_____	_____
Meals, travel, and incidentals—consultants	_____	_____
Meals, travel, and incidentals—client staff	_____	_____
Office supplies and materials	_____	_____
Intervention materials and supplies	_____	_____
Printing and copying	_____	_____
Software and electronic materials	_____	_____
External services	_____	_____
Hardware/equipment expense allocation	_____	_____
Hardware/equipment—rental	_____	_____
Hardware/equipment—maintenance	_____	_____
Fees, licenses and royalties	_____	_____
Facilities expense allocation	_____	_____
Facilities rental	_____	_____
General overhead allocation	_____	_____

Table 12.4 Example of a Cost Estimating Worksheet (Continued)

	Consulting Firm	Client Firm
Other miscellaneous expenses	_____	_____
Total maintenance and monitoring	_____	_____
Evaluation and reporting costs		
Salaries and employee benefits—consultants (Number of people × average salary × employee benefits factor × number of hours on project)	_____	_____
Salaries and benefits—client staff	_____	_____
Meals, travel and incidentals—consultants	_____	_____
Office supplies and materials	_____	_____
Printing and copying	_____	_____
External services	_____	_____
General overhead allocation	_____	_____
Other miscellaneous expenses	_____	_____
Total evaluation costs	_____	_____
Total intervention costs	_____	_____

few formulas that make it easier to estimate the cost. In addition to these worksheets, current charge rates for services, supplies, and salaries are available. These data become outdated quickly and are usually prepared periodically as a supplement.

The most appropriate basis for predicting costs is analyzing the previous costs by tracking the actual costs incurred in all phases of an intervention, from initial analysis to evaluation and reporting. This way it is possible to see how much is spent on the total intervention and how much is being spent in the different categories. Until adequate cost data are available, it may be necessary to use the detailed analysis in the worksheets for cost estimation.

Final Thoughts

Costs are important and should be fully loaded in the ROI calculation. From a practical standpoint, some costs may be optional based on the organization's guidelines and philosophy. However, because of the scrutiny involved in ROI calculations, it is recommended that all costs be included, even if this goes beyond the requirements of the policy.

References

1. Annual Employee Benefits Report, *Nation's Business*, January 1999.

Further Reading

Cascio, Wayne F. *Costing Human Resources: The Financial Impact of Behavior in Organizations.* Kent Human Resource Management Series, Richard W. Beatty (ed.). New York: Van Nostrand Reinhold, 1982.

Donovan, John, Richard Tully, and Brent Wortman. *The Value Enterprise: Strategies for Building a Value-Based Organization.* Toronto: McGraw-Hill/Ryerson, 1998.

Epstein, Marc J., and Bill Birchard. *Counting What Counts: Turning Corporate Accountability to Competitive Advantage.* Reading, MA: Perseus, 1999.

Friedlob, George T., and Franklin J. Plewa Jr. *Understanding Return on Investment.* New York: Wiley, 1991.

Fuller, Jim. *Managing Performance Improvement Projects: Preparing, Planning, and Implementing.* San Francisco: Pfeiffer, 1997.

Hronec, Steven M./Arthur Andersen & Co. *Vital Signs: Using Quality, Time, and Cost Performance Measurements to Chart Your Company's Future.* New York: AMACOM/American Management Association, 1993.

Langley, Gerald J., Kevin M. Nolan, Thomas W. Nolan, Clifford L. Norman, and Lloyd P. Provost. *The Improvement Guide: A Practical Approach to Enhancing Organizational Performance.* San Francisco: Jossey-Bass, 1996.

O'Shea, James, and Charles Madigan. *Dangerous Company: The Consulting Powerhouses and the Businesses They Save and Ruin.* New York: Times Business Random House, 1997.

Schaffer, Robert H. *High-Impact Consulting: How Clients and Consultants Can Leverage Rapid Results into Long-Term Gains.* San Francisco: Jossey-Bass, 1997.

PART
IV

Challenges

How to Build a Business Case for the Consulting Expense

Forecasting ROI

Here is often confusion regarding when it is appropriate to develop the consulting ROI, the types of data to collect, and the level of evaluation that is most suitable for an ROI calculation. The traditional and recommended approach, described in previous chapters, is to base ROI calculations strictly on business results obtained from the consulting intervention. Business performance measures (Level 4 data) are easily converted to monetary values, which are necessary for an ROI calculation. Sometimes these measures are not available, and it is usually assumed that an ROI calculation is out of the question. This chapter will illustrate that ROI calculations are possible at several different stages—even before the project is initiated.

Why Forecast ROI?

Although ROI calculation based on postproject data is the most accurate way to assess and develop an ROI calculation, sometimes it is important to know the forecast before the final results are tabulated. Forecasting during the project, or in some cases even before the project is pursued, is an important issue when critical reasons drive the need for a forecasted ROI.

Reduce Uncertainty

Whenever uncertainty can be reduced in a project, it is to the client's benefit. In a perfect world, the client would like to know the expected payoff before any action is taken. Realistically, knowing the exact payoff may not be possible—and, from a practical standpoint, it may not be feasible. However, there is still the desire to take the uncertainty out of the equation and act on the best data available. This sometimes pushes the project to a forecasted ROI before any resources are expended. Some managers simply will not budge without a preproject forecast; they need some measure of expected success before allocating any resources to the project.

Projects Are Too Expensive to Pursue Without Supportive Data

In some cases even a pilot project is not practical until some analysis has been conducted to examine the potential ROI. For example, if the project involves a significant amount of work in design, development, and delivery, a client may not want to expend the resources, even for a pilot, unless there is some assurance of a positive ROI. Although there may be some trade-offs with a lower-profile and lower-cost pilot, the preproject ROI nevertheless becomes an important issue in these situations, prompting some clients to stand firm until an ROI forecast is produced.

To Compare with Post Data

Whenever there is a plan to collect data on the success of the consulting project regarding application and implementation, impact, and ROI, it is helpful to compare actual results to preproject expectations. In an ideal world, a forecasted ROI should have a defined relationship with the actual ROI, or they should be very similar—or at least one should lead to the other with some adjustments. One important reason for forecasting ROI is to see how well the forecast holds up under the scrutiny of postproject analysis.

Save Costs

There are several cost savings issues prompting the ROI forecast. First, the forecast is often a very inexpensive process because it involves estimations and many different assumptions. Second, if the forecast becomes a reliable predictor of the postproject analysis, then the forecasted ROI might substitute for the actual ROI, at least with some adjustments. This could save money on the postproject analysis. Finally, the forecasted ROI data might be used for comparisons in other areas, at least as a beginning point for other types of projects. Thus, the forecasted ROI might have some transfer potential to other specific projects.

To Comply with Policy

More organizations are developing policy statements and, in the case of government agencies, sometimes even passing laws to require a forecasted ROI before major projects are undertaken. For example, in one organization any project exceeding $300,000 must have a forecasted ROI before it can be approved. In one foreign government, consultants can receive partial payments on a project if the ROI forecast is positive and likely to enhance the organization. This formal policy and legal structure is becoming a frequent reason for developing the ROI forecast.

Collectively, these five reasons are causing more organizations to examine ROI forecasts (or at least to examine ROI during a project) so that the client and the consultant will have some estimate of the expected payoff.

The Trade-Offs of Forecasting

ROI can be developed at different times and at different levels. Unfortunately, the ease, convenience, and low cost involved in capturing a forecasted ROI create trade-offs in accuracy and credibility. As shown in Figure 13.1, there are five distinct time intervals during a consulting project when the ROI can be developed. The relationship of credibility,

ROI with:	Data Collection Timing (Relative to Project)	Credibility	Accuracy	Cost to Develop	Difficulty
1. Preproject forecast	Before project	Not very credible	Not very accurate	Inexpensive	Not difficult
2. Reaction and satisfaction data	During project				
3. Learning data	During project				
4. Application and implementation	After project				
5. Business impact data	After project	Very credible	Very accurate	Expensive	Very difficult

Figure 13.1 ROI at different times and levels.

accuracy, cost, and difficulty is also shown in this figure. The time intervals are as follows:

1. *A preproject forecast* can be developed using estimates of the impact of the consulting intervention. This approach lacks credibility and accuracy, but it is also the least expensive and least difficult ROI to calculate. There is value in developing the ROI on a preproject basis. This will be discussed in the next section.
2. *Reaction and satisfaction data* can be extended to develop an anticipated impact, including the ROI. In this case, participants actually anticipate the chain of impact as a consulting project is applied and implemented and influences specific business measures. While the accuracy and credibility are greater than for the preproject forecast, this approach still lacks the credibility and accuracy desired in most situations.
3. *Learning data* in some projects can be used to forecast ROI. This approach is applicable only when formal testing shows a relationship between acquiring certain skills or knowledge and subsequent business performance. When this correlation is available (it is usually developed to validate the test), test data can be used to forecast subsequent performance. The performance can then be converted to monetary impact and the ROI can be developed. This has less potential as an evaluation tool due to the lack of situations in which a predictive validation can be developed.
4. In some situations, when frequency of skills and actual use of skills are critical, the *application and implementation* of the skills or knowledge can be converted to a value using employee compensation as a basis. This is particularly helpful in situations where competencies are being developed and values are placed on improving competencies, even if there is no immediate increase in pay.
5. Finally, the ROI can be developed from *business impact data* converted directly to monetary values and compared to the cost of the program. This postproject evaluation is the basis for the other ROI calculations in this book and has been the principal approach used in previous chapters. This is the preferred approach, but because of the pressures outlined earlier, it is critical to examine ROI calculations at other times and at levels other than Level 4.

This chapter will discuss in detail preproject evaluation and the ROI calculations based on reactions. ROI calculations developed from learning and application data will be discussed to a lesser degree.

Preproject ROI Forecasting

Perhaps one of the most useful steps in convincing a client that a consulting expense is beneficial is to forecast the ROI for a consulting project. The process is very similar to the postproject analysis, except that the extent of the impact must be estimated along with the forecasted cost.

Basic Model

Figure 13.2 shows the basic model for capturing the necessary data for a preprogram forecast. This model is a modification of the postprogram consulting ROI process model, except that data and influence are projected instead of being collected during different time frames. In place of the data collection is an estimation of the change in impact data expected to be influenced by the intervention. Isolating the effects of the consulting intervention becomes a nonissue, as the estimate of output takes the isolation factor into consideration. For example, when a person is asked to indicate how much of the particular improvement can be driven by a consulting project, the actual response to the isolation factor is already taken into consideration. Only the consulting factor is an issue, as the other factors have been isolated in the estimation process.

The method to convert data to monetary values is exactly the same because the data items examined in a pre- and postproject analysis should be the same. Estimating the project's cost should be an easy step, as costs can easily be anticipated based on previous consulting projects using reasonable assumptions about the current consulting project. The anticipated intangibles are merely speculation in forecasting, but can be reliable indicators of which measures may be influenced in addition to those included in the ROI calculation. The formula used to calculate the ROI is the same as in the postproject analysis. The amount of monetary value from the data conversion is included as the numerator, while the estimated cost of the consulting intervention is inserted as the denominator. The projected cost-benefit analysis can be developed along with the actual ROI. The steps for developing the process are detailed next.

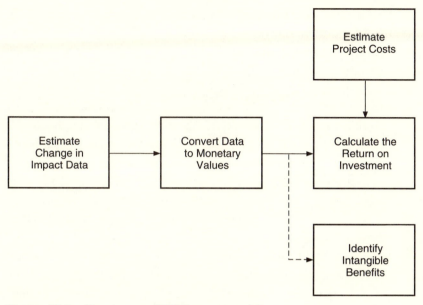

Figure 13.2   Preprogram ROI forecast model.

Steps to Develop the Actual ROI

The detailed steps for developing the preproject ROI forecast are presented in simplified form in the following list.

1. Develop the Level 3 and 4 objectives with as many specifics as possible. These should be developed from the initial needs analysis and assessment. They detail what would actually change in the work setting and identify which measures would actually be influenced. If these are not known, the entire forecasting process is in jeopardy. There must be some assessment of which measures will change as a result of the intervention, and someone must indicate the extent to which this will take place.

2. Estimate or forecast the monthly improvement in the business impact data. This is considered to be the amount of change directly related to the intervention and is denoted by ΔP.

3. Convert the business impact data to monetary values using one or more of the methods described in Chapter 11. These are the same techniques and the same processes as are used in a postproject analysis; this value is denoted by V.

4. Develop the estimated annual impact for each measure. In essence, this is the first-year improvement from the consulting project, showing the value for the change in the business impact measures directly related to the consulting project. In formula form, this is $\Delta I = \Delta P \times V \times 12$.

5. Factor additional years into the analysis if a project will have a significant useful life beyond the first year. When this is the case, these values may be factored to reflect a diminished benefit in subsequent years. The client or owner of the process should give some indication as to the amount of the reduction and the values developed for years two, three, and so on. However, it is helpful to be conservative by using the smallest numbers possible.

6. Estimate the fully loaded consulting project cost. Using all of the cost categories contained in Chapter 12, the fully loaded cost would be estimated and projected for the consulting intervention. This is denoted as C. Again, all direct and indirect costs should be included in the calculation.

7. Calculate the forecasted ROI using the total projected benefits and the estimated cost in the standard ROI formula:

$$\mathrm{ROI}(\%) = \frac{\Delta I - C}{C} \times 100$$

8. Use sensitivity analysis to develop several potential ROI values with different levels of improvement (ΔP). When more than one measure is changing, that analysis would perhaps be performed using a spreadsheet showing different possible scenarios for output and the subsequent ROI.

9. Identify potential intangible benefits by taking input from those most knowledgeable about the situation. These are only anticipated and are based on assumptions from previous experience with this type of consulting intervention.

10. Communicate the ROI projection and anticipated intangibles with much care and caution. The target audience must clearly understand that this is based on several assumptions (clearly defined), and that the values are the best possible estimates. However, there is still much room for error.

These steps enable an individual to forecast ROI. The most difficult part of the process is the initial estimate of performance improvement. Several sources of data are available for this purpose, as described next.

Forecasting/Estimating Performance Improvement

Several sources of input are available when attempting to estimate the actual performance improvement that will be influenced by a consulting project. The following important considerations should be explored:

1. Experience in the organization with similar previous consulting interventions or similar projects can help form the basis of the estimate. Adapting that breadth of experience can be an important factor as comparisons are rarely, if ever, exact.
2. The consulting project team may have experience with similar consulting projects in other organizations or in other situations. Here, the experience of the designers, developers, and implementers involved in the consulting project will be helpful as they reflect on their experiences with other organizations.
3. The input of external experts who have worked in the field or tackled similar projects in other organizations can be extremely valuable. These may be other consultants, suppliers, designers, or others who have earned a reputation as knowledgeable about this type of process in this type of situation.
4. Estimates can be obtained directly from a subject matter expert (SME) in the organization. This is an individual who is very familiar with the internal processes being altered, modified, or improved by the consulting project. Internal SMEs are very knowledgeable and are sometimes the most favored source for obtaining conservative estimates.
5. Estimates can be obtained directly from the client or the sponsor of the project. This is the individual who is ultimately making the purchasing decision and is providing data or input on the anticipated change in a measure linked to the actual consulting project. This influential position makes him or her a very credible source.
6. Individuals who are directly involved in the consulting intervention, often labeled *consulting participants*, are sometimes in a posi-

tion to know how much of a measure can be changed or improved with a particular type of consulting intervention. These individuals understand the processes, procedures, and performance measurements being influenced. Their close proximity to the situation makes them highly credible and often the most accurate sources for estimating the amount of change.

Collectively, these sources provide an appropriate array of possibilities for helping to estimate the value of an improvement. This is the weakest link in the ROI forecasting process and deserves the most attention. It is important that the target audience receive a proposal that includes a forecasted ROI and understands where the estimates came from, as well as who made them. Even more importantly, though, the target audience must view the source as credible. Otherwise, the forecasted ROI will have no credibility.

Case Example

It may be helpful to illustrate how a forecasted ROI can be developed using the processes explained here. A global financial services company was interested in purchasing customer contact management software to enable its sales relationship managers to keep track of routine correspondence and communication with customers. According to the needs assessment and initial analysis, there was a need for such a project. A consulting assignment would involve further detailing of the exact needs, selecting an appropriate software package, and implementing the software along with appropriate job aids, job training, and classroom training if necessary. However, before the project could be pursued and software purchased, a forecasted ROI was needed. Following the steps outlined earlier in this chapter, it was determined that four business impact measures would be influenced by the implementation of this project:

1. Increase in sales to existing customers
2. Reduction in customer complaints due to missed deadlines, late responses, and failure to complete transactions
3. Reduction in response time for customer inquiries and requests
4. Increase in customer satisfaction composite survey index

In examining the potential problem, several individuals provided input. With comprehensive customer contact management software in place, relationship managers would benefit from quick and effective customer communication and have easy access to customer databases. The software would also provide the functionality to develop calendars and to-do lists. Relationship managers would further benefit from features such as built-in contact management, calendar sharing, and the fact that the software is Internet ready. To determine the extent to which the four measures would change, input was collected from four sources:

1. Internal software developers with expertise in various software applications provided input on expected changes in each of the measures.
2. Relationship managers provided input on expected changes in the variables if the software was used regularly.
3. The individual interested in pursuing the project, namely the client, provided some input on what could be expected from the consulting process.
4. Finally, a survey of software developers provided some input.

When input is based on estimates, the actual results may differ significantly. However, this client was interested in a forecast based on very limited analysis but strengthened with the best expert opinions available. After some discussion of the availability of data and examining the techniques to convert data to monetary values, the following conclusions were reached:

- The increase in sales could easily be converted to a monetary value as the margin for this particular project would be applied directly.
- The cost of a customer complaint could be based on a discounted internal value currently in use, thus providing a generally accepted figure.
- The actual customer response time was not tracked accurately, nor was the value of this measure readily available. It was anticipated that this would be an intangible benefit.
- There was no generally accepted value for increasing customer satisfaction, so customer satisfaction impact data would be listed as a potential intangible.

The forecasted ROI calculation was developed for a single division in the organization. After the possible scenarios were reviewed, it was decided that there could be a range of possibilities for increasing sales and reducing complaints. The sales increase should be in the range of 3 to 9 percent. Thus, three scenarios were developed using 3 percent, 6 percent, and 9 percent as the increase in sales. Complaint reduction was expected to be in the range of 10 to 30, so three scenarios were developed for the reduction in actual complaints, using values of 10, 20, and 30 in the ROI calculation.

The increase in sales was easily converted to monetary values using the margin rates, and the reduction in customer complaints was easily converted using the discounted value for a customer complaint. The cost for the project could easily be estimated based upon input from those who examined the situation very briefly. The total cost was developed to include development costs, materials, software, equipment, facilitators, facilities for meetings, lost time for learning activities, and coordination and evaluation. This fully loaded projected cost, when compared to the benefits, yielded a range of expected ROI values. Table 13.1 shows a matrix of the nine possible scenarios using payoffs on the two measures. The ROI values range from a low of 60 percent to a high of 180 percent. With these values in hand, the decision to move forward was a relatively easy one, as even the worst-case scenarios were very positive, and the best case was approximately three times the amount of the worst. Thus, the

Table 13.1   Expected ROI Values for Different Outputs

Potential Sales Increase (Existing Customers, %)	Potential Complaint Reduction (Monthly Reduction)	Expected ROI (%)
3	10	60
3	20	90
3	30	120
6	10	90
6	20	120
6	30	150
9	10	120
9	20	150
9	30	180

decision was made to move forward with the project. As this example illustrates, the process needs to be kept simple, using the most credible resources available to quickly arrive at estimates for the process. Recognizing this is an estimate, its advantage is simplicity and low cost, and these factors should be considered when developing the processes.

Forecasting with a Pilot Program

Although the steps just listed provide a process for estimating the ROI when a pilot program is not conducted, the more favorable approach is to develop a small-scale pilot project and develop the ROI based on postprogram data. This scenario involves the following five steps:

1. As in the previous process, develop Level 3 and 4 objectives.
2. Initiate the consulting project on a very small-scale sample as a pilot project, without all the bells and whistles. This keeps the cost extremely low without sacrificing the fundamentals of the project.
3. Conduct the project, fully implementing it with one or more of the typical groups of individuals who can benefit from the consulting initiative.
4. Develop the ROI using the consulting ROI process model for postproject analysis. This is the ROI process used in the previous chapters.
5. Finally, decide whether to implement the project throughout the organization based on the results of the pilot project.

This provides a much more accurate approach to developing data based on a pilot program and withholding full implementation until results can be developed from the pilot study. In this scenario, data can be developed using all six types of measures outlined in this book.

Forecasting ROI with Reaction Data

When a reaction evaluation includes planned applications from a consulting intervention, the important data can ultimately be used in ROI calculations. With questions concerning how participants plan to use what they learned and the results they expect to achieve, higher-level evaluation information can be developed. The questions presented in

Table 13.2 illustrate how these types of data are collected with an end-of-consulting intervention questionnaire. Participants are asked to state specifically how they plan to use the consulting intervention and the results they expect to achieve. They are asked to convert their planned accomplishments into annual monetary values and show the basis for developing the values. Participants can adjust their responses with a confidence factor to make the data more credible and allow them to reflect their level of uneasiness with the process.

When tabulating data, participants multiply the confidence levels by the annual monetary values, which produces a more conservative estimate for use in the data analysis. For example, if a participant estimated that the monetary impact of the consulting intervention would be $10,000, but was only 50 percent confident in his or her estimation, a $5,000 value would be used in the ROI calculations.

Table 13.2   Important Questions to Ask on Feedback Questionnaires

Planned Improvements

As a result of this consulting intervention, what specific actions will you attempt as you apply what you have learned?

1.

2.

3.

Please indicate what specific measures, outcomes, or projects will change as a result of your actions.

1.

2.

3.

As a result of anticipated changes above, please estimate (in monetary terms) the benefits to your organization over a period of one year. $ _____

What is the basis of this estimate?

What confidence, expressed as a percentage, can you put in your estimate? (0% = no confidence; 100% = certainty)

_____%

To develop a summary of the expected benefits, several steps are taken. First, any data that are incomplete, unusable, extreme, or unrealistic are discarded. Next, an adjustment is made to the estimate for confidence level as previously described. Individual data items are then totaled. Finally, as an optional exercise, the total value is adjusted again by a factor that reflects the subjectivity of the process and the possibility that participants will not achieve the results they anticipate. This adjustment factor can be determined by the consulting team. In one organization, the benefits are divided by 2 to develop a number to use in the equation. Finally, the ROI is calculated using the net benefits from the consulting intervention divided by the consulting intervention costs. This value, in essence, becomes the expected return on investment once the confidence adjustment for accuracy and the adjustment for subjectivity have been made.

This process can best be described using an actual case. M&H Engineering and Construction Co. designs and builds large commercial projects such as manufacturing plants, paper mills, and municipal water systems. Safety is always a critical issue at M&H and usually commands much management attention. To improve the current level of safety performance, a safety improvement consulting project was initiated for project engineers and construction superintendents. The consulting intervention focused on safety leadership, safety planning, safety inspection, safety meetings, accident investigation, safety policy and procedures, safety standards, and workers' compensation. After completing the project, engineers and superintendents were expected to improve the safety performance of their specific construction projects. A dozen safety performance measures used in the company were discussed and analyzed during the consulting intervention. At the end of the consulting intervention, participants completed a comprehensive reaction feedback questionnaire, which probed specific action items planned as a result of the consulting intervention and provided estimated monetary values of the planned actions. In addition, participants explained the basis for estimates and placed a confidence level on their estimates. Table 13.3 presents data provided by the first group of participants. Only 18 of the 24 participants supplied data (experience has shown that approximately 50 to 70 percent of participants will provide usable data on this series of questions). The total cost of the consulting intervention, including participants' salaries, was $29,000. Prorated development costs were included in this figure.

Table 13.3 Level 1 Data for ROI Calculations

Participant Number	Estimated Value ($)	Basis	Confidence Level
1	80,000	Reduction in accidents	90%
2	90,000	OSHA reportable injuries	80%
3	50,000	Accident reduction	100%
4	10,000	First aid visits/visits to doctor	100%
5	50,000	Reduction in lost time injuries	95%
6	Millions	Total accident cost	100%
7	75,000	Workers' compensation	80%
8	7,500	OSHA citations	75%
9	50,000	Reduction in accidents	100%
10	30,000	Workers' compensation	80%
11	150,000	Reduction in total accident costs	90%
12	20,000	OSHA fines/citations	70%
13	40,000	Accident reductions	100%
14	4 million	Total cost of safety	95%
15	65,000	Total workers' compensation	50%
16	Unlimited	Accidents	100%
17	2,000	Visits to doctor	100%
18	45,000	Injuries	90%

The monetary value of the planned improvements was extremely high, reflecting the participants' optimism and enthusiasm at the end of a very effective consulting intervention from which specific actions were planned. As a first step in the analysis, extreme data items such as *millions, unlimited,* and *$4 million* were discarded, and each remaining value was multiplied by the confidence value and totaled. This adjustment is one way of reducing highly subjective estimates. The resulting tabulations yielded a total improvement of $655,125. Because of the subjective nature of the process, the values were adjusted by a factor of 2, an arbitrary number suggested by the principal consultant and supported by the management group. This "adjusted" value was $327,563, or $328,000 once rounded. The projected ROI, which was based on the feedback questionnaire at the end of the intervention but before job application, is as follows:

$$\text{ROI} = \frac{\$328,000 - \$29,000}{\$29,000} \times 100 = 1,031\%$$

The consultant communicated these projected values to the CEO but cautioned that the data were very subjective, although they had twice been adjusted downward. The consultant also emphasized that the forecasted results were generated by the participants in the consulting intervention, who were presumably aware of what they could accomplish. In addition, the consultant mentioned that a follow-up was planned to determine the results actually delivered by the group.

A word of caution is in order when using Level 1 ROI data: the calculations are highly subjective and may not reflect the extent to which participants will apply what they have learned to achieve results. A variety of influences in the work environment can enhance or inhibit the participants' attainment of performance goals. Having high expectations at the end of the consulting intervention is no guarantee that those expectations will be met. Disappointments are documented regularly in consulting interventions throughout the world and are reported in research findings.

While the process is subjective and possibly unreliable, it does have some usefulness. First, if evaluation must stop at Level 1, the approach provides more insight into the value of the consulting intervention than data from typical reaction questionnaires. Managers usually find these data more useful than a report stating that "Forty percent of participants rated the consulting intervention above average." Unfortunately, there is evidence that a high percentage of evaluations stop at this first level of evaluation. Reporting Level 1 ROI data provides a more useful indication of the potential impact of the consulting intervention than the alternative, which is to report attitudes and feelings about the consulting intervention and the consultants.

Second, these data can form a basis for comparing different projects of the same type (i.e., safety). If one consulting intervention forecasts an ROI of 300 percent and another projects 30 percent, then it would appear that one consulting intervention may be more effective than the other. The participants in the first consulting intervention may have more confidence in the planned application of the consulting intervention.

Third, collecting these type of data focuses increased attention on consulting intervention outcomes. Participants involved in the intervention will have an understanding that specific behavior change is expected, which produces results for the organization. This issue becomes very clear to participants as they anticipate results and convert them to monetary values. Even if this projected improvement is ignored, the exercise is productive because of the important message sent to participants.

Fourth, if a follow-up is planned to pinpoint postconsulting intervention results, the data collected in the Level 1 evaluation can be very helpful for comparison. The data collection helps participants plan the implementation of what they have learned. Incidentally, when a follow-up is planned, participants are more conservative with their projected estimates.

The calculation of the ROI at Level 1 is increasing, and some organizations have based many of their ROI calculations on Level 1 data. Although the calculations may be very subjective, they do add value, particularly if they are included as part of a comprehensive evaluation system.

Forecasting ROI with Learning Data

Testing for changes in skills and knowledge in a consulting project is a very common technique for Level 2 evaluation. In many situations, participants are required to demonstrate their knowledge or skills at the end of the consulting intervention, and their performance is expressed as a numerical value. When this type of test is developed, it must be reliable and valid. A reliable test is one that is stable over time and produces consistent results. A valid test is one that measures what it purports to measure. Since a test should reflect the content of the consulting project, successful mastery of consulting intervention content should be related to improved job performance. Consequently, there should be a relationship between test scores and subsequent on-the-job performance. Figure 13.3 illustrates the potential relationship between test scores and job performance in a perfect correlation. This relationship, expressed as a correlation coefficient, is a measure of validity for the test.

This testing situation provides an excellent opportunity for an ROI calculation with Level 2 data using valid test results. When there is a statistically significant relationship between test scores and on-the-job performance (output), and the performance can be converted to monetary units, then it is possible to use test scores to estimate the ROI from the consulting intervention using the following six steps:

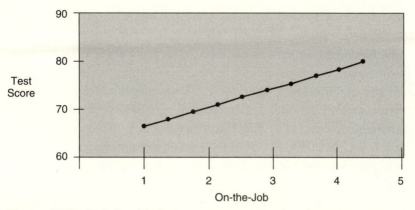

Figure 13.3 Relationship between test scores and performance.

1. Ensure that the consulting intervention content reflects desired on-the-job performance.
2. Develop an end-of-consulting intervention test that reflects consulting intervention content.
3. Establish a statistical relationship between test data and output performance of participants.
4. Predict performance levels for each participant with given test scores.
5. Convert performance data to monetary values.
6. Compare the total predicted value of the consulting intervention with intervention costs.

This approach enjoys the best application when there is significant learning taking place or when the consulting project focuses almost entirely on developing learning solutions. The absence of validated tests is a problematic issue, as the instruments cannot be used to project actual performance unless there have been some steps to ensure validity.

An example illustrates this approach. Consumer Products Marketing (CPM) is the marketing division of a large consumer products company. Sales representatives for CPM make frequent sales calls to large retail food and drug companies with the objective of increasing sales and market share of CPM products. Sales representatives must ensure that retailers understand the advantages of CPM products, provide adequate display space for their products, and assist in promotional and advertising efforts.

CPM has developed a strong sales culture and recruits highly capable individuals for sales assignments. A consulting project was initiated to cultivate new sales representatives. Newly recruited sales representatives rotate through different divisions of the company in a two-month assignment to learn where and how the products are made and their features and benefits, as well as specific product-marketing strategies. This initial assignment culminates with an intensive one-week professional marketing program that focuses on sales techniques, marketing strategies, and customer service skills. At the end of the one-week assignment, participants complete a comprehensive exam that reflects the knowledge and skills learned in the consulting intervention. As part of the exam, participants analyze specific customer service and sales situations and decide on specific actions. The test also covers product features, policies, and marketing practices.

To validate the test, CPM developed a correlation between test scores and actual on-the-job performance measured by sales volumes, sales growth, and market shares for sales representatives. The correlation was statistically significant with each variable. As a quick way of calculating the expected ROI for a consulting intervention, CPM estimates output levels for each item using the test scores, converts them to monetary values, and calculates the ROI.

As with the previous ROI estimate in end-of-intervention questionnaires, some cautions are in order. This is a forecast of the ROI and not the actual value. Although participants acquired skills and knowledge from the consulting intervention, there is no guarantee that they will apply the techniques and processes successfully or that positive results will be achieved. This process assumes that the current group of participants has the same relationship to output performance as previous groups. It ignores a variety of environmental influences, which can alter the situation. And finally, the process requires calculating the initial correlation coefficient, which may be difficult to develop for many tests.

Although this approach develops an estimate based on historical relationships, it can be useful in a comprehensive evaluation strategy and has several advantages. First, if postconsulting intervention evaluations (Level 4) are not planned, this process will yield more information about the projected value of the consulting intervention than could be obtained from raw test scores. This process represents an expected return on investment based on the historical relationships involved. Second, by developing individual ROI measurements and communicating them to participants, the process provides reinforcement potential. It communicates to participants that increased sales and market share are expected to result from the application of what was learned in the consulting intervention. Third, this process can have considerable credibility with management and can preclude expensive follow-ups and postconsulting intervention monitoring. If these relationships are statistically sound, the estimate should have credibility with the target group.

Forecasting ROI with Application of Skills and Competencies

In almost every consulting project, participants are expected to change their on-the-job behaviors by applying what was learned in the intervention. On-the-job applications are very critical to consulting intervention success, particularly with the focus on competencies. Although the use of skills on the job is no guarantee of results, it is an underlying assumption for most consulting interventions that if the knowledge and skills are applied, results will follow. A few organizations attempt to take this process a step further and measure the value of on-the-job behavior changes and calculate the ROI. In these situations, estimates are taken from participants, their supervisors, the management group, or experts in the field. The following six steps are used to develop the ROI:

1. Develop competencies for the target job.
2. Indicate the percentage of job success that is represented by the competencies included in the consulting intervention.
3. Determine the monetary values of competencies using salaries and employee benefits of participants.
4. Compute the worth of pre- and postconsulting intervention skill levels.
5. Subtract postconsulting intervention values from preconsulting intervention values.
6. Compare the total added benefits with the consulting intervention costs.

Perhaps an example will help illustrate one technique for measuring the value of on-the-job applications. With the help of consultants, the United States government redesigned its introduction to supervision course, a five-day learning solution for newly appointed supervisors.[1] The consulting intervention focuses on eight competencies:

1. Role and responsibilities of the supervisor
2. Communications
3. Planning, assigning, controlling, and evaluating work
4. Ethics
5. Leadership
6. Analyzing performance problems
7. Customer service
8. Managing diversity

The immediate managers of the new supervisors indicated that these eight competencies accounted for 81 percent of first-level supervisors' jobs. For the target group being evaluated, the average annual salary plus benefits for the newly appointed supervisors was $42,202. Thus, multiplying this figure by the amount of job success accounted for by the competencies (81 percent) yielded a dollar value of $34,184 per participant. In other words, if a person performed successfully in these eight competencies for one year, the value to the agency would be $34,184. Of course, this assumes that employees are paid an amount equal to their contribution when they are fully competent.

Using a scale of 0 to 9, managers rated the skills for each of the competencies before the consulting intervention was conducted. The average level of skills required to be successful in the job was determined to be 6.44. The skill rating prior to the job was 4.96, which represented 77 percent of the 6.44 (i.e., participants were performing at 77 percent of the level required to be successful in the competencies). After the consulting intervention, the skill rating was 5.59, representing 87 percent of the level necessary to be successful.

Monetary values were assigned based on the participants' salaries. Performance at the required level was worth $34,184. At a 77 percent proficiency level, the new supervisors were performing at a contribution value of $26,322. After the application of the learning, this value had reached 87 percent, representing a contribution value of $29,740.

The difference in these values, $3418, represents the gain per participant attributable to the course. The consulting intervention cost was $1368 per participant. Thus, the ROI is:

$$\text{ROI} = \frac{\$3418 - \$1368}{\$1368} = \frac{\$2050}{\$1368} \times 100 = 150\%$$

As with other estimates, a word of caution is in order. These results are subjective because the rating systems used are subjective and may not necessarily reflect an accurate assessment of the value of the consulting intervention. Also, since a consulting intervention is usually implemented to help the organization achieve its objectives, some managers insist on tangible changes in hard data such as quantity, quality, cost, and time. For them, a Level 3 evaluation is not always a good substitute for Level 4 data, if Level 4 data are available. In this example, an assumption is made that competencies acquired and applied will influence Level 4 business measures.

Although this process is subjective, it has several useful advantages. First, if there are no plans to track the actual impact of the consulting intervention in terms of specific, measurable business results (Level 4), then this approach represents a credible substitute. In many consulting interventions, particularly with skill building for supervisors, it is difficult to identify tangible changes on the job. Therefore, alternate methods of determining the worth of a consulting intervention are needed. Second, this approach results in data that are usually credible with the management group if management understands how the data are developed and the assumptions behind the data. An important point regarding the projected ROI for the U.S. government course is that the data on the changes in competence level came from the managers who rated their supervisors. In this specific project, the numbers were large enough to make the process statistically significant.

ROI with Business Impact Data

For most consulting interventions evaluated with ROI calculations, the focus is on the business impact measures (Level 4 data) influenced by the consulting project. These measures are usually expressed in terms of cost reduction, productivity increases, improved quality, increased customer service, or reduced response times. It is relatively easy to convert them to monetary values for an ROI calculation. Earlier chapters focused on this type of data for ROI calculations, so additional detail is not needed here.

ROI calculations on business results are very credible and reliable if appropriate steps have been taken to isolate the effects of the consulting intervention and accurately convert the results to monetary units. When ROI data are needed, this level of evaluation should always be sought if at all possible. Thus, ROI with Level 4 data becomes the fifth level of evaluation—the ultimate level of accountability.

Shortcut Ways for Forecasting ROI

This chapter presents the techniques for forecasting the ROI at four different time frames using four different levels of evaluation data. Two of these techniques are useful for very simple and inexpensive projects. Forecasting using learning data at Level 2 and application data at Level 3 is rare and should be reserved only for large-scale projects involving significant learning events. There are two very useful techniques that may be helpful even in short-term, low-profile, inexpensive projects.

Preproject Forecasting

Preproject forecasting may be necessary and actually desired even if it is not required. Because Level 4 data are the drivers of the consulting project, business impact measures should be identified up front. Estimating the actual change in these measures is a recommended and highly useful exercise, as it begins to show the client and the consultant the perceived value of the project. This is a simple exercise that should take no more than one or two days. The result can be extremely valuable in communicating to the client and in providing some clear direction and focus for the consultant.

Forecasting with Reaction Data

In almost every consulting assignment, reaction data are collected from the participants involved in a consulting project. A worthwhile extension of reaction data is to include several questions that allow those individuals to project the success of the project. This was discussed as an option in Chapter 4. Here it is recommended as another simple tool for forecasting the actual ROI. This provides some additional insight into the potential worth of the project and alerts the consultant and consulting staff to potential problems or issues that may need attention as the remaining issues are addressed in the consulting intervention. The additional questions are very simple and can easily be obtained with 15 to 20 minutes of the participants' time. For the process to be successful and usable, participants must be committed to it. This can usually be achieved by exploring ways to increase the response rate for the various instruments described in this book.

Final Thoughts

This chapter illustrates that ROI calculations can be developed at different times and different levels of evaluation, although most consultants and clients focus only on Level 4 data for ROI calculations. While postconsulting intervention data are desired, there are situations where Level 4 data are not available in a postintervention time frame or where evaluations at that level are not attempted or planned. ROI estimates developed at Levels 1, 2, and 3 can be useful to management and the consulting staff while at the same time focusing the participants' attention on the economic impact of the consulting intervention. Using ROI estimates at Levels 1 and 2 may give a false sense of accuracy. Figure 13.1 shows the relationship of ROI at the different levels. As would be expected, ROI calculations with Level 1 data are the lowest in terms of credibility and accuracy but have the advantage of being inexpensive and relatively easy to develop. ROI calculations using Level 4 data are rich in credibility and accuracy but are very expensive and difficult to develop. Although ROI calculations at Level 4 are preferred, ROI development at other levels is an important part of a comprehensive and systematic evaluation process.

References

1. Broad, Mary L, Lisa Szymanski, Alex Douds, and Jack J. Phillips. "Built-in Evaluation: U.S. Government," in *In Action: Measuring Return on Investment* (vol. 1), Jack J. Phillips (ed.). Alexandria, VA: American Society for Training and Development, 1994, pp. 55–70.

Further Reading

Dean, Peter J., Ph.D., and David E. Ripley (eds.). *Performance Improvement Interventions: Performance Technologies in the Workplace: Volume Three of the Performance Improvement Series: Methods for Organizational Learning*. Washington, DC: The International Society for Performance Improvement, 1998.

Esque, Timm J., and Patricia A. Patterson. *Getting Results: Case Studies in Performance Improvement* (vol. 1). Washington, DC: HRD/International Society for Performance Improvement, 1998.

Friedlob, George T., and Franklin J. Plewa Jr. *Understanding Return on Investment*. New York: Wiley, 1991.

Hale, Judith. *The Performance Consultant's Fieldbook: Tools and Techniques for Improving Organizations and People*. San Francisco: Jossey-Bass/Pfeiffer, 1998.

Kaufman, Roger, Sivasailam Thiagarajan, and Paula MacGillis. *The Guidebook for Performance Improvement: Working with Individuals and Organizations*. San Francisco: Jossey-Bass/Pfeiffer, 1997.

Phillips, Jack J. *Return on Investment in Training and Performance Improvement Programs*. Houston, TX: Gulf, 1997.

Price Waterhouse Financial & Cost Management Team. *CFO: Architect of the Corporation's Future*. New York: Wiley, 1997.

Swanson, Richard A. *Analysis for Improving Performance: Tools for Diagnosing Organizations & Documenting Workplace Expertise*. San Francisco: Berrett-Koehler, 1994.

How to Provide Feedback and Communicate Results to the Client

WITH DATA IN hand, what's next? Should the data be used to modify the project, change the process, show the contribution, justify new projects, gain additional support, or build goodwill? How should the data be presented? The worst course of action is to do nothing. Communicating results is as important as achieving them. Achieving results without communicating them is like planting seeds and then failing to fertilize and cultivate the seedlings—the yield simply won't be as great. This chapter provides useful information about presenting evaluation data to the various audiences using both oral and written reporting methods.

Why Be Concerned About Communicating Results?

Communicating results is a critical issue in consulting interventions. While it is important to communicate achieved results to interested stakeholders once the project is complete, it is also important to communicate throughout the intervention. This ensures that information is flowing so that adjustments can be made and so that all stakeholders are aware of the success and issues surrounding the consulting project. There are at least five key reasons for being concerned about communication in a consulting project.

Measurement and Evaluation Mean Nothing Without Communication

As Mark Twain once said, "Collecting data is like collecting garbage—pretty soon we will have to do something with it." Measuring success and collecting evaluation data mean nothing unless the findings are communicated promptly to the appropriate audiences so that they will be aware of what is occurring and can take action if necessary. Communication allows a full loop to be made from the project results to necessary actions based on those results.

Communication Is Necessary for Making Improvements

Because information is collected at different points during the process, the communication or feedback to the various groups that will take action is the only way adjustments can be made. Thus, the quality and timeliness of communication become critical issues for making necessary adjustments or improvements. Even after a project is completed, communication is necessary to make sure the target audience fully understands the results achieved and how those results could be enhanced either in future projects or in the current project, if it is still operational. Communication is the key to making these important adjustments at all phases of the project.

Communication Is Necessary for Explaining Contributions

The contribution of the consulting project surrounding the six major types of measures is a confusing issue at best. The different target audiences will need a thorough explanation of the results. A communication strategy including techniques, media, and the overall process will determine the extent to which the audiences understand the contribution. Communicating results, particularly with business impact and ROI, can quickly become confusing for even the most sophisticated target audiences. Communication must be planned and implemented with the goal of making sure the audiences understand the full contribution.

Communication Is a Sensitive Issue

Communication is one of those important issues that can cause major problems. Because the results of an intervention can be closely linked to the political issues in an organization, communication can upset some individuals while pleasing others. If certain individuals do not receive the information or if it is delivered inconsistently from one group to another, problems can quickly surface. Not only is it an understanding issue, it is also a fairness, quality, and political correctness issue to make sure communication is properly constructed and effectively delivered to all key individuals who need the information.

A Variety of Target Audiences Need Different Information

Because there are so many potential target audiences for communication on the success of a consulting project, it is important for the communication to be tailored directly to their needs. A varied audience will command varied needs. Planning and effort are necessary to make sure the audience receives all of the information it needs, in the proper format, and at the proper time. A single report for all audiences may not be appropriate. The scope, size, media, and even the actual information of different types and different levels will vary significantly from one group to another, making the target audience the key to determining the appropriate communication process.

Collectively, these reasons make communication a critical issue, although it is often overlooked or underestimated in consulting interventions. This chapter builds on this important issue and shows a variety of techniques for accomplishing all types of communication for various target audiences.

Principles of Communicating Results

The skills required to communicate results effectively are almost as delicate and sophisticated as those needed to obtain results. The style is as important as the substance. Regardless of the message, audience, or medium, a few general principles apply and are explored next.

Communication Must Be Timely

Usually, consulting results should be communicated as soon as they are known. From a practical standpoint, it may be best to delay the communication until a convenient time, such as the publication of the next client newsletter or the next general management meeting. Questions about timing must be answered. Is the audience ready for the results in light of other things that may have happened? Is it expecting results? When is the best time for having the maximum effect on the audience? Are there circumstances that dictate a change in the timing of the communication?

Communication Should Be Targeted to Specific Audiences

Communication will be more effective if it is designed for a particular group. The message should be specifically tailored to the interests, needs, and expectations of the target audience.

The results of a consultant's projects are used in this chapter and reflect outcomes at all levels, including the six types of data developed in this book. Some of the data are developed earlier in the project and communicated during the project. Other data are collected after the project's implementation and communicated in a follow-up study. Thus, the results, in their broadest sense, may involve early feedback in qualitative terms to ROI values in varying quantitative terms.

Media Should Be Carefully Selected

For particular groups, some media may be more effective than others. Face-to-face meetings may be better than special bulletins. A memo distributed exclusively to top management may be more effective than the company newsletter. The proper method of communication can help improve the effectiveness of the process.

Communication Should Be Unbiased and Modest

It is important to separate fact from fiction and accurate statements from opinions. Various audiences may accept communication from consultants with skepticism, anticipating biased opinions. Boastful statements sometimes turn off recipients, and most of the content is lost. Observable, believable facts carry far more weight than extreme or sensational claims. Although such claims may get audience attention, they often detract from the importance of the results.

Communication Must Be Consistent

The timing and content of the communication should be consistent with past practices. A special communication at an unusual time during the consulting intervention may provoke suspicion. Also, if a particular group, such as top management, regularly receives communication on consulting outcomes, it should continue receiving communication—even if the results are not positive. If some results are omitted, it might leave the impression that only positive results are reported.

Testimonials Are More Effective Coming from Individuals the Audience Respects

People's opinions are strongly influenced by those of others, particularly others who are respected and trusted. Testimonials about consulting results, when solicited from individuals respected by others in the organization, can influence the effectiveness of the message. This respect may be related to leadership ability, position, special skills, or knowledge. A testimonial from an individual who commands little respect and is regarded as a substandard performer can have a negative impact on the message.

The Audience's Opinion of the Consulting Firm Will Influence the Communication Strategy

Opinions are difficult to change, and a negative opinion of the consulting firm may not be altered by the mere presentation of facts. However, the presentation of facts alone may strengthen the opinions held by those who already agree with the consulting results. It helps reinforce their position and provides a defense in discussions with others. A consulting firm with a high level of credibility and respect may have a relatively easy time communicating results. Low credibility can create problems when trying to be persuasive. The reputation of the firm is an important consideration in developing the overall strategy.

These general principles are important to the overall success of the communication effort. They should serve as a checklist for the consulting team during dissemination of program results.

A Model for Communicating Results

The process of communicating program results must be systematic, timely, and well planned, as illustrated in the model in Figure 14.1. The model represents seven components of the communication process that should normally occur in the sequence shown.

The first step is one of the most important and consists of an analysis of the need to communicate results from a consulting intervention. Possibly, a lack of support for the consulting effort was identified, and perhaps the need for making changes to or continuing to fund the project was uncovered. There may be a need to restore confidence or build credibility for the consulting project. Regardless of the triggering events, an important first step is to outline the specific reasons for communicating the results of the program.

The second step focuses on a plan for communication. Planning is very important and usually involves three types of plans rather than an overall plan for communicating results in all types of consulting projects. The first plan includes numerous issues to be addressed in all communication about the project. The second plan covers the communication around the project, detailing exactly what will be communicated, when, and to which groups. The third plan covers communicating specific types of data, such as the results at the end in terms of an impact study.

The third step involves selecting the target audiences for communication. Audiences range from top management to past participants, all of whom have their own special communication needs. All groups should be considered in the communication strategy. An artfully crafted, targeted communication may be necessary to win the approval of a specific group.

The fourth step involves developing written material to explain program results. This can include a wide variety of possibilities, from a brief summary of the results to a detailed research report on the evalu-

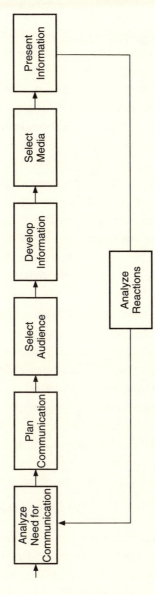

Figure 14.1 Communications model.

ation effort. Usually, a complete report is developed, and then selected parts or summaries from the report are used for different media.

Selecting the medium is the fifth step. Some groups respond more favorably to certain methods of communication. A variety of approaches, both oral and written, are available to the consulting professional.

Information is presented in the sixth step. The product is delivered with the utmost care, confidence, and professionalism.

The last step, but not the least significant, is analyzing reactions to the communications. Positive reactions, negative reactions, and a lack of comments are all indicators of how well the information was received and understood. An informational but unscientific analysis may be appropriate for many situations. Tuning in to the reaction of a specific group may often suffice. For an extensive and more involved communication effort, a formal and structured feedback process may be necessary. Reactions could trigger an adjustment to the communication of the same project results or provide input to make adjustments for future project communications.

This communications model is not intended to make the process complicated. Rather, it is a method of ensuring that clear, accurate information is provided to the appropriate audiences. More than one audience usually receives the results of a consulting intervention, and each audience has its own unique needs. Each of the components in the model should be given consideration, if only informally, before the communications strategy is developed. Otherwise, the full impact of the effort may be diminished. The various steps in the model are amplified in the remainder of this chapter.

Analyzing the Need for Communication

Because there may be other reasons for communicating results, a list should be tailored to the organization and adjusted as necessary. The reasons for communicating consulting results depend on the specific project, the setting, and the unique needs of the client. The most common reasons are:

- *To secure approval for the consulting project and allocate resources of time and money.* The initial communication presents a proposal, a projected ROI, or other data that are intended to secure the project approval. This communication may not contain very much data but rather may anticipate what is to come.

- *To gain support for the project and its objectives.* It is important to have support from a variety of groups. This communication is intended to build the necessary support to make the project work successfully.

- *To secure agreement on the issues, solutions, and resources.* As the project begins, it is important for all those directly involved to have some agreement and understanding of the important elements and requirements surrounding the project.

- *To build credibility for the consulting firm, its techniques, and the finished products.* It is important early in the process to make sure that those involved understand the approach and reputation of the consulting firm, and, based on the approach taken, the commitments made by all parties.

- *To reinforce the processes used in the consulting intervention.* It is important for key managers to support the intervention and reinforce the various processes used in the consulting project. This communication is designed to enhance those processes.

- *To drive action for improvement in the consulting project.* This early communication is designed as a process improvement tool to effect changes and improvements as the needs are uncovered and suggestions are made by various individuals.

- *To prepare participants for the consulting project.* It is necessary for those most directly involved in the project—the consulting participants—to be prepared for assignments, roles, and responsibilities that will be required of them as they bring success to the project.

- *To enhance results throughout the project and the quality of future feedback.* This communication is designed to show the status of the project and to influence decisions, seek support, or communicate events and expectations to the key stakeholders. In addition, it will enhance both the quality and quantity of information as stakeholders see the feedback cycle in action.

- *To show the complete results of the consulting intervention.* This is perhaps the most important communication, where all of the results involving all six types of measures are communicated to the appropriate individuals so that they have a full understanding of the success or shortcomings of the project.

- *To underscore the importance of measuring results.* Some individuals need to understand the importance of measurement and evaluation and see the need for collecting important data on different measures.
- *To explain techniques used to measure results.* Several individuals on the client team and support staff need to understand the techniques used in measuring results. In some cases, these techniques may be transferred internally for use with other projects. In short, these individuals need to understand the soundness and theoretical framework of the process used.
- *To stimulate desire in participants to be involved in the project.* Ideally, consulting participants want to be involved in the consulting project. This communication is designed to pique their interest in the project, the assignment, and their importance to the project.
- *To stimulate interest in the consulting firm's products.* From a consulting firm perspective, some communications are designed to create client interest in all of the products and services based on the results obtained by the current product or process.
- *To demonstrate accountability for client expenditures.* It is important for a broad group to understand the need for accountability and the approach of the consultant or the consulting firm. This ensures accountability for expenditures on the project.
- *To market future consulting projects.* From a consulting firm perspective, it is important to build a database of successful projects to use in convincing others that the consulting process can add value.

Because there may be other reasons for communicating results, the list should be tailored to the individual organization.

Planning the Communication

Any type of successful activity must be carefully planned to produce the maximum results. This is a critical part of communicating the results of consulting assignments. The planning of the communications is important to ensure that each audience receives the proper information at the right time and that appropriate actions are taken. Three separate issues are important in planning the communication of results, as presented next.

Communication Policy Issues

In examining the complete consulting process, policy issues need to be developed around the communication of results. These range from providing feedback during a project to communicating the ROI from an impact study. Policy issues rest with both the client and the consultant. Internally, the client group may want to develop the policy regarding communication results as part of an overall policy on consulting assignments. From the consulting firm standpoint, the policy may be developed as part of the overall results-based approach to consulting interventions. Seven different areas will need some attention as the policies are developed:

1. *What will actually be communicated?* It is important to detail the types of information communicated throughout the consulting project—not only the six types of data from the consulting ROI process model, but the overall progress with consulting may be a topic of communications as well.

2. *When will the data be communicated?* With communications, timing is critical. If adjustments in the project need to be made, the information should be communicated quickly so that swift actions can be taken.

3. *How will the information be communicated?* This shows the preferences toward particular types of communication media. For example, some organizations prefer to have written documents sent out as reports, while others prefer face-to-face meetings, and still others want electronic communications utilized as much as possible.

4. *The location for communication.* Some prefer that communication take place close to the consulting assignment, others prefer client offices, and still others prefer the consulting firm's facilities. The location can be an important issue in terms of convenience and perception.

5. *Who will communicate the information?* Will the consulting group, an independent person, or an individual involved on the client

team communicate the information? The person communicating must have credibility so that the information is believable.

6. *The target audience.* Identify specific target audiences that should always receive information and others that will receive information when appropriate.

7. *The specific actions that are required or desired.* When information is presented, in some cases no action is needed; in others, changes are desired and sometimes even required.

Collectively these seven issues frame the policy around communication as a whole.

Planning the Communication Around the Entire Project

When a project is approved, the communication plan is usually developed. This details how specific information is developed and communicated to various groups and the expected actions. In addition, this plan details how the overall results will be communicated, the time frames for communication, and the appropriate groups to receive information. The client and consultant need to agree on the extent of detail in the plan. Additional information on this type of planning is provided later.

Communicating an Impact Study

The third type of plan is aimed at presenting the results of an impact study. This occurs when a major consulting project is completed and the overall, detailed results are known. One of the major issues is who should receive the results and in what form. This is more specialized than the plan for the entire project because it involves the final study from the project. Table 14.1 shows the communication plan for a major team-based consulting intervention that had a stress reduction solution. Teams were experiencing high levels of stress; then, through a variety of activities and job changes, stress began to diminish among the teams. The same process was made available to other teams who were experiencing similar symptoms.

Five different communication pieces were developed for different audiences. The complete report was an ROI impact study, a 75-page report that served as the historical document for the project. It went to the client, the consulting staff, and the particular manager of each of the

Table 14.1 Consulting Project Communication Plan

Communication Document	Communication Target(s)	Distribution Method
Complete report with appendices (75 pages)	• Client team • Consulting staff • Intact team manager	Distribute and discuss in a special meeting
Executive summary (8 pages)	• Senior management in the business units • Senior corporate management	Distribute and discuss in routine meeting
General interest overview and summary without actual ROI calculation (10 pages)	• Participants	Mail with letter
General interest article (1 page)	• All employees	Publish in company publication
Brochure highlighting project, objectives, and specific results	• Team leaders with an interest in the project • Other clients	Include with other marketing materials

teams involved in the studies. An executive summary—a much smaller document—went to some of the higher-level executives. A general interest overview and summary without the ROI calculation went to the participants. A general interest article was developed for company publications, and a brochure was developed to show the success of the consulting project. The brochure was used in marketing the same process internally to other teams and served as additional marketing material for the consulting firm. This detailed plan may be part of the overall plan for the consulting assignment but may be fine-tuned during the actual consulting process.

Collectively, these three types of plans underscore the importance of organizing the communication strategy for a particular consulting project or the overall consulting process in an organization.

Selecting the Audience for Communications

When approaching a particular audience, the following questions should be asked about members of each potential group:

- Are they interested in the project?
- Do they really want to receive the information?
- Has someone already made a commitment to them regarding communication?
- Is the timing right for this audience?
- Are they familiar with the project?
- How do they prefer to have results communicated?
- Do they know the consultants? The consulting firm?
- Are they likely to find the results threatening?
- Which medium will be most convincing to them?

For each target audience, three actions are needed:

1. To the greatest extent possible, the consultants should know and understand the target audience.
2. The consultants should find out what information is needed and why. Each group will have its own needs relative to the information desired. Some want detailed information, while others want brief encapsulations. Rely on the input from others to determine audience needs.
3. The consultants should try to understand audience bias. Each group will have a particular bias or opinion. Some will quickly support the results, whereas others may be against them or be neutral. The staff should be empathetic and try to understand differing views. With this understanding, communications can be tailored to each group. This is especially critical when the potential exists for the audience to react negatively to the results.

Basis for Selecting the Audience

The potential target audiences to receive information on consulting results are varied in terms of job levels and responsibilities. Determining which groups will receive a particular communication piece deserves careful thought, as problems can arise when a particular group receives inappropriate information or is omitted altogether. A sound basis for proper audience selection is analyzing the reason for communication, as discussed earlier. Table 14.2 shows common target audiences and the basis for selecting the audience.

Perhaps the most important audience is the client or client team. This group (or individual) initiates the project, reviews data, selects the consultant, and weighs the final assessment of the effectiveness of the project. Another important target audience is the top management group. This group is responsible for allocating resources to the consulting intervention and needs information to help justify expenditures and gauge the effectiveness of the efforts.

Selected groups of managers (or all managers) are also important target audiences. Management's support and involvement in the con-

Table 14.2 Common Target Audiences

Reason for Communication	Primary Target Audiences
To secure approval for the project	Client, top executives
To gain support for the project	Immediate managers, team leaders
To secure agreement with the issues	Participants, team leaders
To build credibility for the consulting firm	Top executives
To enhance reinforcement of the processes	Immediate managers
To drive action for improvement	Consultants
To prepare participants for the project	Team leaders
To enhance results and the quality of future feedback	Participants
To show the complete results of the project	Client team
To underscore the importance of measuring results	Client, consultants
To explain techniques used to measure results	Client, support staff
To create desire for a participant to be involved	Team leaders
To stimulate interest in the consulting firm's products	Top executives
To demonstrate accountability for client expenditures	All employees
To market future consulting projects	Prospective clients

sulting process and the department's credibility are important to success. Effectively communicating program results to management can increase both support and credibility.

Communicating with the participants' team leaders or immediate managers is essential. In many cases, these people must encourage participants to implement the project. Also, they often support and reinforce the objectives of the project. An appropriate return on investment improves the commitment to consulting interventions and provides credibility for the consulting staff.

Occasionally, results are communicated to encourage participation in the project. This is especially true for those projects offered on a volunteer basis. The potential participants are important targets for communicating results.

Consulting participants need feedback on the overall success of the effort. Some individuals may not have been as successful as others in achieving the desired results. Communicating the results adds additional pressure to effectively implement the project and improve results for the future. For those achieving excellent results, the communication will serve as a reinforcement of the consulting intervention. Communicating results to project participants is often overlooked, under the assumption that since the project is over, the participants do not need to be informed of its success.

The consulting staff must receive information about program results. Whether for small projects where consultants receive a project update or for larger projects where a complete team is involved, those who design, develop, facilitate, and implement the project must be given information on the project's effectiveness. Evaluation information is necessary so adjustments can be made if the program is not as effective as it could be.

The support staff should receive detailed information about the process for measuring results. This group provides support services to the consulting team, usually in the department where the project is conducted.

Company employees and stockholders may be less likely targets. General interest news stories may increase employee respect. Goodwill and positive attitudes toward the organization may also be by-products of communicating project results. Stockholders, on the other hand, are more interested in the return on their investment.

While Table 14.2 shows the most common target audiences, there can be others in a particular organization. For instance, management or employees could be subdivided into different departments, divisions, or even subsidiaries of the organization. The number of audiences can be large in a complex organization. At a minimum, four target audiences are always recommended: a senior management group, the participants' immediate manager or team leader, the consulting participants, and the consulting staff.

Developing the Information: The Impact Study

The type of formal evaluation report depends on the extent of detailed information presented to the various target audiences. Brief summaries of project results with appropriate charts may be sufficient for some communication efforts. In other situations, particularly with significant consulting interventions requiring extensive funding, the amount of detail in the evaluation report is more crucial. A complete and comprehensive impact study report may be necessary. This report can then be used as the basis of information for specific audiences and various media. The report may contain the following sections.

Management/Executive Summary

The management summary is a brief overview of the entire report, explaining the basis for the evaluation and the significant conclusions and recommendations. It is designed for individuals who are too busy to read a detailed report. It is usually written last but appears first in the report for easy access.

Background Information

The background information provides a general description of the project. If applicable, the needs assessment that led to the implementation of the project is summarized. The solution is fully described, including the events that led to the consulting intervention. Other specific items necessary to provide a full description of the project are included. The extent of detailed information depends on the amount of information the audience needs.

Objectives

The objectives for both the project and the solutions are outlined. Sometimes they are the same, but they may be separate: this distinction is presented in Chapter 3. The report details the particular objectives of the study itself so that the reader clearly understands desired accomplishments for the assignment or intervention. In addition, if specific consulting solutions have been implemented during this process, they are detailed here, as these are the issues or objectives from which the different types or levels of data will be collected.

Evaluation Strategy/Methodology

The evaluation strategy outlines all of the components that make up the evaluation process. Several components of the results-based model and the ROI process presented in this book are discussed in this section of the report. The specific purposes of evaluation are outlined, and the evaluation design and methodology are explained. The instruments used in data collection are also described and presented as exhibits. Any unusual issues in the evaluation design are discussed. Finally, other useful information related to the design, timing, and execution of the evaluation is included.

Data Collection and Analysis

This section explains the methods used to collect data as outlined in earlier chapters. The data collected are usually presented in the report in summary form. Next, the methods used to analyze data are presented with interpretations.

Program Costs

Program costs are presented in this section. A summary of the costs by category is included. For example, analysis, development, implementation, and evaluation costs are recommended categories for cost presentation. The assumptions made in developing and classifying costs are discussed in this section of the report.

Reaction and Satisfaction

This section details the data collected from key stakeholders, particularly the participants involved in the process, to measure reactions to the consulting project and levels of satisfaction with various issues and parts of the process. Other input from the client group is also included to show levels of satisfaction.

Learning

This section shows a brief summary of the formal and informal methods for measuring learning. It explains how participants have learned new processes, skills, tasks, procedures, and practices from the consulting project.

Application and Implementation

This section shows how the project was actually implemented and the degree of success achieved with the application of new skills and knowledge. Implementation issues are addressed, including any major success and/or lack of success.

Business Impact

This section shows the business impact measures representing the business needs that initially drove the project. This shows the extent to which performance has changed during the implementation of the consulting intervention.

Return on Investment

This section shows the ROI calculation along with the benefit-cost ratio. It compares the value to what was expected and provides an interpretation of the calculation.

Intangible Measures

This section shows the various intangible measures directly linked to the consulting intervention. Intangibles are those measures not converted to monetary values or included in the ROI calculation.

Barriers and Enablers

In this section, the various problems and obstacles affecting the success of the project are detailed and presented as barriers to implementation. Also, those factors or influences that have had a positive effect on the project are included as enablers. Together, these provide tremendous insight into what can hinder or enhance projects in the future.

Conclusions and Recommendations

This section presents conclusions based on all of the results. If appropriate, brief explanations are presented of how each conclusion was reached. A list of recommendations or changes in the program, if appropriate, is provided with brief explanations for each recommendation. It is important that the conclusions and recommendations be consistent with one another and with the findings described in the previous section.

These components make up the major parts of a complete evaluation report.

Developing the Report

Table 14.3 shows the table of contents from a typical evaluation report for an ROI evaluation. This specific study was conducted for a large financial institution and involved an ROI analysis on a consulting project for commercial banking. The typical report provides background information, explains the processes used, and—most importantly—presents the results.

While this report is an effective, professional way to present ROI data, several cautions need to be followed. Since this document reports the success of a consulting intervention involving a group of employees, complete credit for the success must go to the participants and their

Table 14.3   Format of an Impact Study Report

- General information
  - Background
  - Objectives of study
- Methodology for impact study
  - Levels of evaluation
  - ROI process
  - Collecting data
  - Isolating the effects of consulting
  - Converting data to monetary values
- Data analysis issues
- Costs
- Results: general information
  - Response profile
  - Success with objectives
- Results: reaction and satisfaction
  - Data sources
  - Data summary
  - Key issues
- Results: learning
  - Data sources
  - Data summary
  - Key issues
- Results: application and implementation
  - Data sources
  - Data summary
  - Key issues
- Results: business impact
  - General comments
  - Linkage with business measures
  - Key issues
- Results: ROI and its meaning
- Results: intangible measures
- Barriers and enablers
  - Barriers
  - Enablers
- Conclusions and recommendations
  - Conclusions
  - Recommendations
- Exhibits

immediate leaders, whose performance generated the success. Another important caution is to avoid boasting about results. Although the ROI process may be accurate and credible, it still may have some subjective issues. Huge claims of success can quickly turn off an audience and interfere with the delivery of the desired message.

A final caution concerns the structure of the report. The methodology should be clearly explained, along with assumptions made in the analysis. The reader should readily see how the values were developed and how the specific steps were followed to make the process more conservative, credible, and accurate. Detailed statistical analyses should be placed in the appendix.

Selecting the Communication Media

There are many options available for communicating program results. In addition to the impact study report, the most frequently used media are meetings, interim and progress reports, the organization's publications, and case studies.

Meetings

If used properly, meetings are fertile opportunities for communicating program results. All organizations have a variety of meetings, and in each the proper context and consulting results are an important part. A few examples illustrate the variety of meetings.

Staff Meetings
Throughout the chain of command, staff meetings are held to review progress, discuss current problems, and distribute information. These meetings can be an excellent forum for discussing the results achieved in a consulting intervention when it relates to the group's activities. Project results can be sent to executives for use in staff meetings, or a member of the consulting team can attend the meeting to make the presentation.

Manager Meetings
Regular meetings with the first-level management group are quite common. Typically, items are discussed that will possibly help their

work units. A discussion of a consulting project and the subsequent results can be integrated into the regular meeting format.

Panel Discussions
Although not common in all organizations, panel discussions can be very helpful in showing how a problem was solved. A typical panel might include two or more managers or team leaders discussing their approach to a solution of a problem common to other areas. A successful discussion based on the results of a recent project can provide convincing data to other managers.

Best Practices Meetings
Some organizations have best practices meetings or video conferences to discuss recent successes and best practices. This is an excellent opportunity to learn and to share methodologies and results.

Business Update Meetings
A few organizations have initiated periodic meetings for all members of management, in which the CEO reviews progress and discusses plans for the coming year. A few highlights of consulting project results can be integrated into the CEO's speech, showing top executive interest, commitment, and support. Consulting results are mentioned along with operating profit, new facilities and equipment, new company acquisitions, and next year's sales forecast.

Whenever a management group convenes in significant numbers, evaluate the appropriateness of communicating consulting project results.

Interim and Progress Reports

Although interim and routine memos and reports are usually limited to large projects, they can be a highly visible way to communicate results. Published or disseminated via the computer intranet on a periodic basis, these reports usually have several purposes:

- To inform management about the status of the project
- To communicate the interim results achieved in the consulting intervention
- To activate needed changes and improvements

A more subtle reason for these reports is to gain additional support and commitment from the management group and to keep the project intact. These reports are produced by the consulting staff and distributed to a select group of managers in the organization. Format and scope vary considerably. Common topics are presented here.

Schedule of Activities
A schedule of planned steps/activities should be an integral part of this report. A brief description should be presented.

Reactions from Consulting Participants
A brief summary of reaction evaluations may be appropriate to report initial success. Also, brief interviews with participants might be included.

Project Results
A key focus of this report is the results achieved from the consulting project. Significant results that can be documented should be presented in an easily understood format. The method(s) of evaluation should be briefly outlined, along with the measurement data.

Support Team Member Spotlight
A section that features a key support team member can be very useful. Emphasis is placed on the member's efforts and involvement in consulting activity. Statements or interview comments may be useful.

Change in Responsibility
Occasionally, people involved in planning, developing, implementing, or evaluating the project are reassigned, transferred, or promoted. It is important to communicate how these changes affect responsibilities and the project.

Participant Spotlight
A section that highlights a member of the client team can focus additional attention on results. This is an opportunity to recognize outstanding participants responsible for excellent results with the project and bring attention to unusual achievements.

While the preceding list may not be suited for every report, it represents topics that should be presented to the management group.

When produced in a professional manner, the report can improve management support and commitment to the effort.

The Organization's Publications and Standard Communication Tools

To reach a wide audience, consultants can use in-house publications. Whether newsletters, magazines, newspapers, or electronic files, these types of media usually reach all employees. The information can be quite effective if communicated appropriately. The scope should be limited to general interest articles, announcements, and interviews. Following are types of issues that should be covered in these publications.

Program Results
Results communicated through these types of media must be significant enough to arouse general interest. For example, a story with the headline, "Safety Project Helps Produce 1 Million Hours Without a Lost-Time Accident," will catch the attention of many people because they may have participated in the project and can appreciate the significance of the results. Reports on the accomplishments of a group of participants may not create interest unless the audience relates to the accomplishments.

In many consulting interventions, results are achieved weeks or even months after the project is completed. Participants need reinforcement from many sources. If results are communicated to a general audience, including participants' subordinates or peers, there is additional pressure to continue the project or similar ones in the future.

Building Interest
Stories about participants involved in a consulting intervention and the results they achieve create a favorable image. Employees are made aware that the company is investing time and money to improve performance and prepare for the future. This type of story provides information about projects that employees otherwise may not have known about and sometimes creates a desire to participate if given the opportunity.

Participant Recognition
General audience communication can bring recognition to project participants, particularly those who excel in some aspect of the project.

When participants deliver unusual performance, public recognition can enhance their self-esteem.

Human Interest Stories

Many human interest stories can come out of consulting interventions. A rigorous project with difficult requirements can provide the basis for an interesting story on participants who implement the project.

In one organization, the editor of the company newsletter participated in a very demanding consulting project and wrote a stimulating article about what it was like to be a participant. The article gave the reader a tour of the entire project and its effectiveness in terms of results achieved. It was an interesting and effective way to communicate about a challenging activity.

The benefits are many and the opportunities endless for consultants to utilize in-house publications and company-wide intranets to let others know about the success of projects.

E-mail and Electronic Media

Internal and external Web pages on the Internet, company-wide intranets, and e-mail are excellent vehicles for releasing results, promoting ideas, and informing employees and other target groups of consulting results. E-mail, in particular, provides a virtually instantaneous means with which to communicate and solicit response from large numbers of people.

Project Brochures and Pamphlets

A brochure might be appropriate for projects conducted on a continuing basis, where participants have produced excellent results. It should be attractive and present a complete description of the project, with a major section devoted to results obtained with previous participants, if available. Measurable results and reactions from participants, or even direct quotes from individuals, could add spice to an otherwise dull brochure.

Case Studies

Case studies represent an effective way to communicate the results of a consulting project. Consequently, it is recommended that a few projects be developed in a case format. A typical case study describes the situation, provides appropriate background information (including the events that led to the intervention), presents the techniques and strategies used to develop the study, and highlights the key issues in the project. Case studies tell an interesting story of how the evaluation was developed and the problems and concerns identified along the way.

Case studies have many useful applications in an organization. First, they can be used in group discussions, where interested individuals can react to the material, offer different perspectives, and draw conclusions about approaches or techniques. Second, they can serve as self-teaching guides for individuals trying to understand how evaluations are developed and utilized in the organization. Finally, case studies provide appropriate recognition for those involved in the actual cases. More importantly, they recognize the participants who achieved the results, as well as the managers who allowed the participants to be involved in the project. The case study format has become one of the most effective vehicles for learning about project evaluation.

A Case Example

The various methods for communicating results can be creatively combined to fit any situation. Here is an effective example utilizing three approaches: a case study, management meetings, and a brochure.

The production division of a manufacturing company had achieved outstanding results through a consulting intervention involving processes and work flow. The results were in the form of key bottom-line measures, such as lost-time accidents, grievances, scrap rate, and unit hours. The unit hour was a basic measure of individual productivity.

These results were achieved through the efforts of the supervisors applying and implementing several consulting solutions. This fact was discreetly mentioned at the beginning of a presentation made by two of the supervisors. In a panel discussion format with a moderator, the two supervisors outlined the accuracy of the results. This was presented in a question-and-answer session during a monthly meeting for all supervisors. The supervisors mentioned that the results were linked to the consulting project.

The comments were published in a brochure and distributed to all supervisors through their department managers. The title of the publication was *Getting Results: A Success Story.* On the inside cover, specific results were detailed, along with additional information on the project. A close-up photograph of each supervisor, taken during the panel discussion, was included on this page. The next two pages presented a summary of the techniques used to secure the results. The brochure was used in staff meetings as a discussion guide to cover the points from the panel discussion. Top executives were also sent copies. In addition, the discussion was videotaped and used in subsequent interventions as a model of application for workplace changes to improve performance. The brochure also served as a handout.

The communication effort was a success. All levels of management had favorable responses and top executives asked the consultants to implement similar projects in other areas.

Communicating the Information

Perhaps the biggest challenge of communication is the delivery of the message. This can be accomplished in a variety of ways and settings based on the target audience and the media selected for the message. Three particular approaches deserve additional coverage. The first is providing insight into how to give feedback throughout the consulting project to make sure information flows so changes can be made. The second is presenting an impact study to a senior management team. This may be one of the most challenging tasks for the consultant. The third is communicating regularly and routinely with the executive management group. Each of these three approaches is explored in more detail.

Providing Feedback

One of the most important reasons for collecting reaction, satisfaction, and learning data is to provide feedback so that adjustments or changes can be made throughout the consulting project. In most consulting interventions, data are routinely collected and quickly communicated to a variety of groups. Table 14.4 shows a feedback action plan designed to provide information to several feedback audiences using a variety of media.

As the plan shows, data are collected during the project at four specific time intervals and communicated back to at least four audiences—

Table 14.4 Feedback Action Plan

Data Collection Item	Timing	Feedback Audience	Media	Timing of Feedback	Action Required
1. Preproject survey	Beginning of project	Client team participants	Meeting	1 week	None
• Climate/environment		Team leaders	Survey summary	2 weeks	None
• Issue identification		Consultants	Survey summary	2 weeks	Communicate feedback
			Meeting	1 week	Adjust approach
2. Implementation survey	Beginning of implementation	Client team participants	Meeting	1 week	None
• Reaction to plans		Team leaders	Survey summary	2 weeks	None
• Issue identification		Consultants	Survey summary	2 weeks	Communicate feedback
			Meeting	1 week	Adjust approach
3. Implementation reaction survey/interviews	One month into implementation	Client team participants	Meeting	1 week	Comments
		Support staff	Study summary	2 weeks	None
• Reaction to solution		Team leaders	Study summary	2 weeks	None
• Suggested changes		Immediate managers	Study summary	2 weeks	Support changes
			Study summary	3 weeks	Support changes
		Consultants	Meeting	3 days	Adjust approach
4. Implementation feedback questionnaire	End of implementation	Client team participants	Meeting	1 week	Comments
		Support staff	Study summary	2 weeks	None
• Reaction (satisfaction)		Team leaders	Study summary	2 weeks	None
• Barriers		Immediate managers	Study summary	2 weeks	Support changes
• Projected success			Study summary	3 weeks	Support changes
		Consultants	Meeting	3 days	Adjust approach

and sometimes six. Some of these feedback sessions result in identification of specific actions that need to be taken. This process becomes comprehensive and needs to be managed in a very proactive way. The following steps are recommended for providing feedback and managing the feedback process. Many of the steps and issues follow the recommendations given by Peter Block in his successful consulting book, *Flawless Consulting*.

1. *Communicate quickly.* Whether it is good news or bad news, it is important to let individuals involved in the project have the information as soon as possible. The recommended time for providing feedback is usually a matter of days and certainly no longer than a week or two after the results are known.

2. *Simplify the data.* Condense data into a very understandable, concise presentation. This is not the format for detailed explanations and analysis.

3. *Examine the role of the consultants and the client in the feedback situation.* Sometimes the consultant is the judge, and sometimes the consultant is the jury, prosecutor, defendant, or witness. On the other hand, sometimes the client is the judge, jury, prosecutor, defendant, or witness. It is important to examine the respective roles in terms of reactions to the data and the actions that need to be taken.

4. *Use negative data in a constructive way.* Some of the data will show that things are not going so well, and the fault may rest with the consulting firm or the client. In either case, the story basically changes from "Let's look at the success we've made," to "Now we know which areas to change."

5. *Use positive data in a cautious way.* Positive data can be misleading, and if they are communicated too enthusiastically they may create expectations beyond what may materialize later. Positive data should be presented in a cautious way—almost in a discounting mode.

6. *Choose the language of the meeting and communication very carefully.* Use language that is descriptive, focused, specific, short, and simple. Avoid language that is too judgmental, general, stereotypical, lengthy, or complex.

7. *Ask the client for reactions to the data.* After all, the client is the number one customer, and the client's reaction is critical since it is most important that the client is pleased with the project.

8. *Ask the client for recommendations.* The client may have some very good recommendations as to what needs to be changed to keep a project on track or put it back on track if it derails.

9. *Use support and confrontation carefully.* These two issues are not mutually exclusive. There may be times when support and confrontation are needed for the same group. The client may need support and yet be confronted for lack of improvement or sponsorship. The consulting group may be confronted on problem areas that have developed but may need support as well.

10. *React and act on the data.* Weigh the different alternatives and possibilities to arrive at the adjustments and changes that will be necessary.

11. *Secure agreement from all key stakeholders.* This is essential to make sure everyone is willing to make adjustments and changes that seem necessary.

12. *Keep the feedback process short.* Don't let it become bogged down in long, drawn-out meetings or lengthy documents. If this occurs, stakeholders will avoid the process instead of being willing to participate in the future.

Following these 12 steps will help move the project forward and provide important feedback, often ensuring that adjustments are supported and made.

Presenting Impact Study Data to Senior Management

Perhaps one of the most challenging and stressful communications is presenting an impact study to a senior management team that also serves as the client in a consulting project. The challenge is convincing this highly skeptical and critical group that outstanding results have been achieved (assuming they have) in a very reasonable time frame, addressing the salient points, and making sure the managers understand the process. Two particular issues can create challenges. First, if the results are very impressive, it may be difficult to make the managers believe the data. On the other extreme, if the data are negative, it will be a challenge to make sure managers don't overreact to the negative results and look for someone to blame. Following are guidelines that can help make sure this process is planned and executed properly:

- Plan a face-to-face meeting with senior team members for the first one or two major impact studies. If team members are unfamiliar with the complete consulting ROI process, a face-to-face meeting is necessary to make sure they understand the process. The good news is that they will probably attend the meeting because they have not seen ROI data developed for this type of project. The bad news is that it takes a lot of time—usually one to two hours—for this presentation.
- After a group has had a face-to-face meeting with a couple of presentations, an executive summary may suffice. At this point the team understands the process, so a shortened version may be appropriate.
- After the target audience is familiar with the process, a brief version may be necessary. This will involve a one- to two-page summary with charts and graphs showing all six types of measures.
- In making the initial presentation, the results should not be distributed beforehand or even during the session, but should be saved until the end of the session. This will allow enough time for presentation of the process and reaction to it before the target audience sees the actual ROI number.
- Present the process step by step, showing how and when the data were collected, who provided the data, how the data were isolated from other influences, and how the data were converted to monetary values. The various assumptions, adjustments, and conservative approaches are presented along with the total cost of the project. The costs are fully loaded so that the target audience will begin to buy into the process of developing the actual ROI.
- When the data are actually presented, the results are presented step by step, starting with Level 1, moving through Level 5, and ending with the intangibles. This allows the audience to see the reaction and satisfaction, learning, application and implementation, business impact, and ROI. After some discussion on the meaning of the ROI, the intangible measures are presented. Allocate time to each

level as appropriate for the audience. This helps overcome potentially negative reactions to a very positive or negative ROI.
- Show the consequences of additional accuracy if it is an issue. The
trade-off for more accuracy and validity often means more
expense. Address this issue whenever necessary, agreeing to add
more data if required.
- Collect concerns, reactions, and issues for the process and make
adjustments accordingly for the next presentation.

Collectively, these steps will help in preparing for and presenting
one of the most critical meetings in the consulting ROI process.

Communicating with Executive Management and Clients

No group is more important than top executives when it comes to communicating consulting results. In many situations, this group is also the
client. Improving communications with this group requires developing an
overall strategy, which may include all or part of the actions outlined next.

Strengthen the Relationship with Executives

An informal and productive relationship should be established between
the consultant responsible for the project and the top executive at the
location where the project is taking place. Each should feel comfortable
discussing needs and project results. One approach is to establish frequent, informal meetings with the executive to review problems with current projects and discuss other performance problems/opportunities in
the organization. Frank and open discussions can provide the executive
with insight not possible from any other source and can be very helpful to
the consulting firm in determining the direction of the initiative.

Show How Consulting Projects Have Helped Solve Major Problems

While hard results from recent projects are comforting to an executive,
solutions to immediate problems may be more convincing. This is an
excellent opportunity to discuss a possible future intervention.

Distribute Memos on Project Results

When an intervention has achieved significant results, make appropriate top executives aware of them. This can easily be done with a brief

memo or summary outlining what the project was supposed to accomplish, when it was implemented, who was involved, and the results achieved. This should be presented in a for-your-information format that consists of facts rather than opinions. A full report may be presented later.

All significant communications on consulting projects, plans, activities, and results should include the executive group. Frequent information on consulting projects, as long as it is not boastful, can reinforce credibility and accomplishments.

Ask the Executive to Be Involved in the Review

An effective way to enhance commitment from top executives is to ask them to serve on a consulting review committee. A review committee provides input and advice to the consulting staff on a variety of issues, including needs, problems with the present project, and project evaluation issues. This committee can be helpful in letting executives know what the projects are achieving.

Conduct a Consulting Review

A consulting review meeting is an effective way to communicate results to top executives. While this review can be conducted more frequently, an annual basis is common. The primary purpose is to show top management what has been accomplished with consulting and what is planned for the future. The meeting can last from two hours to two days depending on its scope and the amount of consulting activity. This meeting is best suited for situations in which there are long-term projects, long-term relationships, and/or multiple projects with the same firm. A typical agenda for this review meeting is shown in Table 14.5.

This meeting may be the single most important event on the consulting firm's calendar during the year. It must be carefully planned, timely, well executed, and controlled to accomplish its purpose. This approach has been used in many organizations, and the reaction has been extremely favorable. Executive managers want to know what the organization is accomplishing, what results have been achieved—and, most of all, they want to have input on the decisions for new projects.

Table 14.5   Annual Consulting Review Agenda

Time	Annual Review Meeting Topic
8:00 A.M.	Review of consulting for the past year
8:30	Evaluation strategy for each project and results achieved
9:30	Significant deviations from the expected results (both positive and negative)
10:00	Break
10:15	Basis for determining needs for the next year
10:30	Anticipated projects for the coming year (secure support and approval)
10:45	Proposed evaluation strategy and potential payoffs
11:00	Problem areas in the consulting process (lack of support, where management involvement is needed, or other potential problems that can be corrected by executive management)
11:30	Concerns of executive management
Noon	Adjourn

Analyzing Reactions to Communication

The best indicator of how effectively the results of a consulting project have been communicated is the level of commitment and support from the management group. The allocation of requested resources and strong commitment from top management are tangible evidence of management's perception of the results. In addition to this macro-level reaction, there are a few techniques consultants can use to measure the effectiveness of their communication efforts.

Whenever results are communicated, the reactions of the target audiences can be monitored. These reactions may include nonverbal gestures, oral remarks, written comments, or indirect actions that reveal how the communication was received. Usually, when results are presented in a meeting, the presenter will have some indication of how the results were received by the group. The interest and attitude of the audience can usually be quickly evaluated.

During the presentation, questions may be asked, or, in some cases, information may be challenged. A tabulation of these challenges and questions can be useful in evaluating the type of information to include in future communications. Positive comments about the results are certainly desired and, when they are made—formally or informally—they should also be noted and tabulated.

Consulting staff meetings are an excellent arena for discussing the reaction to communicating results. Comments can come from many sources depending on the particular target audiences. Input from different members of the staff can be summarized to help judge the overall effectiveness of the project.

When major program results are communicated, a feedback questionnaire may be used for an entire audience or a sample of the audience. The purpose of this questionnaire is to determine the extent to which the audience understood and/or believed the information presented. This is practical only when the effectiveness of the communication has a significant impact on the future actions of the consulting firm.

Another approach is to survey the management group to determine its perceptions of the results. Specific questions should be asked about results. What does the management group know about the results? How believable are the results? What additional information is desired about the project? This type of survey can help provide guidance in communicating results.

The purpose of analyzing reactions is to make adjustments in the communication process—if adjustments are necessary. Although the reactions may involve intuitive assessments, a more sophisticated analysis will provide more accurate information to make these adjustments. The net result should be a more effective communication process.

Shortcut Ways to Provide Feedback and Communicate with Clients

While this chapter has presented a full array of possibilities for all types of projects, a simplified and shortcut approach may be appropriate for small-scale projects and inexpensive consulting assignments. The following five issues can be addressed with minimal time.

1. Planning can be very simple and occupy only one block in the evaluation planning document. It is helpful to reach an agreement as to who will see the data and when those individuals will receive data.

2. Feedback during a project should be simplified using a question-naire, followed by a brief meeting to communicate the results. This is almost informal but should address as many of the issues outlined in this chapter as possible. Most importantly, it should be kept simple and should lead to action if action is needed.

3. An impact study should be developed showing the actual success of the project, preferably with all six types of data. If certain types of data have been omitted, the impact study should be developed with the data that are available, following the appropriate areas or topics contained in an impact study as outlined in this chapter.

4. The impact study results should be presented in a face-to-face meeting with the clients and perhaps with the executive group if the two are not the same. This is usually a meeting that will be easy to schedule and necessary from the perspectives of both the client and the consultant. A one-hour meeting can show the results of the project and allow the parties to respond to various issues. Using suggestions for conducting this meeting, as out-lined in this chapter, would be helpful in this situation.

5. Keep impact study data for marketing purposes. From the per-spective of the consultant, this is excellent marketing data that can be used in a generic way to convince others that the consult-ing project is successful. From the client's perspective, this is a historical document that leaves a permanent record of success and can be used as a reference in the future. When communicat-ing results from past studies, client confidentiality and protection of sensitive information should be honored.

Final Thoughts

This chapter has presented the final step in the results-based approach to consulting accountability. Communicating results is a crucial step in the overall evaluation process. If this step is not taken seriously, the full impact of the results will not be realized. The chapter began with gen-eral principles for communicating program results. A communications model has been presented that can serve as a guide for any significant communication effort. The various target audiences have been dis-cussed and, because of its importance, emphasis has been placed on the executive group. A suggested format for a detailed evaluation report has also been provided. Much of the remainder of the chapter has been devoted to a detailed presentation of the most commonly used media for communicating program results, including meetings, client publications, and electronic media. Numerous examples have illustrated these concepts.

Further Reading

Bleech, J.M., and D.G. Mutchler. *Let's Get Results, Not Excuses!* Hollywood, FL: Lifetime, 1995.

Block, Peter. *Flawless Consulting*. San Diego: Pfeiffer, 1981.

Connors, R., T. Smith., and C. Hickman. *The OZ Principle*. Englewood Cliffs, NJ: Prentice Hall, 1994.

Fradette, Michael, and Steve Michaud. *The Power of Corporate Kinetics: Create the Self-Adapting, Self-Renewing, Instant-Action Enterprise*. New York: Simon & Schuster, 1998.

Fuller, Jim. *Managing Performance Improvement Projects: Preparing, Planning, and Implementing*. San Francisco: Pfeiffer, 1997.

Hale, Judith. *The Performance Consultant's Fieldbook: Tools and Techniques for Improving Organizations and People*. San Francisco: Jossey-Bass/Pfeiffer, 1998.

Kaufman, Roger. *Strategic Thinking: A Guide to Identifying and Solving Problems*. Washington, DC: American Society for Training and Development/International Society for Performance Improvement, 1996.

Kaufman, Roger, Sivasailam Thiagarajan, and Paula MacGillis. *The Guidebook for Performance Improvement: Working with Individuals and Organizations*. San Francisco: Pfeiffer, 1997.

Kraut, A.I. *Organizational Surveys*. San Francisco: Jossey-Bass, 1996.

Labovitz, George, and Victor Rasansky. *The Power of Alignment: How Great Companies Stay Centered and Accomplish Extraordinary Things*. New York: Wiley, 1997.

Langdon, Danny G. *The New Language of Work*. Amherst, MA: HRD, 1995.

Sujansky, J.C. *The Power of Partnering*. San Diego: Pfeiffer, 1991.

Overcoming Resistance and Barriers to Measuring Consulting ROI

E VEN THE BEST-DESIGNED process, model, or technique is worthless unless it is effectively and efficiently integrated into the organization. Often there is resistance to the consulting ROI process from both the client and the consultant. Some of this resistance is based on fear and misunderstanding. Some is based on real barriers and obstacles. Although the consulting ROI process presented in this book is a step-by-step, methodical, and simple procedure, it can fail if it is not properly integrated and fully accepted and supported by those who must make it work in the organization. This chapter focuses on the key issues needed to overcome resistance to implementing the ROI process in the client organization and the consulting firm.

Why Be Concerned About Overcoming Resistance?

With any new process or change, there is resistance. Resistance may be especially great during implementation of a process as complex as consulting ROI. There are four key reasons why there should be a detailed plan for overcoming resistance.

Resistance Is Always Present

There is always resistance to change. Sometimes there are good reasons for resistance, but often it exists for the wrong reasons. The goal is to sort out both types and try to dispel the myths. When legitimate barriers are the basis for resistance, trying to minimize them or remove them altogether is the challenge.

Implementation Is Key

As with any process, effective implementation is the key to success. This occurs when the new technique or tool is integrated into the routine framework. Without effective implementation, even the best process will fail. A process that is never removed from the shelf will never be understood, supported, or improved. There must be clear-cut steps for designing a comprehensive implementation process that will overcome resistance.

Consistency Is Needed

As this process is implemented from one study to another, consistency is an important consideration. With consistency come accuracy and reliability. The only way to make sure consistency is achieved is to follow clearly defined processes and procedures each time the consulting ROI is tackled. Proper implementation will ensure that this occurs.

Efficiency

Cost control and efficiency will always be an issue in any major undertaking, and the consulting ROI process is no exception. Implementation must ensure that tasks are done efficiently as well as effectively. It will help ensure that process cost is kept to a minimum, that time is utilized appropriately, and that the process remains affordable.

The Approach to Overcoming Resistance

Resistance shows up in many ways—as comments, remarks, actions, or behaviors. Table 15.1 shows some comments that reflect open resistance to the ROI process. Each of these represents issues that need to be resolved or addressed in some way. A few of the comments are based on realistic barriers, while others are based on myths that must be dispelled. Sometimes resistance reflects underlying concerns. The individuals involved may fear losing control of their processes, or may feel that they are vulnerable to actions that may be taken if the process is not successful. Some may be concerned about any process that brings change or requires additional learning efforts.

Resistance can appear in both major audiences addressed in this book. It can appear in consulting firms, as many consultants may resist the consulting ROI process and openly make comments similar to those listed in Table 15.1. Heavy persuasion and evidence of tangible benefits may be needed to convince those in a consulting firm that this is a process that must be undertaken, should be undertaken, and is in their best interest to undertake. The other major audience—client organizations—will also experience resistance. Although most clients would like to see the results of the consulting project, they may have concerns

Table 15.1   Typical Objections to the Consulting ROI Process

Open Resistance
1. It costs too much.
2. It takes too much time.
3. Who is asking for this?
4. It is not in my job duties.
5. I did not have input on this.
6. I do not understand this.
7. What happens when the results are negative?
8. How can we be consistent with this?
9. The ROI process is too subjective.
10. Our managers will not support this.
11. ROI is too narrowly focused.
12. This is not practical.

about the information they are asked to provide and about whether their performance is being judged along with the evaluation of the entire project. In reality, they may express the same fears listed in Table 15.1.

The challenge is to implement the process in both organizations methodically and consistently so that it becomes normal business behavior and a routine and standard process built into consulting interventions. The implementation necessary to overcome resistance covers a variety of areas. Figure 15.1 shows actions outlined in this chapter that are presented as building blocks to overcoming resistance. These are all necessary to build the proper base or framework to dispel myths and remove or minimize barriers. The remainder of this chapter presents specific strate-

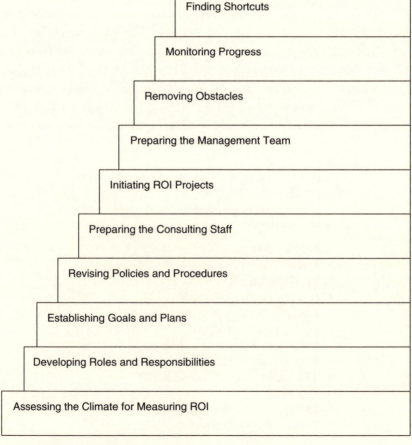

Figure 15.1　Building blocks for overcoming resistance.

gies and techniques for each of the 10 building blocks identified in Figure 15.1. They apply equally to the consulting firm and the client organization, and no attempt is made to separate the two in this presentation. In some situations, a particular strategy would work best in a consulting firm, while others may work best in client organizations. In reality, all 10 may be appropriate for both groups in certain cases.

Assessing the Climate

As a first step toward implementation, some organizations assess the current climate for achieving results. One useful tool, presented in the Appendix, reflects a results-based assessment. This instrument—or some version of it—can serve as an initial assessment of how the consulting staff and managers perceive the consulting intervention and its results. This instrument is an excellent tool for determining the current perspectives. In some organizations, annual assessments are completed to measure progress as the consulting process is implemented. Others take the assessment instrument to the management group to determine the extent to which managers perceive consulting as effective. The use of an assessment process provides an excellent understanding of the current status. With this awareness, the organization can plan for significant changes, pinpointing particular issues that need support as the consulting ROI process is implemented.

Developing Roles and Responsibilities

Defining and detailing specific roles and responsibilities for different groups and individuals addresses many of the resistance factors and helps pave a smooth path for implementation. In this section, four key issues are addressed.

Identifying a Champion

As an early step in the process, one or more individual(s) should be designated as the internal leader or champion for the process. As in most change efforts, someone must take responsibility for ensuring that the process is implemented successfully. This leader serves as a champion for ROI and is usually the one who understands the process best and sees vast potential for its contribution. More importantly, this leader is willing to teach others and will work to sustain sponsorship.

The ROI leader is a member of the consulting staff who usually has this responsibility full time in larger consulting firms or part time in smaller organizations. Client organizations may also have an ROI leader who pursues the ROI process from the client's perspective. The typical job title for a full-time ROI leader is manager of measurement and evaluation. Some organizations assign this responsibility to a team and empower it to lead the ROI effort.

Developing the ROI Leader

In preparation for this assignment, individuals usually obtain special training that builds specific skills and knowledge for the ROI process. The role of the implementation leader is quite broad and serves a variety of specialized duties. In some organizations, the implementation leader can take on as many as 14 roles, as shown in Table 15.2.

Leading the ROI effort is a difficult and challenging assignment that requires special skill building. Fortunately, there are programs available that teach these skills. For example, one such program is designed to certify individuals who are assuming a leadership role in the implementation of the ROI process. This certification is built around 10 specific skill sets linked to successful consulting ROI implementations. These are:

1. Planning for ROI calculations
2. Collecting evaluation data
3. Isolating the effects of consulting
4. Converting data to monetary values

Table 15.2 Roles of the ROI Leader

Technical expert	Cheerleader
Consultant	Communicator
Problem solver	Process monitor
Initiator	Planner
Designer	Analyst
Developer	Interpreter
Coordinator	Teacher

5. Monitoring intervention costs
6. Analyzing data, including calculating the ROI
7. Presenting evaluation data
8. Implementing the ROI process
9. Providing internal consulting on ROI
10. Teaching others the ROI process

This process is quite comprehensive but may be necessary to build the appropriate skills for tackling this challenging assignment.

Establishing a Task Force

Making the process work well may require the use of a task force. This is usually a group of individuals from different parts of the consulting process who are willing to develop the consulting ROI process and implement it in the organization. The selection of the task force may involve volunteers, or participation may be mandatory depending on specific job responsibilities. The task force should represent the necessary cross section for accomplishing stated goals. Task forces have the additional advantage of bringing more people into the process and developing more ownership and support for the consulting ROI process. The task force must be large enough to cover the key areas but not so large that it becomes cumbersome and difficult to manage. A good size is 6 to 12 members. For the client organization, the same approach may be necessary—utilizing a task force for evaluating consulting activities as well as other processes.

Assigning Responsibilities

Determining specific responsibilities is a critical issue because confusion can arise when individuals are unclear about their specific assignments in the ROI process. Responsibilities apply to two areas. The first is the measurement and evaluation responsibility of the entire consulting staff. It is important for everyone involved in consulting interventions to have some responsibility for measurement and evaluation. These responsibilities include providing input on the design of instruments, planning specific evaluations, analyzing data, and interpreting the results. Typical responsibilities include:

- Ensuring that the needs assessment includes specific business impact measures
- Developing specific application objectives (Level 3) and business impact objectives (Level 4) for each intervention
- Focusing the content of the intervention on the performance improvement, ensuring that exercises, case studies, and skill practices relate to the desired objectives
- Keeping participants focused on application and impact objectives
- Communicating rationale and reasons for evaluation
- Assisting in follow-up activities to capture application and business impact data
- Providing technical assistance for data collection, data analysis, and reporting
- Designing instruments and plans for data collection and analysis

While it may be inappropriate to have each member of the staff involved in all of these activities, each individual should have at least one or more responsibilities as part of his or her routine job duties. This assignment of responsibility keeps the ROI process from being disjointed and separated from major consulting activities. More importantly, it brings accountability to those directly involved in interventions.

Another issue involves the technical support function. Depending on the size of the consulting firm or client organization, it may be helpful to establish a group of technical experts who provide assistance with the ROI process. When this group is established, it must be clear that the experts are not there to relieve others of evaluation responsibilities but to supplement technical expertise. Some firms have found this approach to be effective. For example, one of the top five consulting firms has a measurement and evaluation staff of 32 individuals who provide technical support for evaluating consulting interventions. This is an extreme situation. When this type of support is developed, responsibilities revolve around six key areas:

1. Designing data collection instruments
2. Providing assistance for developing an evaluation strategy
3. Analyzing data, including specialized statistical analyses
4. Interpreting results and making specific recommendations

5. Developing an evaluation report or case study to communicate overall results
6. Providing technical support in all phases of the ROI process

The assignment of responsibilities for evaluation is also an issue that needs attention throughout the evaluation process. Although the consulting staff must have specific responsibilities during an evaluation, it is not unusual to require others in support functions to have responsibility for data collection. These responsibilities are defined when a particular evaluation strategy plan is developed and approved.

Establishing Goals and Plans

Establishing goals, targets, and objectives is critical to the implementation. This includes detailed planning documents for the overall process as well as individual ROI projects. Several key issues relating to goals and plans are covered here.

Setting Evaluation Targets

Establishing specific targets for evaluation levels is an important way to make progress with measurement and evaluation. Targets enable the staff to focus on improvements needed at specific evaluation levels. In this process, the percentage of projects planned for evaluation at each level is developed. The first step is to assess the present situation. The number of all consulting projects, including repeated projects of a similar nature, is tabulated along with the corresponding level(s) of evaluation presently conducted for each project. Next, the percentage of projects using reaction questionnaires is calculated. This is probably 100 percent now. The process is repeated for each level of the evaluation.

After detailing the current situation, the next step is to determine a realistic target within a specific time frame. Many organizations set annual targets for changes. This process should involve the input of the entire consulting staff to ensure that targets are realistic and that the staff is committed to the process. If the consulting staff does not develop ownership for this process, targets will not be met. The improvement targets must be achievable, while at the same time challenging and motivating. Table 15.3 shows the targets established in a large consulting firm for five levels. In some organizations, half of the business impact evaluations are taken to Level 5, while in others every evaluation is taken to this level. Most organizations plan for the gradual improvement of increasing evaluation activity at Levels 3, 4, and 5, with a profile such as the one outlined in Table 15.3 being achieved in two years.

Target setting is a critical implementation issue. It should be completed early in the process with the full support of the consulting staff. Also, if practical and feasible, the targets should have the approval of key managers—particularly the senior management team.

Developing a Project Plan for Implementation

An important part of implementation is to establish timetables for the complete implementation process. These timetables become a master plan for the completion of the different elements presented in this chapter, beginning with assigning responsibilities and concluding with meeting the targets previously described. From a practical standpoint, this schedule is a project plan for transitioning from the present situation to the desired future situation. The items on the schedule include—but are not limited to—developing specific ROI projects, building staff skills, developing policy, teaching managers the process, analyzing ROI data, and communicating results. The more detailed the document, the more useful it becomes. The project plan is a living, long-range document that should be reviewed frequently and adjusted as necessary. More importantly, it should always be familiar to those who are working on the ROI process. Figure 15.2 shows an ROI implementation project plan for a large petroleum company.

Table 15.3   Evaluation Targets in a Large
Consulting Firm

Level	Target
Level 1, reaction and satisfaction	100%
Level 2, learning	80%
Level 3, application and implementation	40%
Level 4, business impact	25%
Level 5, ROI	10%

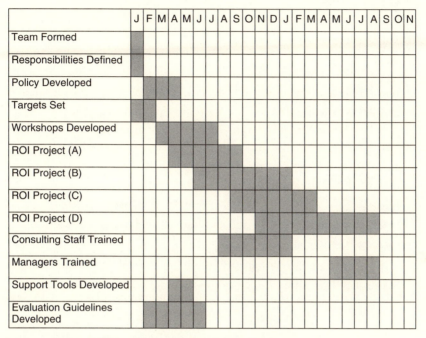

Figure 15.2   ROI implementation project plan.

Revising/Developing Policies and Guidelines

Another key part of planning is revising (or developing) the organization's policy concerning measurement and evaluation for consulting interventions, which is often a consulting function. The policy statement contains information developed specifically for the measurement and evaluation process. It is frequently developed with the input of the consulting staff and key managers or clients. Sometimes policy issues are addressed during internal workshops designed to build skills for measurement and evaluation. The policy statement addresses critical issues that will influence the effectiveness of the measurement and evaluation process. Typical issues include adopting the five-level framework presented in this book, requiring Level 3 and 4 objectives for some or all interventions and defining responsibilities for the consulting intervention's development. Figure 15.3 shows the topics in the measurement and evaluation policy for a large electric utility firm.

Policy statements are very important because they provide guidance and direction for the staff and others who work closely with the ROI

1. Purpose

2. Mission

3. Evaluate all interventions, which includes the following levels:
   a. Participant satisfaction (100%)
   b. Learning (no less than 70%)
   c. Job applications (50%)
   d. Results (usually through sampling, 10%; highly visible, expensive)
   e. ROI 5% (by request)

4. Evaluation support group (corporate) will provide assistance and advice in measurement and evaluation, instrument design, data analysis, and evaluation strategy.

5. Interventions are developed following logical steps, beginning with needs analysis and ending with communicating results.

6. Evaluation instruments must be designed or selected to collect data for evaluation. They must be valid, reliable, economical, and subject to audit by the evaluation support group.

7. Responsibility for results rests with consultants and participants or participants' team leaders.

8. An adequate system for collecting and monitoring consulting costs must be in place. All direct costs should be included.

9. At least annually, the management board will review the status and results of consulting. The review will include consulting plans, strategies, results, costs, priorities, and concerns.

10. Line management shares in the responsibility for the consulting success. Evaluation through follow ups, pre-intervention commitments, and overall support.

11. Managers/supervisors must declare competence achieved through interventions. When not applicable, the consulting staff should evaluate.

12. External consultants must be selected based on evaluation data from previous projects. A central data/resource base should exist.

Figure 15.3 Results-based internal consulting policy (excerpt from an actual policy).

13. Consulting results must be communicated to the appropriate target audiences. At a minimum, this includes management (participants' leaders), participants, and the entire consulting staff.

14. The consulting staff should be qualified to do an effective needs analysis and evaluation.

15. Central database must be maintained for consulting projects to prevent duplication and serve as a consulting resource.

16. Union involvement in consulting plan.

Figure 15.3 Results-based internal consulting policy (excerpt from an actual policy). (*Continued*)

process. These individuals keep the process clearly focused and enable the group to establish goals for evaluation. Policy statements also provide an opportunity to communicate basic requirements and fundamental issues regarding performance and accountability. More than anything else, they serve as tools for teaching others, especially when they are developed in a collaborative and collective way. If policy statements are developed in isolation and do not enjoy ownership from the staff and management, they will not be effective or useful.

Guidelines for measurement and evaluation are important for showing how to utilize the tools and techniques, guide the design process, provide consistency in the ROI process, ensure that appropriate methods are used, and place the proper emphasis on each of the areas. The guidelines are more technical than policy statements and often contain detailed procedures showing how the process is actually undertaken and developed. They often include specific forms, instruments, and tools necessary to facilitate the process.

Preparing the Consulting Staff

Consultants often resist the ROI process. They may see evaluation as an unnecessary intrusion into their responsibilities that absorbs precious time and stifles their freedom to be creative. The cartoon character Pogo perhaps characterized it best when he said, "We have met the enemy, and he is us." This section outlines some important issues that must be addressed when preparing the consulting staff for the implementation of ROI.

Involving the Staff

On each key issue or major decision, the staff should be involved in the process. As policy statements are prepared and evaluation guidelines are developed, staff input is absolutely essential. It is difficult for the staff to resist something it helped design and develop. Using meetings, brainstorming sessions, and task forces, the staff should be involved in every phase of developing the framework and supporting documents for ROI.

Using ROI as a Learning Tool

One reason the consulting staff may resist the ROI process is that the effectiveness of its interventions will be fully exposed, putting the consulting firm's reputation on the line. Consultants may have a fear of failure. To overcome this, the ROI process should be clearly positioned as a tool for learning and not a tool for evaluating consulting staff performance—at least during its early years of implementation. Consultants will not be interested in developing a process that can be used against them.

Evaluators can learn as much from failures as from successes. If the consulting intervention is not working, it is best to find out quickly in order to understand the issues firsthand, not from others. If a consulting intervention is ineffective and not producing the desired results, it will eventually be known to clients and/or members of the management group—if they are not aware of it already. A lack of results will cause managers to become less supportive of consulting interventions. If the weaknesses of interventions are identified and adjustments are made quickly, not only will more effective interventions be developed, but the credibility of and respect for consulting will be enhanced.

Teaching the Staff

The consulting staff usually has inadequate skills in measurement and evaluation and thus will need to develop some expertise in the process. Measurement and evaluation is not always a formal part of the preparation in becoming a consultant. Consequently, each consultant must be provided training on the ROI process to learn its systematic steps. In addition, consultants must know how to develop an evaluation strategy and specific plan, how to collect and analyze data from the evaluation, and how to interpret results from data analysis. Sometimes a one- to two-day workshop is needed to help consultants build adequate skills and knowledge to understand the process, appreciate what the process can do for the consulting firm and client organization, see the necessity for it, and participate in a successful implementation.

Initiating ROI Project

The first tangible evidence of the consulting ROI process may be the initiation of the first project in which an ROI calculation is planned. This section outlines some of the key issues involved in identifying the projects and keeping them on track.

Selecting Initial Interventions

Selecting an intervention for ROI analysis is an important and critical issue. Only specific types of interventions should be selected for comprehensive, detailed analysis. Typical criteria for identifying interventions for analysis are to select interventions that:

- Involve large groups of employees
- Are expected to have a long life cycle
- Are linked to major operational problems/opportunities
- Are important to overall strategic objectives
- Are expensive
- Are time consuming
- Have high visibility
- Have management's interest in evaluation

Using these or similar criteria, the consultant must select the appropriate projects to consider for ROI evaluation. Ideally, management should concur with or approve the criteria.

The next major step is determining how many projects to undertake initially and in which particular areas. Small numbers of initial projects—perhaps two or three interventions—are recommended. The selected interventions may represent the functional areas of the business such as operations, sales, finance, engineering, and information systems. Another approach is to select interventions representing functional areas of consulting, such as productivity improvement, re-engineering, quality enhancement, technology implementation, and major change. It is important to select a manageable number so the process will be implemented.

Developing the Planning Documents

Perhaps the two most useful ROI documents are the data collection plan and the ROI analysis plan discussed in an earlier chapter. These plans show which data will be collected, at what time and by whom, and how specific analyses will be conducted, including isolating the effects of consulting and converting data to monetary values. Each consultant should know how to develop, understand, and use these plans.

Reporting Progress

As the projects are developed and the ROI implementation is under way, status meetings should be conducted to report progress and discuss critical issues with appropriate team members. For example, if an intervention for operations is selected as one of the ROI projects, the key staff involved in the intervention should meet regularly to discuss the status of the project. This keeps the project team focused on the critical issues, generates the best ideas for tackling particular problems and barriers, and builds a knowledge base for better implementation evaluations in future interventions. Sometimes this group is facilitated by an external consultant, perhaps an expert in the ROI process. In other cases, the internal ROI leader may facilitate the group.

In essence, these meetings serve three major purposes: reporting progress, learning, and planning. The meeting usually begins with a status report on each ROI project, describing what has been accomplished since the previous meeting. Next, the specific barriers and problems encountered are discussed. During the discussions, new issues are interjected in terms of possible tactics, techniques, or tools. Also, the entire group discusses how to remove barriers to success and focuses on suggestions and recommendations for next steps, including developing specific plans. Finally, the next steps are determined.

Establishing Discussion Groups

Because the ROI process is considered difficult to understand and apply, it is sometimes helpful to establish discussion groups to teach the process. These groups could supplement formal workshops and other learning activities and are often very flexible in their format. Groups are usually facilitated by an external ROI consultant or the internal ROI leader. In each session, a new topic is presented and discussed thoroughly. Concerns and issues about the topic are discussed, including how they apply to the organization. The process can be adjusted for different topics as the needs of the group drive the issues. Ideally, participants in group discussions should have an opportunity to apply, explore, or research the topics between sessions. Assignments such as reviewing a case analysis or reading an article are also appropriate between sessions to further the development of knowledge and skills associated with the process.

Preparing the Management Team

Perhaps no group is more important to the ROI process than the management team that must allocate resources for consulting and support the interventions. In addition, the management team often provides input and assistance for the ROI process. Specific actions for training and developing the management team should be carefully planned and executed.

A critical issue that must be addressed before a consulting intervention is the relationship between the consulting staff and key managers. A productive partnership is needed, which requires each party to understand the concerns, problems, and opportunities of the other. Developing this type of relationship is a long-term process that must be deliberately planned and initiated by key consultants. Sometimes the decision to commit resources and support for consulting is based on the effectiveness of this relationship.

Workshop for Managers

One effective approach for preparing managers for the ROI process is to conduct a workshop on consulting accountability. Varying in duration from half a day to two days, this practical workshop shapes critical skills and changes perceptions to enhance support for the consulting ROI process. Managers leave the workshop with an improved perception of the impact of consulting and a clearer understanding of their roles in the consulting process. More importantly, they often develop a renewed commitment to making consulting interventions work in their organization.

Due to the critical need for understanding of this topic in managing consulting interventions, this workshop should be required for many if not all managers, unless they have previously demonstrated strong support for the consulting intervention function. Because of this requirement, it is essential for executives to be supportive of this workshop and in some cases to take an active role in conducting it. To tailor the intervention to specific organizational needs, a brief needs assessment may be necessary to determine the specific focus and areas of emphasis for the workshop.

Because convincing top management to embrace the consulting intervention may be a difficult task, three approaches should be considered:

- *Discuss and illustrate the consequences of inadequate management support for consulting.* For example, the statistics on wasted time and money are staggering.
- *Show how current support is lacking.* An evaluation of a recent consulting intervention will often reveal barriers to the successful application of consulting. Lack of management support is often the main reason, which brings the issue close to home.
- *Demonstrate how money can be saved and results achieved with the ROI process.*

The endorsement of the top management group is very important. In some organizations, top managers actually attend the workshop to explore firsthand what is involved and what they must do to make the process work. At a minimum, top management should support the workshop by signing memos describing the workshop or by approving policy statements regarding the workshop.

The Overall Importance of Consulting

Managers need to be convinced that consulting is a mainstream function that is growing in importance and influence in modern organizations. They need to understand the results-based approach of today's progressive consulting firms. Managers should perceive consulting interventions as a critical process in the organization and should be able to describe how the process contributes to strategic and operational objectives. Data from the organization should be presented to show the full scope of consulting in the organization. Tangible evidence of top management's commitment to the process should be presented in the form of memos, directives, or policies signed by the CEO or other appropriate top executives. Also, external data should be shared to illustrate the growth of consulting budgets and the increasing importance of consulting.

The Impact of Consulting

Too often, managers are unsure about the success of consulting. Managers need to be able to identify the steps for measuring the impact of consulting on important output variables. Reports and studies should be presented that show the impact of the consulting intervention using measures such as productivity, quality, cost, response time, and customer satisfaction. Internal evaluation reports, if available, should be presented to managers, revealing convincing evidence that consulting is making a significant difference in the organization. If internal reports are not available, success stories or case studies from other organizations can be utilized. Managers need to be convinced that consulting is a successful, results-based tool—not only to help with change, but to meet critical organizational goals and objectives as well.

Responsibility for Consulting

Defining who is responsible for what areas of the consulting intervention is important to the success of the project. Managers should know their specific responsibilities, see how they can influence consulting, and understand the degree of responsibility they must assume in the future. Multiple responsibilities for consulting are advocated, including specific responsibilities for managers, participants, participant supervisors, and consultants. In some organizations, job descriptions are revised to reflect consulting responsibilities. In other organizations, major job-related goals are established to highlight management's responsibility for consulting.

Active Involvement

One of the most important ways to enhance managers' support for consulting is to actively involve them in the process, having them commit to one or more ways to become actively involved in the future. Figure 15.4 shows several forms of manager involvement identified in one company. The information in the figure is presented to managers with

---

The following are areas for present and future involvement in the consulting. Please check your areas of planned involvement.

	In Your Area	Outside Your Area
■ Provide input on a consulting needs analysis	☐	☐
■ Serve on a consulting advisory committee	☐	☐
■ Provide input on an intervention design	☐	☐
■ Serve as a subject matter expert	☐	☐
■ Serve on a task force to develop an intervention	☐	☐
■ Provide reinforcement to employees as they participate in a consulting intervention	☐	☐
■ Coordinate an intervention program	☐	☐
■ Assist in an intervention evaluation or follow-up	☐	☐

Figure 15.4   Management involvement in consulting.

a request for them to commit to at least one area of involvement. After these areas are fully explained and discussed, each manager is asked to select one or more ways in which he or she will be involved in consulting in the future. A commitment to sign up for at least one involvement role is required. If used properly, these commitments are a rich source of input and assistance from the management group. There will be many offers for involvement, and a quick follow-up on all offers is recommended.

Removing Obstacles

As the consulting ROI process is implemented, there will be obstacles to its progress. Many of the objections discussed in this chapter may be valid, while others may be based on unrealistic fears or misunderstandings. As part of the implementation, attempts should be made to dispel the myths and remove or minimize the barriers or obstacles described in the Introduction. These myths should be discussed and debated in the organization so that they can be dispelled, at least in the eyes of the consultants or other support staff.

Monitoring Progress

A final part of the implementation process is monitoring the overall progress made and communicating that progress. Although it is an often overlooked part of the process, an effective communication plan can help keep the implementation on target and let others know what the consulting ROI process is accomplishing for the consulting firm and the client organization.

The initial schedule for implementation of the ROI process provides a variety of key events or milestones. Routine progress reports should be developed to communicate the status and progress of these events or milestones. Reports are usually developed at six-month intervals, but may be more frequent for short-term projects. Two target audiences—the consulting staff and senior managers—are critical for progress reporting. The entire consulting staff should be kept informed of the progress, and senior managers need to know the extent to which ROI is being implemented and how it is working in the organization.

Shortcut Ways to Make the ROI Process Work

To address concerns about excessive time and resources for the consulting ROI process, it is important to constantly pursue shortcut ways to make the ROI process work. Throughout this book in practically every chapter, shortcut ways have been presented that will help you save time and cost as a consulting ROI process is applied and implemented. Chapter 2 presents 10 shortcuts for using the process in your organization. Those serve as a helpful summary of the key issues involved in developing these shortcuts. It may be helpful to review those shortcuts now, as they are not reprinted here. In addition, at the end of each chapter is a section on shortcut ways to accomplish the objective of the chapter. Those chapter presentations provide an amplification of the 10 ways presented in Chapter 2. Collectively, there are many shortcut ways through which time can be saved and cost can be reduced without seriously damaging the effectiveness of the process.

Final Thoughts

In summary, the implementation of the ROI process is a very critical issue. If it is not approached in a systematic, logical, and planned way, the ROI process will not become an integral part of consulting and, consequently, the accountability of consulting interventions will suffer. This final chapter has presented the different elements that must be considered and issues that must be addressed to ensure that implementation is smooth and uneventful. This is the most effective way to overcome resistance to ROI. The result provides a complete integration of consulting ROI as a mainstream activity in the consulting process.

Further Reading

Esque, Timm J., and Patricia A. Patterson. *Getting Results: Case Studies in Performance Improvement* (vol. 1). Washington, DC: HRD/International Society for Performance Improvement, 1998.

Fuller, Jim. *Managing Performance Improvement Projects: Preparing, Planning, and Implementing.* San Francisco: Pfeiffer, 1997.

Kaufman, Roger, Sivasailam Thiagarajan, and Paula MacGillis. *The Guidebook for Performance Improvement: Working with Individuals and Organizations.* San Francisco: Pfeiffer, 1997.

Labovitz, George, and Victor Rasansky. *The Power of Alignment: How Great Companies Stay Centered and Accomplish Extraordinary Things.* New York: Wiley, 1997.

LaGrossa, Virginia, and Suzanne Saxe. *The Consultative Approach: Partnering for Results!* San Francisco: Jossey-Bass/Pfeiffer, 1998.

Langley, Gerald J., Kevin M. Nolan, Thomas W. Nolan, Clifford L. Norman, and Lloyd P. Provost. *The Improvement Guide: A Practical Approach to Enhancing Organizational Performance.* San Francisco: Jossey-Bass, 1996.

Rackham, Neil, Lawrence Friedman, and Richard Ruff. *Getting Partnering Right: How Market Leaders Are Creating Long-Term Competitive Advantage.* New York: McGraw-Hill, 1996.

Redwood, Stephen, Charles Goldwasser, and Simon Street/PricewaterhouseCoopers. *Practical Strategies for Making Your Corporate Transformation a Success: Action Management.* New York: Wiley, 1999.

Segil, Larraine. *Intelligent Business Alliances: How to Profit Using Today's Most Important Strategic Tool.* New York: Times Business/Random House, 1996.

Trout, Jack, and Steve Rivkin. *The Power of Simplicity: A Management Guide to Cutting Through the Nonsense and Doing Things Right.* New York: McGraw-Hill, 1999.

Do Your Consulting Projects Focus on Results?

A Self-Assessment

A Survey for Clients

Instructions. For each of the following statements, please circle the response that best matches the consulting activities and philosophy in your organization. If none of the answers describe the situation, select the one that best fits. Please be candid with your responses.

Select the most correct response.

1. The direction and goals of the consulting process at your organization:
   a. Shifts with trends, fads, and industry issues.
   b. Is determined by managers of departments and adjusted as needed.
   c. Is based on a mission and a strategic plan for the consulting function.

2. The primary mode of operation of the consulting function is:
   a. To respond to requests by managers and other employees to deliver solutions.
   b. To help management react to crisis situations and reach solutions.
   c. To implement solutions in collaboration with management to prevent problems and crisis situations.
3. Consulting solutions usually focus on:
   a. Changing perceptions and opinions.
   b. Enhancing skills and job performance.
   c. Driving business measures and enhancing job performance.
4. Most new consulting solutions are initiated:
   a. When a solution appears to be successful in another organization.
   b. By request of management.
   c. After analysis has indicated that the solution is needed.
5. To determine solutions:
   a. Management is asked to choose a solution from a list of existing packaged solutions.
   b. Employees and unit managers are asked about needs.
   c. Needs are systematically derived from a thorough analysis of performance problems and issues.
6. When determining the consulting solutions needed for target audiences:
   a. Nonspecific solutions for large audiences are offered.
   b. Specific needs of specific individuals and groups are addressed.
   c. Very focused projects are implemented only for those people who need them.
7. The responsibility for results from consulting:
   a. Rests primarily with the consultants.
   b. Is shared with consultants and managers, who jointly ensure that results are obtained.
   c. Rests with consultants, participants, and managers all working together to ensure accountability.
8. Systematic, objective evaluation, designed to ensure that consulting participants are appropriately implementing the consulting project:
   a. Is never accomplished. Evaluations are conducted during the project and they focus on how much the participants are satisfied with the project.

     b. Is occasionally accomplished. Participants are asked if the consulting project was effective on the job.

     c. Is frequently and systematically pursued. Performance is evaluated after the project is completed.

9. Consulting projects are staffed:

     a. Primarily with internal consultants.

     b. With one preapproved major consulting firm.

     c. In the most economical and practical way to meet deadlines and cost objectives, using internal staff and a variety of consulting firms.

10. The objectives for consulting solutions are:

     a. Nonspecific and based on subjective input.

     b. Based on learning, application, and implementation.

     c. Based on business impact, application, implementation, and satisfaction.

11. Costs for consulting are accumulated:

     a. On a total aggregate basis only.

     b. On a project-by-project basis.

     c. By specific process components such as initial analysis and implementation, in addition to a specific project.

12. Management involvement in consulting is:

     a. Very low, with only occasional input.

     b. Moderate, usually by request, or on an as-needed basis.

     c. Deliberately planned for all major consulting projects, to ensure a partnership arrangement.

13. To ensure that consulting projects are translated into performance on the job, we:

     a. Encourage participants to apply what they have learned and report results.

     b. Ask managers to support and reinforce consulting project results.

     c. Utilize a variety of transfer strategies appropriate for each situation.

14. The consulting staff's interaction with management is:

     a. Rare. Consultants almost never discuss issues with them.

     b. Occasional; during activities such as needs analysis or project coordination.

     c. Regular; to build relationships, as well as to develop and deliver solutions.

15. The investment in consulting projects is measured primarily by:
    a. Subjective opinions.
    b. Observations by management, reactions from consulting participants.
    c. Monetary return through improved productivity, costs, quality, or customer service.

16. New consulting projects, with no formal method of evaluation, are implemented at my organization:
    a. Regularly.
    b. Seldom.
    c. Never.

17. The results of consulting projects are communicated:
    a. When requested, to those who have a need to know.
    b. Occasionally, to members of management only.
    c. Routinely, to a variety of selected target audiences.

18. Management responsibilities for consulting:
    a. Are minor, with no specific responsibilities.
    b. Consist of informal responsibilities for selected consulting projects.
    c. Are very specific. Managers have some responsibilities for projects in their business units.

19. During a business decline at my organization, the consulting function will
    a. Be the first to have its budget reduced.
    b. Be retained at the same budget level.
    c. Go untouched in reductions and possibly be increased.

20. Budgeting for consulting is based on:
    a. Last year's budget.
    b. Whatever the consultant can "sell."
    c. A zero-based system based on the need for each project.

21. The principal group that must justify consulting expenditures is:
    a. The consultants.
    b. The consultants and managers of the unit where the project is initiated.
    c. Senior management over the area where the consulting project is implemented.

22. Over the last two years, the consulting budget as a percent of oper-
    ating expenses has:
    a. Decreased.
    b. Remained stable.
    c. Increased.

23. Senior management's involvement in consulting projects:
    a. Is limited to introductions, announcements, and extending con-
       gratulations.
    b. Includes reviewing status, opening/closing meetings, discus-
       sions of status, presentation on the outlook of the organization,
       and so on.
    c. Includes participation in the project, monitoring progress,
       requiring key managers to be involved, and so on.

24. When an employee is directly involved in a consulting project, he
    or she is required to:
    a. Do nothing unless instructed.
    b. Ask questions about the project and use the projects materials
       and learning.
    c. Implement the project successfully, encourage others to imple-
       ment it, and report success.

25. Most managers in your organization view the consulting function as:
    a. A questionable activity that wastes too much time of employees.
    b. A necessary function that probably cannot be eliminated.
    c. An important resource that can be used to improve the organi-
       zation.

Score the assessment instrument as follows. Allow:

> 1 point for each (a) response.
> 3 points for each (b) response.
> 5 points for each (c) response.

The total will be between 30 and 100 points

The interpretation of scoring is provided below. The explanation is
based on the input from dozens of organizations.

Score Range	*Analysis of Score*
99–125	*Outstanding environment* for achieving results with consulting. Great management support. A truly successful example of results-based consulting.
76–100	*Above average* in achieving results with consulting. Good management support. A solid and methodical approach to results-based consulting projects.
51–75	*Needs improvement* to achieve desired results with consulting. Management support is ineffective. Consulting projects do not usually focus on results.
25–50	*Serious problems* with the success and status of consulting. Management support is nonexistent. Consulting projects are not producing results.

Index